fasces p. 25

The Lost Worlds
of
Ancient America

Compelling Evidence of Ancient Immigrants,
Lost Technologies, and Places of Power

THE LOST WORLDS OF
ANCIENT
AMERICA

Edited by Frank Joseph
Foreword by John DeSalvo, PhD

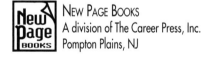
NEW PAGE BOOKS
A division of The Career Press, Inc.
Pompton Plains, NJ

THE LOST WORLDS OF ANCIENT AMERICA
EDITED BY JODI BRANDON
TYPESET BY EILEEN MUNSON
Cover design by Lucia Rossman/Digi Dog Design
Printed in the U.S.A.

To order this title, please call toll-free 1-800-CAREER-1 (NJ and Canada: 201-848-0310) to order using VISA or MasterCard, or for further information on books from Career Press.

The Career Press, Inc.
220 West Parkway, Unit 12
Pompton Plains, NJ 07444
www.careerpress.com
www.newpagebooks.com

Library of Congress Cataloging-in-Publication Data

The lost worlds of ancient America : compelling evidence of ancient immigrants, lost technologies, and places of power / edited by Frank Joseph ; foreword by John DeSalvo.
    p. cm.
Includes bibliographical references and index.
ISBN 978-1-60163-204-3 -- ISBN 978-1-60163-614-0 (ebook) 1. America--Antiquities. 2. America--Discovery and exploration--Pre-Columbian. 3. America--Civilization. 4. America--History--To 1810. 5. Excavations (Archaeology)--America. 6. Historic sites--America. 7. Prehistoric peoples--America. 8. Visitors, Foreign--America--History--To 1500. 9. Technology--America--History--To 1500. I. Joseph, Frank.

E21.5.L67 2012
970.01--dc23

                                                            2012000063

To the memory of
Fred Rydholm,
whose love of America's prehistory translated into high wisdom,
which continues to nourish us, as it must future generations.

Contents

Part I
Physical Proof

Part II
Sites

Part III
Ancient American Hi-Tech

Part IV
Foreigners in Prehistoric America

A New Voyage Into
Prehistory

My good friend Frank Joseph has put together a most significant compilation of intriguing information about the exploration of the Americas long before Christopher Columbus dropped anchor off the shore of San Salvador. These revelations will change our perceptions of the past, as we have come to know it. History books will have to be rewritten to accommodate such new information. We can no longer take for granted and with faith versions of the past we were taught in school. These previous notions must be discarded in favor of a new historical paradigm provide by independent investigators.

Frank is one of these pioneers who researched prehistory for decades. His publications and expertise qualify him as the perfect editor for such an eclectic anthology. I nonetheless suggest and urge readers to keep an open mind while reading it. *The Lost Worlds of Ancient America* offers them a new way of seeing the history of their country, and a fresh appreciation of the wonderful accomplishments achieved here before the arrival of modern Europeans. Numerous pre-Columbian explorers may have traversed the Atlantic, as evidenced in their surviving archaeological sites and artifacts. These finds are being researched, studied, and evaluated by experts—professional and avocational—from all over the world.

The Lost Worlds of Ancient America is additionally valuable for its power to stimulate public interest in the subject and encourage professional research into it. Certainly, more scholars with open minds are needed to address and investigate possibilities for overseas' influences at work on our country in pre-Columbian times. Science as a tool collects data for honest evaluation, minus any preconceived notions or biases. Sadly, such scientific objectivity is currently missing from orthodox scholars. Accordingly, it is my hope that this new book will serve as a catalyst for a new kind of research, free from the narrow-mindedness and academic mind-set that have so far hobbled the healthy growth of archaeology in our country.

In any case, readers of *The Lost Worlds of Ancient America* are sure to embark on their own voyage of discovery into the remote past. I wish them a safe and enlightening journey.

John DeSalvo, PhD

Director of the Great Pyramid of Giza Research Association, and author of *Power Crystals: Spiritual and Magical Practices, Crystal Skulls, and Alien Technology*

Unlocking America's Forbidden Past
by Frank Joseph

"New opinions often appear first as jokes and fancies, then as blasphemies and treason, then as questions open to discussion, and finally, as established truths."

—George Bernard Shaw[1]

When publisher Wayne May asked me to edit a new magazine he wanted to release in summer 1993, our chief purpose was to challenge a predominant dogma we knew was false. Until then, the belief that America had been hermetically sealed off from the rest of the outside world before the arrival of Christopher Columbus went unquestioned throughout our country's public information and educational systems. Scattered groups and societies of a few, mostly amateur scholars collected what evidence they could to the contrary.

But these avocational antiquarians only passed information back and forth among themselves; none of it ever so much as leaked outside the small, isolated circles of home-grown enthusiasts. *Ancient American* magazine shattered that impotent anonymity by preaching the cause of cultural diffusionism—the position that our continent's pre-Columbian past has been richly endowed by overseas visitors—to the public at large. America, we know, has been a melting pot long before the Statue of Liberty was set up in New York Harbor.

From *Ancient American*'s very first issue, and every one of the nearly 100 that followed without a break throughout the last 18 years, it popularized non-conformist archaeology with simple, clear text, illustrated by abundant, photographic evidence that confronted scientific orthodoxy, not with unsubstantiated theories or personal opinions, but dramatic documentation in the form of artifacts from the ancient Old World and the latest breakthroughs in the genetic and forensic sciences.

Some of the best writers to ever grace the pages of *Ancient American* are represented in this, New Page Books' third collection of our magazine's outstanding articles. These men and women have devoted many years, sometimes decades, in pursuit of the real prehistory of our continent. They comprise university-trained geologists, college professors, science writers for prominent periodicals, award-winning investigators, physicists, engineers, zoologists, radio broadcasters, artists, newspaper columnists, society presidents, and so on—but no mainstream archaeologists. One of them, Dr. Cyrus Gordon, subsequently labeled a "rogue professor" by his conventional colleagues for questioning their No-Pre-Columbian-Foreigners-in-America Paradigm, explained, "No politically astute member of the Establishment who prizes his professional reputation is likely to risk his good name for the sake of a truth that his peers (and therefore the public) may not be prepared to accept for fifty or a hundred years."[2]

Our efforts on behalf of that shunned truth were made chiefly possible by growing numbers of superb researchers and authentic discoverers, whose contributions comprise the flesh and blood of *Ancient American*. Without its publication, their paradigm-shattering finds would have sunk into oblivion, because our magazine is the only such venue allowing independent investigators an otherwise-unavailable public forum. Some of their most persuasive proofs are presented in the following pages. They make up enough evidence to blow the lid off Establishment Archaeology, and compel a thorough reorientation of our true origins.

When did the first humans enter America? Who were they? Where did they come from? How did they get here? Why is an enormous stone wall, conservatively dated to 2,000 years ago, buried in Texas? How can we account for evidence for manned flight or applied electricrical energy during pre-Columbian times? Who built a super-highway across West Virginia long before the first pioneers arrived? How do we dismiss thousands of 1,500-year-old inscribed tablets unearthed in Michigan during the course of seven decades, or hundreds of Roman coins scattered across the Midwest? These and similar questions, assiduously side-stepped by mainstream archaeologists, are authoritatively answered here with hard facts.

Geological testing of an stone discovered in Eastern Tennessee by Smithsonian archaeologists more than 100 years ago, and ever since officially condemned as a "fake," proves it does, in fact, bear a first-century Hebrew inscription. Analysis of an Inca mummy discovered in the Andes Mountains shows it constitutes the remains of a girl who was part-Caucasian. Corn grown only in North America is graphically portrayed on the walls of 3,500-year-old Egyptian tombs and temples. A monumental monolith identical to counterparts in Stone Age Europe has been uncovered at the base of Ohio's serpentine earthwork. A fourth-century helmet from Wales was excavated in Indiana. Genes from ancient Western Europe and the Near East are being traced in several of today's Native American tribes.

These irrefutable proofs represent a sampling of evidence conclusively establishing foreign influences at work centuries and millennia before the arrival of modern Europeans. These hitherto-unacknowledged visitors did not constitute occasional anomalies, but formed and shaped the prehistory of our country. They also disclose a vaster, richer panorama of ancient America than ever previously imagined.

Part I

Physical Proof

CHAPTER 1

California's Buried Altar and Monument to the Great Flood
by Frank Joseph

The recent and dramatic find of a foreign, pre-Columbian artifact in western America is also among the most convincing of its kind ever made. The stone block's discovery under conditions beyond all possibilities of fraud, plus the nature of its identity, represent a truly revealing discovery. Not very far away, another monolith is inscribed with one of the largest, most complex examples of rock art. Both objects are clues to the mysterious prehistory of the Golden State.

Frank Joseph was editor-in-chief of Ancient American magazine from its founding in 1993 until his retirement in 2007. In 1995, the Midwestern Epigraphic Society (Columbus, Ohio) presented him with the Victor Moseley Award. Seven years later, he became a professor of world archaeology with the Savant Institute of Japan (Osaka). Joseph has published nine books about the lost civilizations of Atlantis, more than any other writer in history.

Shortly after the turn of the 21st century, an old house was being torn down in a western neighborhood of Los Angeles, California. After its demolition, workers began digging up the backyard in preparation for new construction. At 5 feet beneath the surface, their shovels struck something unexpectedly bulky and solid. Persistent excavation brought to light a sculpted monolith 3.4 feet tall with a base measurement of 1.7 by 1.6 feet. The reddish, igneous block is almost perfectly rectangular in shape, weighs 228 pounds, and shows the effects of having been buried in acidic soil for many centuries.

Abstract lines and semi-circles identically cover either side, while, more than half-way up the broader front, the likeness of a human head partially emerges from the center in bas relief, surrounded by engraved ridges suggesting a hair style terminating below the head in large, twin curls. The oblate facial features are carefully molded, although details are sparse. Small eyes and mouth are depicted, with possible remnants of nose

The Los Angeles Monolith.

and brow. These carvings resemble nothing similar to indigenous Californian or even North American tribal imagery. They are utterly unlike anything found in native Native American art, either prehistoric or contemporary. Indian material culture did not include monumental stone sculpture.

After a cursory examination during a recent exhibition of the Public Broadcasting System's well-known "Antiques Roadshow" television program, an appraiser/archaeologist could offer no opinion, save that the large object, judging from its soil stains, was at least 500 years old, but probably much older. Curators from the archaeology department at the Natural History Museum of Los Angeles have not been able to add anything to the appraiser's limited assessment. Although they did not question the unique artwork's pre-Columbian provenance, its precise age, original purpose, significance of its illustrated surface, or identity of its creators escaped them. Owners of the monolith shared what little they know of their accidental find with *Ancient American* on conditions of personal anonymity and privacy concerning the undisclosed whereabouts of their discovery.

It must forever remain an insoluable mystery, so long as mainstream scholars restrict their investigation within the borders of pre-Columbian North America. In the light of the outside world, however, the artifact stands revealed. Its full-face, sculpted relief with stylized headdress and crude, though effective execution finds its close likeness in an ancient Old World deity. Beginning with the mid-16th century BC, the Phoenicians began to assert their separate identity and emerge from the other, Semitic peoples of Canaan, a kingdom roughly corresponding to the region encompassing modern-day Israel, Palestinian territories, western parts of Syria, and Lebanon. In fact, most of today's Lebanese are more or less directly descended from the Phoenicians. According to the 2011 census, only 12 percent of today's population in Lebanon are Arab.[1] DNA studies reveal "overwhelming" genetic similarities between Phoenicians and most modern Lebanese.

"They argue that Arabization merely represented a shift to the Arabic language as the vernacular of the Lebanese people," states Wikipedia, "and that, according to them, no actual shift of ethnic identity, much less ancestral origins, occurred.... Thus, Phoenicianists emphasize that the Arabs of Lebanon, Syria, Palestine, Egypt, Sudan, Tunisia, Iraq, and all other 'Arabs', are different peoples, each descended from the indigenous pre-Arab populations of their respective regions, with their own histories and lore, and that therefore they do not belong to the one pan-Arab ethnicity, and thus such categorisation is erred or inapplicable."[2] The globe-trotting proclivity of modern Lebanese is part of their character-heritage from Phoenician ancestors, whose large, sturdy ships built with "the cedars of Lebanon" enabled the establishment of a mercantile empire that spanned the Mediterranean Sea and carried colonists around the African continent more than 1,000 years before Vasco da Gama.

Among the Phoenicians' most beloved deities was Ashtart, their version of the much-earlier Sumerian Inanna. She was the divine patroness of both fertility and war—life and death—twin aspects embodied in her celestial light, the planet Venus, rising in the east as the Morning Star and setting in the west as the Evening Star. Eleventh-century BC Phoenician cosmologist Sanchuniathon portrayed her as "the Mighty One, wandering through the world," an appropriate conception for the far-ranging Phoenicians, whose sailors prayed to her as "Our Lady of the Sea."[3]

When they arrived in Egypt as traders and settlers, Ashtart was welcomed as a popular import by their hosts, assuming some features of an indigenous goddess, Hathor, particularly her iconic headdress, with its bouffant configuration ending in two close-fitting curls on either side of the head. Thereafter, Ashtart was usually portrayed wearing the stylized headdress wherever the Phoenicians traveled, as evidenced by one of their bronze figures of the goddess from Carranzo, Spain.

The Egyptians worshipped her as Qadashu during the 18th and 19th Dynasties, from 1550 until 1200 BC, when the two peoples had a falling out. A prayer to Ashtart-Qadashu found in Egypt at a Phoenician burial was probably a standard text dedicated to the deity wherever she was venerated: "Praise, Lady of the Stars of Heaven, Mistress of All the Gods. May She grant life, welfare, prosperity, and health. Mayest thou grant that I behold thy beauty daily."[4]

Although the countenance protruding from the Los Angeles monolith wears a Hathor headdress, it does not belong to that Egyptian goddess or

Qadashu, because neither deity was ever so crudely depicted in the Nile Valley. Phoenician divinities, on the contrary, were often coarsely portrayed, such as the photograph example included here from eighth-century BC Hadrumetum, a Phoenician colony in Tunisia, North Africa, of Ashtart's

Stone representation of Phoenician goddess Ashtart, from Hadrumetum, North Africa, c. 850 BC.

engraved image. Its resemblence to the California figure, wholly unlike any other representation of this goddess, is unmistakeable. Moreover, the face-forward style was diagnostic of Phoenician sculpted art.

With the decline of Egyptian and Mycenaean Greek influence on the Aegean World after the 13th century BC, the Phoenicians were free to exploit the rest of the Mediterranean Sea and beyond, throughout the Atlantic realm, where colonies were established in western Morocco and Iberia. They are known to have brought back oranges from the Canary Islands, together with a costly purple dye—the *purpura murex* found in a rare sea-snail shell—from Madeira, and they left a horde of coins on the even more remote Azore island of Corvu. The Los Angeles monolith is physical proof they sailed further. Like other objects of its kind, the sculpted block conforms in size and rectangular-cubic shape to a stone altar for the worship of Ashtart, the "Lady of the Sea," who safely brought Phoenician visitors to the west coast of our continent more than 2,000 years ago.

Another California monolith is better known, but hardly less revealing of foreign travelers to our continent in prehistory. Standing alone on the side of a boulder-strewn mountain, one of America's most perfect works of ancient rock art faces a broad valley. Just west from the town of Hemet, some 90 miles southeast of the Los Angeles's Ashtart monolith, a massive, gray, egg-shaped stone is emblazoned with the intricate design of a labyrinthine maze enclosed in a 3.5-foot square. Although rarely visited, the large image is surrounded by a metal fence topped with barbed wire in the center of a 5.75-acre public preserve set up more than 40 years ago known as "Maze Stone County Park." Even so, few Americans are aware of its existence.

The anciently illustrated boulder is covered with a light patina referred to by locals as "desert varnish." This results from a process of natural oxidation and may be used for dating the Maze someday, after scientists are able to more precisely evaluate the percentage of change in mineral elements laid down on hard surfaces over time. Desert varnish likewise appears within the carving itself, although to a lesser extent than occurs over the rest of the boulder, which geologists estimate has been exposed in its present location after tumbling down from higher up the mountain about 15,000 years ago.

Comparisons between the two accumulations of patina give a rough date of 3,000 to 4,000 Years Before Present, although conventional archaeologists are known to gag at such figures offered by other sciences over which they have no control. Typical is University of California archaeologist Daniel F. McCarthy, who says it is much younger, although his reasons for contradicting the geological evidence seem unconvincing: "Based on pottery shards, ancient tools and other artifacts found at a prehistoric village site in the immediate area, the Hemet Maze Stone has to be a minimum of five hundred years."[5]

He was unable, however, to demonstrate any connection whatsoever between his pottery shards and the Maze Stone, which was executed with a geometrical precision too sophisticated for the hunter-gatherers of McCarthy's 16th-century villagers, who left no designs of any kind behind at their site. Local Indians appear to be genuinely ignorant of the Stone's origins or significance, and were as surprised as everyone else when it was discovered by Irish homesteaders before World War I.

The Maze is actually a Swastika, a symbol known to numerous Native American tribes across the continent from at least Hopewellian times, beginning around 200 BC, when some of the earliest surviving examples were made of copper. What it meant to these prehistoric peoples has not come down to us, but the modern-day Hopi preserve among their most important oral traditions an account of ancestral origins from a Great Flood that practically annihilated mankind. They believe that relatively few survivors migrated from the eastern location of the Deluge, finally settling in the American southwest.

To the Hopi, this mass-migration of their "grandfathers" is signified by the counter-clockwise hooked cross, signifying the mass-migration of their ancestors from the East. Whether or not it is the same symbolism that motivated the ancient carvers of the Hemet Maze is not known. But whatever it represents, it must have stood for something of real importance to merit such high, artistic efforts, to say nothing of its prominent placement on a mountainside. Clearly, it was originally meant to be seen and appreciated by many people.

California archaeologist William Donato, at the Hemet Maze Stone.

Outstanding art as the Hemet petroglyph may be, it is neither the only nor the largest (though perhaps the most finely executed) of its kind in southern California. There are several other stone mazes in the immediate vicinity. Something similar in nearby Ramona was accidentally found by hikers in 1977 after heavy rains exposed the design. They took it to the San Jacinto town hall, where it was displayed until politicians, ignorant of what else to do with the discovery, presented it to gracious, if perplexed, tribal leaders of the neighboring Soboda Indians, who continue to preserve the maze as the heirloom of a distant past of which they know nothing. So far, about 50 maze-stones have been identified throughout Orange, Riverside, Imperial, and San Diego counties. At least 14 examples of labyrinthine rock art are known in a remote area of Palm Springs. Contributing to their mystery, all of them have been found within 150 miles of each other. And virtually every one is rectangular, although varying in size from 4 inches to several feet in diameter. They are invariably located on mountainsides remarkably alike in their boulder-dotted settings. Here, too, Hopi myth seems to fit the evidence, because the Flood story recounts that, as the waters rose to cover the ancestral island, its residents climbed mountainsides to escape drowning.

The largest and most intricate design occurs 10 miles north of Hemet. As an example of the Dark Age mentality abroad in our land, the magnificent, 4-foot-square relic was partially obliterated by four shotgun blasts in the early 1960s. But enough of it survived to yield faint traces of red, mineral-based paint that originally filled the glyph. Subsequent investigation of other maze carvings showed they likewise bore hints, in varying degrees, of red paint, an important discovery that may assist further in dating their creation, at least relative to each other: the less obvious the presence of red paint, the older the petroglyph. The Hemet Stone evidences no indication of red, so it was either never painted, or it is the oldest maze, its paint having been weathered away over time.

In the Hopi "Crown Dance," the Flood is recounted by a "chief speaker," who begins, "I remember the Old Red Land," the birthplace of his ancestors before it went under the waves. Every Indian tribe recounted its own version of a global inundation and the flight of ancestral survivors from the East, over the Atlantic Ocean. Remarkably, this foundation myth was not imported along with the proselytizing efforts of 16th- through 19th-century Christian missionaries, but predated their arrival by unknown generations. Accordingly, Native American recollection of the cataclysm did not originate in the biblical Genesis, although both share some details.

Interestingly, as the Swastika signified North American Hopi predecessor migration from that catastrophe, the hooked cross was likewise the symbol of pre-Columbian Mexico's Chalchiuhtlicue, the Aztec goddess of the Deluge. Her myth told how she changed its victims into fish, the same transformation recounted by the flood-myths of the Babylonians and American Lakota Sioux. Chalchiuhtlicue, "Our Lady of the Turquoise Skirt," a reference to the sea, was commemorated during an annual ceremony in which priests collected reeds, dried them out, then placed them inside her shrine. As writing utensils, the reeds symbolized wisdom for which her lost, overseas' homeland, "the Place of Reeds," was renowned as Aztlan. Phoenetic and mythic resemblences to the Greek Atlantis are inescapeable. Indeed, temple art represented Chalchiuhtlicue seated on a throne surrounded by men and women drowning in huge whirlpools.

Perhaps California's formerly red mazes were meant to preserve that same tradition as ceremonial markers for ritual pilgrimages in imitation of a great migration from some natural disaster undertaken by its survivors.

CHAPTER 2

Ancient Roman Figurine in
New Jersey Waters
by Wayne May *and*
Roman Coins Found in Kentucky
by Lee Pennington

Discovery in 1990 of a freighter that sank during the early years of Imperial Rome off the Mediterranean coast of south France took archaeologists by surprise. Their hitherto-low opinion of Roman seamanship was overturned by the well-preserved vessel's rugged construction and sophisticated design. With such a ship, sailors of Caesar's time could have successfully completed transatlantic voyages to America. That they actually did so is attested by some of their surviving artifacts found from New Jersey to the Middle West.

Wayne May is the publisher of Ancient American magazine, which he founded in 1993, and author of This Land (Hay House Publishers). He is a professional lecturer, guiding archaeological tours to many of our country's most significant prehistoric locations.

On April 15, 2003, a scuba diver searched the sea floor off New Jersey for shark fossils known to strew the sands near River Redbank. In fact, it had been known earlier as Shark River for an abundance of the animal's remains found in the area, some 10 miles south of Sandy Hook. But what

Check

Nelson Jecas discovered was more than a common fossil. Approximately 15 feet beneath the surface, in limited visibility, the 55-year old Bernardsville resident fetched a small, strange object from the ocean bottom.

town

A Roman figurine found on the shores of New Jersey.

Returning with it to dry land, he saw that the small item was a 4-inch-long figurine weighing about 18 ounces and carved from a reddish stone of some kind. Although severely eroded through apparently long exposure to underwater conditions, the object still clearly represented a woman atop a man engaged in sexual intercourse.

Mr. Jecas took his find for professional appraisal to New York's Arteprimitivo Auction House, where expert examiners specialize in classifying, buying, and selling ancient artifact collections. Divulging nothing about the circumstances concerning its discovery, he showed the figurine to the auction house's gallery curator. Mr. Howard Rose easily identified the Shark River artifact as a common fertility image made in Roman Egypt during the early third century AD. Jecas believes it probably belonged to a Egypto-Roman sailor who reached the New Jersey shore about 1,800 years ago.

The graphic figurine is important, physical evidence for ancient Old World contact in North America supporting related discoveries along the eastern shores of our continent. Away from the location where Jecas made his discovery, a man combing the Massachusetts coast with a metal-detector near Beverly found eight Roman coins within a single square yard of the beach. The relatively well-preserved coins were all minted during the fouth century AD and identified by numismatologists as belonging to the reigns of emperors Constantius II (337–361), Valentinianus I (364–375), Valens (364–378), and Gratianus (367–383).

According to Dr. Barry Fell:

> As there were fifty-eight emperors of Rome, who issued some three thousand kinds of coins commonly found in Europe, the chances of a single find-site yielding coins of consecutive rulers spanning only four decades can be estimated as roughly one in one hundred thousand. Thus the coins are not being found as a result of accidental losses by collectors, but are strongly correlated with some factor linked to a short time-span of 337 to 383 AD, and linked also to a single, very restricted find-site. The only reasonable explanation is that these coins are coming from the money-chest of a merchant-ship carrying current coin in use around 375 AD. Over the past sixteen hundred years, the coins have gradually drifted inshore on the bottom current, and are now being thrown up by waves in heavy weather.[1]

Thanks to Nelson Jecas, an important piece of America's prehistoric puzzle has been fitted into place.

Roman Coins Found in Kentucky
by Lee Pennington

Lee Pennington is a retired college professor from the University of Kentucky and Jefferson Community College in Louisville. He taught creative writing at Murray State University, Ohio University, Marshall University, Morehead State University, Eastern State University, and Ball State University. A playwright in residence at the University of Kentucky in Lexington, Pennington is the author of 19 books, including I Knew a Woman and Thigmotropism, both nominated for the Pulitzer Prize in Poetry, respectively, in 1977 and 1993. He has published hundreds of articles in more than 300 magazines in America and abroad, among them Appalachian Journal, Writer's Digest, The Alaska Review, and Kansas Review. He is also a film maker and the owner of JoLe Productions, which during the past 20 years has produced 21 documentaries, many of them dealing with archaeology.

Lightning has struck once again for a Charlestown, Indiana, man. The chances are rather slim, one might think, of anyone finding a single hoard of Roman coins. The chances of finding two sets might be considered off the charts. Yet, that's exactly what has happened to David Wells, as reported in *Ancient American* magazine in June 2009. Wells, using a metal detector, found eight Roman coins along the Ohio River near Louisville, Kentucky, in the early part of 2009. Wells found a second hoard of coins, containing an additional eleven coins, June 14, 2009, a few miles east from where Wells found the first set.

"My brother, Don, and I," Wells said, "were exploring along the riverbank about a mile beyond Bethlehem (a small Indiana town 31 miles east of Louisville). Don went up the river and I started exploring downstream using my metal detector. Before we went to lunch, I found three coins. After lunch, I decided to go back to the same spot, and found eight more." Wells said the coins were about 4 to 6 inches deep in the sandy soil, located in a serpentine line stretching about 30 feet along the bank parallel with the river. "They looked just like they had been washed up there by a wave or something," he said.[2] An immediate response might be that no one is going to find two hoards of Roman coins, and a report of such a thing is suspicious. Although rare, such a thing does happen. As stated by the British Broadcasting Corporation on October 30, 2008, in *Ancients, Shipwrecks & Treasure,* "a local metal-detector enthusiast in Sully, Vale of Glamorgan, Wales, found not one, but two, very large hoards of Roman coins on successive days. One hoard contained 2,366 coins; the other, 3,547." The BBC also reported that a similar find was uncovered in the same area during 1899.[3]

The Wells' find does not include the first Roman coins found along the Ohio River in the Falls of the Ohio area. During 1963, when the Sherman Minton Bridge was being built across the river between Louisville, Kentucky, and New Albany, Indiana, an engineer digging out a pier for the span found some 20 Roman coins about 3 feet beneath the surface. Two of the coins were given to another engineer, who has since died. The widow of the engineer who received the two coins donated them to the Falls of the Ohio Interpretive Center, where they remain. The engineer who originally found the bridge coins moved out of town, and his whereabouts, as well as the coins he took with him, are unknown. The two Wells' discoveries containing 19 Roman coins (eight in the first hoard, 11 in the second) may be just part of the picture. Another Roman coin was reportedly found about 25 years ago along the river just west of Louisville at Corydon, Indiana. Accordingly, more than 70 Roman coins may have been found in the immediate vicinity.

Many dozens of Roman coins, such as this 2009 Kentucky find, have been found from New England to the Midwest.

Considered by mainstream archaeologists to be the definitive article on pre-Columbian coins found in America is a nearly 30-year-old piece by Jeremiah Epstein, "Pre-Columbian Old World Coins in America: An Examination of Evidence," in the February 1980 issue of *Current Anthropology* magazine. Epstein discussed 40 different coins found in North America between 1533 and 1977, dismissing them all as no evidence of prehistoric contact, instead attributing them to "losses by modern day collectors," or, in some cases, "deliberate fraud."

He writes: "… insofar as the coins are concerned, no case can be made for pre-Columbian contact between America and the Mediterranean."[4] Epstein points out that of his list of 40 coin finds, 31 of them were made during the 20th century—25 following World War II. He suggests the imbalance of coin finds up to the 20th century and those found afterward, especially following the war, resulted from Americans traveling to Europe and purchasing the coins. "This coincides," he stated, "with the time when Americans, whether as inductees or as tourists, traveled to Europe in great numbers, and it seems reasonable to suppose that most of the coins found since 1914 had been lost by Americans who brought them back from Europe."[5]

But it is just as reasonable to suppose the increase in coin finds is the direct result of the invention of the metal detector. Gerhard Fisher applied for, and was granted, the first patent for such a device in 1937. Since then, literally millions of enthusiasts are out using metal detectors daily, and one would expect the discovery of lost coins to increase exponentially, just as is the case. Interestingly, of the 40 coins Epstein describes, 32 of them are Roman. The other eight are identified as Phoenician, Greek, and Hebrew. Another interesting thing that Epstein's article shows is that exactly half of the 40 coins under discussion were minted during the second and third centuries AD.

Likewise, the majority of coins in the two David Wells collections fall into this time period. The same date parameters bracket the 10 coins in the Kingman collection found along the Wisconsin River during the 1970s, as reported by Professor James P. Scherz.[6] The same holds true for 12 coins found by Michael Wayne Griffith in a cave shelter at Breathitt County, Kentucky.[7] Many of the Roman coins found in the United States are easily identifiable regarding the century of their manufacture by their depiction of a solar crown, called a "radiate." Radiate coins were only minted between 215 and 295 AD.

A strong supporter of Epstein's conclusions is Professor Miguel Rivera Dorado, Departamento de Antropologia de America, Universidad Complutense, Ciudad Universitaria, in Madrid, Spain. Commenting on Epstein's conclusion that none of the pre-Columbian coins found in America are legitimate, Rivera says, "…a relatively great number of ancient coins have been found, while, in contrast, there is a lack of amphorae, votive offerings, candlesticks, swords, and belt buckles. None of these latter articles can be easily acquired on a tourist trip, there are few collectors of them, and they do not get lost easily because of their form and volume."[8]

Dorado's mention of "Roman swords," however, may be premature. In 1999, Buddy Lemon of Reidland, Kentucky (near Paducah), dug up a sword afterward positively identified as a second-century Roman artifact. Lemon found the weapon using his metal detector along a bank near the mouth of the Tennessee River, which empties into the Ohio River. Members of the Ancient Kentucky Historical Association (Louisville) interviewed Lemon and photographed his find. "I was just below Kentucky Dam," he told them, "when my metal-detector went off. I started digging with a shovel, and found it about two feet down."[9]

Discovered in Kentucky, this "radiate" form of ancient coin portrays a Roman emperor.

The late Michael Paul Henson reported for *Lost Treasure* magazine in 1993 that Lemon's discovery was identical to a specimen picked up earlier near Cincinnati, likewise along the Ohio River.[10] Two more Roman swords have been retrieved from the Mississippi River at St. Paul, Minnesota, and 532 miles down its banks southward to St. Louis, Missouri, with yet another example found near Nashville, Tennessee, on the Cumberland, which empties into the Ohio River. Described by Henson as "an intricately engraved Roman sword of about 100 AD."[11]—the same period he escribed to the weapon found by Lemon—the St. Paul blade particularly underscores the Fred Kingman coin collection's prehistoric authenticity, because both discoveries occurred in general proximity to each other.

The Cincinnati, St. Louis, and Nashville swords were recovered from 4 feet beneath the surface of the ground, suggesting they were all buried at the same time, and could not, therefore, have been accidentally deposited in modern times somehow or hoaxed. Ancient visitors traveling up the Mississippi River would likely explore other major connecting waterways in touch with the Ohio and Wisconsin rivers off the Mississippi, Cumberland, and Tennessee rivers—all places where Roman coins or Roman swords have been discovered. Epstein apparently was not aware of the Sherman Minton Bridge coins (1963), nor the Fred Kingman coins of the1970s. Although found previous to Epstein's article, these coins evidently were not reported in the literature until after the publication of his article in 1980. Despite the great number of Roman coins found in North

America, many more, perhaps most, never even get reported. As the late Norman Totten, professor of history at Bentley College and an authority on pre-Columbian coins, pointed out in commenting on Epstein's report, "...clearer distinctions need to be made between finds and published reports of finds...most coins, wherever found, are never officially reported, much less published. The same is true of other kinds of ancient artifacts discovered outside archaeological excavations."[12]

A revealing picture emerges when all the locations of Roman coins reportedly found in our country are plotted on a map of North America. It shows that virtually all of them were discovered at or near waterways, mostly along the Mississippi and Ohio rivers, together with their watersheds. Six related finds took place on the eastern seaboard: in 1950 on Plum Island, Massachusetts; circa 1965 at Long Island Sound, Connecticut; around 1970 at Princeton, New Jersey; about 1960 in Queen Anne's County, Maryland; 1956 in Gloucester County, Virginia; and circa 1970 on St. Simons Island, Georgia. Two other Roman coins were found in the Gulf of Mexico area: around 1970 at Baton Rouge, Louisiana, and about 1970 on St. Joseph Island, Texas. No such coins are reported to have been found west of the Rocky Mountains. That fact alone weakens Epstein's argument assigning the lost coins to careless collectors. These enthusiasts reside, in fact, on both sides of the Continental Divide.

Individually, the ancient coins found in North America may be little more than anomalous curiosities. But when seen in the aggregate, they form a recognizable pattern left by visitors from Imperial Rome in those areas of our continent where they passed into prehistory.

CHAPTER 3

Tennessee's Ancient Hebrew Inscription
by Scott Wolter

Since its discovery by Smithsonian Institution archaeologists more than 100 years ago, the Bat Creek Stone has been the subject of heated debate. Although it is officially condemned as a transparent hoax by Establishment scholars, independent investigators wonder if it might constitute wrongfully neglected evidence of first-century AD Jews in North America. The argument was finally settled by scientific testing published for the first time in Ancient American's September 10s issue (volume 14, Number 88. Author Scott Wolter, who performed the Bat Creek Stone examination, is a university-trained geologist and president of American Petrographic Services (St. Paul, Minnesota) for the analysis of construction materials, cited for professional excellence by the American Association for Laboratory Accreditation.

This report presents the results of a microscopic examination of the physical and geological features of an archaeological artifact called the Bat Creek Stone that American Petrographic Services Inc. performed at the McClung Museum on the campus of the University of Tennessee, in Knoxville, on May 28, 2010 and June 29, 2010. The scope of our work was limited to:

1. Performing petrographic observations using reflected light microscopy and microphoto documentation on the artifact.

2. Performing Scanning Electron Microscopy (SEM) analysis.

3. Conducting a document review of the Smithsonian Institute field reports written by John W. Emmert, who discovered the artifact on February 14, 1889.

American Petrographic Services, Inc. transported its microscopic equipment to the museum, where staff members, registrar Bob Pennington, and museum director Jefferson Chapman, graciously provided access to their facilities and the artifact. Present during the examination were Dr. Barbara Duncan, education director at the Museum of the Cherokee Indian; Sharon Littlejohn, Eastern Band of Cherokee Indian; and Leslie Kalen, Eastern Band of Cherokee Indian.

The Bat Creek Stone.

On June 29, 2010, American Petrographic Services, Inc. returned to the Science and Engineering Research Facility at the University of Tennessee to complete the examination of the artifact using the Scanning Electron Microscopy equipment on campus.

The Bat Creek Stone was discovered by John W. Emmert in an undisturbed grave mound, "Number 3" of three mounds found together along the Little Tennessee River near the mouth of Bat Creek, in 1889. Emmert was working on behalf of the Smithsonian Institution's Bureau of Ethnology's Mound Survey Project and reported to his immediate supervisor, Cyrus Thomas, a U.S. ethnologist and entomologist prominent during the late 19th century for his studies of the natural history of the American West. Thomas originally identified the Bat Creek inscription as "Paleo-Cherokee."

In 1964, it was brought to the attention of a Chicago patent attorney, Henriette Mertz, who discovered that a photograph of the object had been erroneously published upside down by Washington, D.C.'s Smithsonian Institution, the nation's foremost repository for anthropological and archaeological materials. She additionally suspected that the characters inscribed on the object were not "Paleo-Cherokee," but Phoenician.[1]

In 1971, the inscription was described as "Paleo-Hebrew Judean" from the Roman Era by Dr. Cyrus Gordon (1908–2001), an American scholar of Near Eastern cultures and ancient languages.

Much has been made by previous investigators of earlier correspondence between Emmert and Thomas relevant to the former's supposed struggles with alcoholism and suspicions that he forged the inscription to curry favor with Thomas. Because we have discovered no direct evidence to support these allegations, which casts doubt on the veracity of the discovery, we dismiss them as unfounded. On the contrary, Emmert's fieldwork and documentation appear to be more than competent by the standards of his time, and should be allowed to stand on their own merit.

Typical of many mainstream archaeologists' discussion of other controversial artifacts, they cite speculation and opinion in place of factual evidence to "prove" the artifact fraudulent. Here are just a few examples of their arguments:

1. The authors begin by labeling those who take seriously the idea of pre-Columbian contact with the Old World as "cult archaeologists."[2] This term promotes a negative connotation to the subject matter at the outset. At the same time, name-calling strategies undermine objectivity and credibility.

2. They also undermine their own argument by attempting to associate the Bat Creek inscription with other allegedly fraudulent artifacts, such as the Kensington Rune Stone. I have extensive experience investigating the Minnesota object, which has now been found to be a genuine, medieval artifact.

3. The crux of their argument was to accuse John Emmert of faking the inscription to curry favor with his supervisor, Cyrus Thomas. What is also disturbing and unethical, in this case, is that Emmert's credibility was never questioned until the 1970s, when it was first realized that the inscription was in fact Paleo-Hebrew.

More recent arguments by archaeologists Mainfort and Kwas, who initially argued the inscription was not Hebrew, eventually conceded in

2004 that the inscription was in fact Hebrew after all, but insisted that Freemasons must have been responsible for making the inscription. Another recently proposed theory is that the mound was intruded by the Cherokee during the 18th century.

The Bat Creek Stone was examined on May 28, 2010, using an Olympus SZX12 Zoom microscope with a Spot digital camera system transported to the McClung Museum on the University of Tennessee campus. The artifact was again examined on the University of Tennessee campus with a Scanning Electron Microscope on June 29, 2010. I took photographs of the object during the examinations of May 28, 2010 and June 29, 2010. They revealed that the inscribed side of the Bat Creek Stone with nearly all of the dark brown-colored, approximately 1- to 2-millimeters-thick iron-oxide-rich weathering rind was intact.

Areas along the top edge and in the lower right corner have spalled off, exposing the light brown-colored, un-weathered, iron-cemented, clayey siltstone. In the upper left area are two roughly parallel, approximately 1-centimeter-long, vertical lines scratched into the stone sometime between 1894 (Cyrus Thomas) and 1970 (Cyrus Gordon).

The backside of the Bat Creek Stone has the original Smithsonian identification names and numbers. Virtually all but a few remnants along the top and bottom edges, and the small arrowhead-shaped portion on the lower right side of the approximately 1- to 2-millimeters-thick iron oxide-rich weathering rind has peeled off, exposing the light brown-colored, unweathered, iron-cemented, clayey siltstone.

The scratch made by Emmert with the metal prod at the time of the excavation is on the far right. An approximately 27-millimeter-long scratch is present on the far middle-right end of the backside of the stone. The long, thinning scratch has relatively sharp and jagged edges, and appears to be consistent with contact with a sharp prod, as reported by John Emmert at the time of discovery. The brittle nature of the deposits within the groove comprised of greater than 50 percent clay minerals, with the remaining silica material comprised of quartz (SiO^2).

The following points are factual observations made upon completion of our geological microscopic examination of the Bat Creek Stone artifact, plus a detailed review of the historical letters by John W. Emmert:

1. The Bat Creek inscription was carved into what appears to be a dark brown to light tan-colored, iron-oxide-rich, clayey, siltstone concretion.

2. The relatively shallow (2 to 3 millimeters average depth) and rounded shape of the grooves suggests the characters were carved with a tool that had a somewhat rounded tip.

3. The iron-oxide-rich, clayey siltstone concretion has a dark brown weathering rind that is approximately 1 to 2 millimeters thick.

4. Nearly the entire dark brown, weathered rind layer has peeled off the backside of the artifact, revealing the light brown-colored, clayey siltstone interior.

5. The entire surface of the inscription of the stone was lightly polished, the action of which rounded the edges of the carved grooves of the inscribed characters. This is consistent with the following comment in John Emmert's letter to Cyrus Thomas in his February 15, 1889 letter, "In the one with nine in it, found a large pair of copper bracelets and a polished stone with letters or characters cut on it unlike anything I have ever seen before."[3]

6. The two roughly parallel scratches that were made sometime after 1891 and before January 1971 have sharp and jagged edges.

7. The two roughly parallel scratches have an orange-colored, silty clay at the bottom of the grooves produced by a tool that cut through and crushed the iron-oxide-rich rind.

8. In his February 25, 1889 letter to Cyrus Thomas, John Emmert included a sketch of the inscribed stone that did not include the two roughly parallel scratches on the inscription side.

9. The two roughly parallel scratches are not present in the 1891 photograph, but are present on the stone in 1971.

10. In his March 7, 1889 letter to Cyrus Thomas, John Emmert wrote, "That any one could have ever worked this mound without leaving some evidence of it, I think it impossible."[4]

11. In his March 7, 1889 letter to Cyrus Thomas, John Emmert also wrote, "The engraved stone was lying just under the back of the skull. I punched it on the rough side with my steel rod in probing before I came to the skeletons. The other side of the stone is exactly as it was taken from the skeleton at the bottom of the mound, about five feet deep."[5]

Our interpretations are as follows:

1. The scratch on the backside of the stone has sharp and jagged edges consistent with an unweathered and unpolished, freshly made surface defect.

2. The presence of the fresh scratch made with a metal prod at the time of discovery on the backside of the artifact indicates that the stone was placed "immediately under the skull and jaw bones of skeleton no. 1..." at the time of burial with the inscription side down.[6]

3. The two roughly parallel, non-weathered and unpolished scratches on the inscribed side of the stone were made sometime between 1891 and 1971, apparently while in the custody of the Smithsonian Institution.

4. Because the profile of the grooves of the original inscription are rounded as opposed to the grooves of the two scratches, which are "V"-shaped, this would be consistent with the scratches being made with a sharper, more pointed tool.

5. Based on a visual review of the images and the physical properties of the material, it is estimated that the deposits within the groove carved into the dark brown, iron-oxide-rich weathered rind layer are comprised of greater than 50 percent clay minerals with the remaining silt-sized material comprised of quartz (SiO_2).

6. Because we did not observe any of the orange-colored silty-clay in the grooves of the inscription, and the overall surface of the stone and the edges of the grooves were polished at the time of discovery, the inscription had to have been made prior to the excavation of the mound by John Emmert.

7. Based upon the results of our investigation, the following sequence of events occurred:

   a. The at-least nine-character inscription was carved into the dark brown, iron-rich siltstone concretion on the side with the weathered rind intact.

   b. The entire inscription side was polished, smoothing out the dark brown surface and rounding the sharp edges of the grooves of the carved characters.

   c.   The inscribed stone was placed behind the skull of the deceased (identified as skeleton No. 1 in Mound No. 3) at the time of burial with the inscription side down.

   d.   The backside of the inscribed stone was hit and scratched by the metal prod used by John Emmert at the time of excavation of the mound.

   e.   The two vertical scratches on the inscribed side of the Stone were made after 1891 and before January 1971.

Based on our review of the historical correspondence and the reflected light and scanning electron microscopic examinations of the artifact on May 28, 2010, the following conclusions are appropriate:

1.   Our geological findings are consistent with the Smithsonian Institution's field report written by John W. Emmert.

2.   The complete lack of the orange-colored, silty-clay residue in any of the characters of the inscription is consistent with many hundreds of years of weathering in a wet earth mound comprised of soil and "hard red clay."

3.   The inscribed stone and all the other artifacts and remains found in the mound with it can be no younger than when the bodies of the deceased were buried inside the mound.

These observations validate the artifact's ancient authenticity, and tend to support Professor Gordon's conclusions, published 40 years ago. He translated the inscription, "for Judah," and dated it from 70 to 135 AD, based on its distinctive letterform. Eastern Tennessee's Bat Creek Stone, Gordon stated, "is not only the oldest text ever discovered in North America, but—more importantly—it is the first time a Mediterranean inscription has been found anywhere in the Western Hemisphere in its original site with all the original objects connected with it in place."[7]

CHAPTER 4

A Fox's Tale of Ancient Romans in Peru
by Frank Joseph

Ancient Rome's impact on the New World went far beyond North America, as attested by a humble, obscure artifact at the Saint Louis Museum of Art, Missouri. Under the light of comparative symbolism, its missed significance stands out in bold relief.

The following article originally appeared in Atlantis Rising magazine (Number 79, January/February 2010; www.atlantisrising.com) and is reproduced here with permission of its publisher, J. Douglas Kenyon.

Although mainstream archaeologists dismiss any suggestion of overseas' visitors to America from the Old World before Christopher Columbus, they were hard put to explain away the discovery this year alone of no less than 19 ancient Roman coins at two separate locations in Kentucky. Almost immediately after the first modern Europeans arrived on the shores of our continent, they began picking up such anomalous loose change from newly ploughed farmers' fields or near river banks.

According to U.S. archaeologist Gunnar Thompson, PhD:

Two Roman coins were found near Fayetteville, Tennessee, in 1819. One was of Antonius Pius (138 to 161 AD.); the other was of Emperor Commodus (180 to 192 AD). They were discovered several feet deep beneath trees thought to be several hundred years old. Archaeologists found a 4th Century Roman coin in a burial mound at Round Rock, Texas. Beach-combers near Beverly, Massachusetts have collected numerous coins embossed with faces of Roman emperors between 337 AD and 383 AD.... Other coins dating between 50 BC and 750 AD have been found in North Carolina, Ohio, Georgia, and Oklahoma.[1]

But proof other than than coins tell of Imperial Rome's impact on pre-Columbian America. For more than 100 years after the Spaniards arrived in Chile, during the early 16th century, rumours abounded of El Ciudad de los Césares. This "City of the Caesars" was also referred to as the "City of Patagonia," allegedly founded by ancient Roman sailors fleeing civil unrest after Julius Caesar's assassination, and later shipwrecked at the Straits of Magellan.

The lost city was supposed to have been awash in gold, silver, and diamonds donated by grateful Indians for Roman expertise in building the Inca ancestors' extensive network of roads. Supporting this legend, an Inca aqueduct at Rodadero, Peru does indeed employ "two tiers of rounded, stone arches often referred to as 'true arches'," according to Dr. Thompson: "This style of architecture was a characteristic of the ancient Mediterranean. Consequently, the Rodadero aqueduct makes a strong argument for Greco-Roman cultural diffusion."[2]

Although El Ciudad de los Césares was never found, it may neverthe-less have paralleled other discoveries of an ancient Roman presence on America's eastern shores, such as a shipwreck investigated by underwa-ter archaeologist Robert Marx, off Rio de Janeiro, in 1976. Amphorae he retrieved from the vessel were scientifically analyzed by Elizabeth Will, a professor in Classical Greek history at the University of Massachusetts. She positively identified them as part of a cargo that left the North African port of Zilis around 250 AD. Marx went on to find a bronze fibula—a gar-ment clasp—in Brazil's Guanabarra Bay.[3]

Further north, near the Mexican Gulf Coast, bricks that went into build-ing the Maya city of Comalcalco were stamped with second-century Roman mason marks, and its terracotta plumbing—unique in all Mesoamerica—was identical to contemporary pipes found in Roman-occupied Israel. These and similar finds—such as the ceramic representation of a bearded European with Roman-style haircut and wearing a typically Roman cap retrieved during the excavation of a second-century pyramid at Caliztlahuaca, Mexico—suggest that accounts of the "City of the Caesars" may have had some factual basis in pre-Columbian contacts.

Marx's discoveries were so persuasive, even a few orthodox archaeolo-gists begrudgingly conceded that his undersea evidence did indeed prove that sailors from Imperial Rome achieved at least one trans-Atlantic crossing to Brazil. These conventional scholars were quick to add though, that the mid-third-century mariners must have been merely a few castaways, without any influence on South American prehistory, and could not have represented any important connection with the Roman world.

Contradicting this mainstream supposition is a humble artifact gathering more dust than attention throughout the decades it has been on public display at Missouri's Saint Louis Museum of Art. It was featured in the 2007 issue of *The Midwestern Epigraphic Journal*, when Dr. John White wrote that "The Pig-Soldier Figurine From Moche Appears To Be A Fox After All."[4] Dr. White's "Figurine" refers to the effigy of a were-fox, its head strapped with a conical helmet, and human hands folded above a disk. A red band running around the shield-like disk is punctuated by 15 evenly spaced, cream-colored dots, and surrounds a central, red hooked cross on cream-colored background. These elements are part of a 29-centimeter-high jar with curving, semi-circular, hollow handle at the back; a tube is connected to and protrudes at an angle from the curved

Peruvian effigy bottle with Greco-Roman symbolism of the lunar goddess.

handle, allowing someone to drink or inhale the bottle's contents.

The artifact's display card reads, "Fox-and-Shield Effigy Bottle, Peru, North Coast, Mochica IV culture, Early Intermediate Period, AD 200–500, red and cream painted earthware. On this stirrup-spout vessel we find an anthropomorphic fox at the top of a large, round, painted shield on the front. The fox wears a conical helmet with chinstrap. The shield has a handle that encircles the conically shaped vessel. Painted zones on the back are separated by grooved incising."

This droll description can be counted upon to ignite something less than passionate interest in visitors to the American Archaeology Gallery, where the object is displayed. They are not informed that it is something more than a mildly curious artifact from some unfamiliar culture predating the rise of the Inca Empire by 13 centuries. Instead, it is overlooked, physical evidence for the arrival of Indo-European voyagers in South America from the ancient Old World more than 1,000 years before Christopher Columbus landed on the beach at Hispaniola.

The were-fox jar was made by the Mochica, usually referred to as the Moche, a seafaring people, who inhabited the northern coastal plain of Peru. Around 100 AD, they established a thriving trading network that eventually grew into a powerful civilization, thanks in large measure to their fleets of far-ranging balsa-wood rafts and boats. Though none of these craft survive, they are commonly depicted on contemporaneous pottery. The Moche were also skilled goldsmiths, and created a broad variety of effigy ware, portraying everything from gods and demons engaged in war, labor, sexual activity, sailing, drunkenness, and human sacrifice.

Water management experts on a grand scale, they made the Peruvian Desert bloom with their vast irrigation networks. The centerpiece of their capital city was the Huaca del Sol, the Pyramid of the Sun, composed of more than 130 million adobe bricks to form the largest pre-Columbian structure of its kind built in all the Americas. It originally towered 150 feet over Rio Moche, where it served as a temple for ritual dramas and an imperial residence containing royal burial chambers filled with gold treasures. These were flushed out by 17th-century Spaniards, who diverted the river into the pyramid.

Interestingly, the Saint Louis Museum's were-fox jar has been dated to the Early Intermediate Period, a time of great outward expansion for the Moche. They were also receptive to outside influences, resulting in a Middle Period (300 to 600 AD) of cultural floresence. It was not to endure, however, and succumbed largely to the effects of a super El Niño. Thirty years of intense rain and flooding were followed by another three decades of drought. Before this calamitous series of events from which the Moche were unable to recover, an Early Intermediate Period of broadening interaction with the outside world saw the creation of their were-fox jar. According to *The Complete Museum of Pre-Columbian Gold* Website, "The Moche considered the fox a lunar symbol because of its nocturnal habits."[5]

At the Pyramid of the Sun's smaller, better preserved companion, the Huaca de la Luna, the Pyramid of the Moon, archaeologists found a ceremonial mask of copper-gold alloy configured to mimic a fox head decorated with lunar symbols. This mask was worn by a priest or shaman who personally strove to merge with the animal's identity or soul, thereby taking on its powers. These included healing and a wide range of psychic abilities—particularly prophesy and clairvoyance—connected with lunar energy.

On page 65 of his authoritative book about Andean Civilization, *Pre-Inca Art and Culture*, Swiss professor Hermann Leicht (University of Zurich) reproduced a northern coastal Peruvian vase illustration depicting the moon-divinity sitting in a litter carried by two men wearing fox masks and tails. These were were-foxes, priests in service to the lunar deity, whose avatar on Earth, the Moche believed, was the fox. "Why should they not look upon him then as a servant of the moon," Leicht asked, "since they saw often enough how the beast held conversations with it in long-drawn-out howls?"[6]

We know neither the name of the Moche lunar deity, nor the substance of its worship. But during this same period, on the other side of the world, the moon goddess was worshipped in Rome as Diana, divine mistress of the hunt, who simultaneously protected wild animals, an apparent contradiction made clear in her precept: Humans must kill game to feed themselves, but in moderation. Diana was synonymous with the Greek Artemis, Olympian patroness of women in labor and of children. In Greco-Roman art, both versions were typically portrayed in the company of a fox, usually following the goddess, thereby signifying her "followers" (priests, priestesses, and/or initiates of her lunar cult). But this animal is not the only cogent connection between the ancient Old World and pre-Inca South America.

Artemis-Diana's brother was Phoebus-Apollo, the sun-god, whose own symbol was a leftward-oriented hooked cross, the Swastika. The name is Sanskrit for "good luck sign," and emblematic of all solar deities—invariably male—known to every Indo-Aryan people, of which the Romans were one. Its inverse—the rightward-oriented sauvastika—was likewise associated with the sun-god's twin sister, the moon-goddess. Classical Era vase paintings and statues of Artemis and Diana were typically adorned with the sauvastika. Appearance of this symbol on a Moche effigy jar depicting the same animal identified with an ancient European moon-goddess is underscored by the 15 dots going around the hooked cross; they correspond to half the number of nights in a lunar month.

Moreover, the vessel's manufacture during the Early Intermediate Period occurred between 200 AD and 500 AD, as Roman imperialism expanded to its greatest extent, and just when the majority of Roman coins found in North America were minted. The Romans excelled in road-building, irrigation, and military science, civilized virtues that likewise chiefly characterized the Moche.

This is not to argue that they were themselves ancient Romans. They were more probably a native South American people whose developing society was fundamentally influenced by visitors from the Mediterranean World, whether as shipwrecked castaways or members of expeditions under orders from their Emperor to bring back something of value from Cattigara, the Roman name for South America, according to Dr. Thompson, Argentine anthropologist Dick Iberra-Grasso, and other independent scholars.[7]

Powerful foreigners impacted not only Moche material culture, but made a lasting impression on Andean metaphysics, as evidenced by the were-fox effigy jar. It was almost certainly the original possession of a priest to the moon-goddess, and may have been used as a container for some hallucinogenic potion or drug that enabled him to enter an altered state of consciousness in the performance of his ritual duties. In any case, the Saint Louis Museum's little artifact comprises a kind of physical proof for the arrival in ancient Peru of Roman culture-bearers, who left their identifiable, enduring mark on early South American civilization.

CHAPTER 5

A Controversial Symbol's Original Meaning
by Dr. John J. White, III

Dr. John J. White, III, is the editor emeritus of the Midwestern Epigraphic Sciety's quarterly journal, with wich he was associated for 20 years. He is an experimental physicist and retired principal research scientist from Battelle Memorial Institute, in Columbus, Ohio. Here, to complement its discussion in our first and previous chapters, he offers special insight into mankind's oldest symbol, found on either side of the Atlantic Ocean in prehistory.

The famous Swastika occurs often in ancient art, but its meaning is elusive. Ice Age archaeological evidence demonstrates, however, that the ancient hooked cross was a double-symbol of the Earth Mother Goddess, indicated by the equal-arm cross, and the Earth Father God, indicated by the attachment of a coiled, serpentine figure to the tip of each cross arm. These are symbols of the gods of the ancient fertility religion known at Earth Mother Culture (EMC). Most of the ancient Swastikas encountered are in abbreviated form that obscures their original meaning. Other examples of the EMC double-symbol usage are mentioned below.

Our purpose here is to establish a very basic observation about the use of symbols in ancient art. The notion offered is that many of our ancestors had a simple, fertility-based religion revealed, in part, by the repeated use of simple signs that we can now believe had relatively fixed meanings. The general pervasiveness of this Earth Mother Culture led eventually to a method of sacred name construction called Earth Mother Sacred Language. All of this took place long before the development of writing, at which time knowledge of the old Earth Mother Culture was retained only in fragments and selected traditions. It is through the preponderance of symbols and words occurring in an acceptable or reasonable cultural context that this firm summary can be made.

Viking Swastika fibula *(a brooch or clasp) from Oseburg, Norway, mid-10th century* AD.

Our approach does not refute the data of thousands of man-years of modern archaeology, but it does state that a simpler, sharper, more focused, more logical method of cultural interpretation has been found. We claim that such is a dominant description of man's spiritual culture down through most of the Bronze Age and some of the Iron and Medieval Ages. The Swastika is the subject of many speculations. We should not be overly distracted by corruptions of interpretation or pronunciation that occur in later times when the original cultural context of a subject idea has become vague at best. And in the case of simple symbols, we cannot allow ourselves to be paralyzed if we locate the use of a favorite symbol for another cultural purpose altogether, such as the hexagram, which was adapted by the Hebrew culture long after its earlier use as a fertility symbol of Earth Mother Culture.

The oldest example of a Swastika as symbol apppears in Joseph Campbell's *Flight of the Wild Gander*.[1] Campbell was a remarkable social-science scholar—in many ways, the best encountered to date. He dominated the Establishment in his role as the grand spokesman for the elucidation of the role of mythology in the history of man. He apparently thought that the scientific and organizational approaches to the study of man, as fumbled around by his history-oriented contemporaries, failed to appreciate the benefits of art insights and the simplified elements of normal psychology. Thus, we were treated to a comprehensive synthesis of the experience of man's pursuit of religious insight and inspiration, a la C.G. Jung, using the historical data to illustrate points of passing interest, but suggesting that the picture is too haphazard to be comprehended in organized societal and historical terms.

For example, a sampling of art of from the Ice Age site at Mezin in the Ukraine may be found approximately 60 miles northeast of Kiev. Its artifacts comprise bird figurines carved from mammoth ivory with inscribed patterns that included elaborate Swastikas, around 10,000 BC. These items are sacred images of the Earth Mother, represented as the Bird Mother, inscribed with symbols indicating her Earth Father consort, the Serpent. This is the essence of the paleolithic Earth Mother Cult, when it was principally a fertility cult. In 1939, Viennese paleo-anthropologist Franz Hancâr compiled a survey of the various paleolithic "Venus" statues that had been discovered.[2]

He included the Mezin bird figurines, but did not make a firm claim for the existence of EMC. The hooked-cross patterns were first recognized by the Russian linguist, V.A. Gorodcov, but it was Hancâr who called them the oldest Swastikas found thus far.[3] Campbell quotes the conservative circa 10,000 BC date for Mezin. The actual layer for the artifacts could be as old as 17,000 BC. The original Swastika was an elaborate form with spiral arms, whereas the more modern symbol is like the gammadion (geometrical) form with short arms. A gammadion is a hooked cross, each arm of which resembles the Greek letter Γ, *gamma*. Truncation to the gammadion form does not change the meaning of this symbol in connection with the Earth Mother or Goddess culture.

The crux of the matter is this: The Swastika is a double-symbol for a fertility religion having two gods, the Earth Mother and the Earth Father. The ancient Swastika was an equal-arm cross with a serpent symbol spiral attached to the tip of each arm. Sacred bird images from ancient Australia and Shang China are inscribed with inscribed snakes. Serious confirmation, indeed! The frequently used *yin/yang* symbol refers to the Swastika gods. The so-called "circle-cross" is a double-symbol alternative to the Swastika.

Mississippian Culture Swastika shell engraving from Spiro Mounds, Oklahoma, mid-10th century AD. Also in Oklahoma are the Poteau Stone and Heavener Rune Stone: Norse inscriptions dated to the same period, just 12 and 25 miles due south, respectively, from Spiro Mounds.

We interpret the circle to be the serpent in the ouroborus configuration (completing a circle when the snake bites the tip of its own tail), implying the protective aspect of the Male Principle. Finally, the hexagram is an ancient symbol of sexual union of the gods, the downward-pointed triangle being the female and the upward-pointed triangle being the male. Most of the ancient connections are quite simple. The Sun was the Son of the Earth Gods in many cultures. That is why Sun and Son have the same sound in our English language! Referring to the old hexagram symbol, so, too, "sex" and "six" have the same sound in many languages (for example, German and Latin).

The word *Swastika* could have great significance, and yet be called by some abstract name with an obscure meaning. An example is the Indo-European word raga, which means "king" or "high person," but is made up of two sounds that give no hint of the correct meaning. Fortunately that is not the case for the very old word *Swastika*. There are three spellings and two pronunciations of our special word. They are "Swastika" and "suastika," pronounced with a w-sound, and "svastika" pronounced with a v-sound. The Indo-Germanic word is pronounced with the v-sound, which is the usual EMSL-sound, with V = B = F = P generally assumed. Asian and Native American languages prefer the w-sound, but with the old v-meaning.

English/Welsh-language speakers pronounce the Germanic w with the w-sound, instead of the v-sound. They have many other w-sounds that are non-Germanic in origin. The point of this discussion is to understand that *svastika* is a double-name EMSL word, naming both male and female gods. Thus, we view the word *svastika* as "S(a)va-stika" with the EMSL translation: the-father (and) the earth. Isn't this exactly what the previous discussion of the double-symbol meaning of the "svastika" claimed? Could it be some outrageous, linguistic accident?

Thousands of 6th-Century Tablets in Michigan?
by David Allen Deal

*T*he Michigan Tablets have never left center stage in a controversy surrounding their authenticity since the first of their prodigious numbers surfaced in the 1840s. Since then, their custodianship fell into the hands of their leading detractor, John R. Halsey, PhD, a Michigan State archaeologist.

In his February 2004 Ancient American article ("Michigan's 'Relics' Come Home"; Volume 9, Number 55), he stated, in part, that the disputable artifacts "are all demonstrably modern fakes.... What Harvard archaeologist, Stephen Williams, has pronounced as 'one of the longest-running scams in prehistory' is still alive today, more than a century after its beginning, unfortunate proof that some people will always believe what they want to believe, no matter how preposterous the circumstances may be." In mid-November 2003, Dr. Halsey put the Michigan Tablets on public display at the Michigan Historical Center (Lansing), where he was its director, "explaining yet again to an innocernt public why they are not what they seem."

David Allen Deal's article was a response to Dr. Halsey's statements. Until his death in 2008, Deal was especially qualified to examine a particular example of what seemed to be an astronomical device of some kind, because he had already determined that an ancient carving in Colorado signified a Saturn-Jupiter conjunction on August 8, 471 AD, as published in Celtic America (Appendix A, page 268). Another book, In Plain Sight, described his interpretation of an Arkansas petroglyph that again defined a conjunction of Jupiter with Saturn, this time adjacent to the star Wasat in the constellation of Gemini, as it appeared on March 30, 710 AD. Deal was a practicing professional artist and designer, which, he said of himself, did "nothing to detract from my ability to interpret design and intent."

The so-called "Soper-Savage Collection" has been put into the hands of John R. Halsey, a highly placed archaeologist for Michigan and curator of this newly returned, but much maligned and grossly misunderstood artifact corpus. It is publicly displayed at a state institution, the Michigan Historical Center, where Mr. Halsey has written a document that conforms perfectly and quite nicely to the long-standing dogma of John Wesley Powell. Powell was the formidable and dictatorial director of the Smithsonian Institution's Bureau of Ethnology, who, in the century before last, set down a dictum that has ruled the academic roost in American anthropology; that is, for more than 100 years. Ever since, no American antiquarian, archaeologist, or anthropologist worth his academic salt ever wavers from Major Powell's hard-core line. In Dr. Halsey's case, the pattern is predictably familiar. He toes the mark precisely.

As positive proof that Dr. Halsey's opinions are simply those of other higher-ups, he has provided a large portion of the standard set of well-known and much disparaged, valid, ancient American artifacts, among them, the Kensington Rune Stone, which has now been supported, contrary to his assertions, by state-of-the-art geological testing.[1] Mr. Halsey is apparently not aware of this new information. To his mind, it is a fake. Neither is it probable that he can actually read runic Norse futhark letters to scientifically demonstrate his conclusion, least of all invalidate laboratory tests confirming the rune stone's 15th-century provenance. Mr. Halsey's "other well known archaeological 'hoaxes,' such as the Newark Holy Stones, the Davenport Tablets, and the Cardiff Giant," are among the most hated relics by Establishment academics in America, proponents of the Powell doctrine.

After lumping the entire Soper-Savage Collection together with these allegedly fraudulent examples, Mr. Halsey goes on to inform us that the "pseudo-cuneiform monogram," which is found on nearly every item in the entire corpus of thousands of Michigan artifacts, represents "IHP," being somehow related to the "HIS" of Roman Christianity. Precisely how, or by what linguistic knowledge, logic, or expertise he employs to conclude this claim, we are left in a state of total darkness. The great, mid-20th-century cryptanalyst Henriette Mertz also made a similar error, but admitted that she might be wrong about it. She did recognize the Coptic nature of the religion, however, which is something more than Mr. Halsey has been able to muster.[2]

He has given nothing more than his opinion. Please remember he is a state archaeologist, trained in America for American tastes and not of, or for, the "Old World," where these languages were studied by academics. Scholars were trained not to expect such things here in America. In fact, American archaeologists refrain from using words such as *necropolis* for New World cemeteries, primarily because they are trained to separate the two worlds, Old and New. A word such as *necropolis* carries with it a hint of ancient Greece, or Egypt. And that would never do in American archaeology. Simply not permitted! The real difficulty is that Mr. Halsey is reading from left to right, and this is his major malfunction.

The text reads from right to left, as does Hebrew. This writer has no accurate knowledge or opinion on the "Cardiff Giant," but we might well add to Mr. Halsey's litany some other, unwanted-by-American-academia, but found-in-America archaeological evidence, which the Establishment continues to sweep under the old, time-worn rug of cultural isolation. We felt compelled to add to Mr. Halsey's list of hated-by-the-Establishment artifacts several others that tend to disprove Powell's near-sighted and limited, pre–Victorian Age ideas—ideas that have become coagulated, solidified, and found so prevalent to this very day in our schools of higher indoctrination. All of these American artifacts are constantly berated by the academics, and have always stood blatantly in the way of the standard and accepted Powell dictum/dogma.

One of the 3,000 or more inscribed, fired-clay tablets removed from prehistoric mounds across Michigan from 1840 to 1911.

First is the infamous Los Lunas inscription in New Mexico, where the oldest recorded star-date in America is found directly associated with a major, Ten Commandment lapidary inscription, inscribed in ancient (paleo-) Hebrew. This artifact site was also fully supported by Dr. Cyrus Gordon, who definitely did not march to Academia's drummer, but was a highly respected linguist around the world. We will definitely add the Ohio

Decalogue to our list. Halsey loosely makes reference to it and a companion artifact as "The Newark Holy Stones." We shall be a little more specific. It was discovered under a huge, dismantled, ancient cairn of rocks 45 feet high and 500 feet wide, about 1860.

The elegant, carved object was found within its own stone coffin/box. It features a figure of Moses and the Ten Commandments carved in "monumental" Hebrew all around it. Immediately dismissed as a "fraud" after a cursory examination by several academic experts, their classification went unchallenged until recent years. Throughout the rest of the 19th century and for half of the next, the Ohio Decalogue inscription was chiefly disregarded by professional epigraphers, because it had been written in a form of Hebrew they could not recognize. Because it was unknown to them, they concluded, it had to be an amateurish fake subsequently discarded as "monumental Hebrew."

Shortly after World War II, an entire series of tablets and pottery shards dating from the fifth century BC newly unearthed in Palestine were covered with the same kind of "monumental Hebrew" appearing on the Ohio Decalogue Stone. Despite this embarrassing discovery, no mainstream archaeologist has credited the Ohio Decalogue Stone as the authentically ancient artifact it is. Both the Los Lunas site and Ohio Decalogue Stone are cited here to show that the Michigan Tablets are not unique, but should be regarded rather in the context of other related finds, the pre-Columbian authenticity of which has been established.

There is a consistent graphic, illustrative theme running throughout the Michigan artifacts, unknown and unrecognized by Mr. Halsey in his blissful state of official, academic ignorance, who sees them merely as casual "biblical scenes." On the overwhelming majority of these tablets, there is a being called YHW—written in a totally discrete, fourth century AD alphabet I deciphered some years ago, as a cuneiform-styled, paleo-Hebrew alphabet, never seen before or since.[3] This highest of beings is usually not shown in full facial likeness.

On most of the tablets, he is called YHW, or Yahw-eh, and nearly always shown above two subordinate deities (Elohym), who are in constant competition—no, actually, warfare, even to the point of death on some tablets. One is a younger son of the right hand; the other is the Son-of-the-Left Hand, finally defeated and burned-on-a-pyre, evil elder of the two subordinate divinities. Both are messiahs intent on winning power over mankind. One for good, and one for evil. This is not a recognizable, trinitarian, Christian doctrine. In common parlance, we might say YHW is a great, mighty one who created the universe, whose son (the good one) created all life on earth, and whose brother is trying to defeat him, as graphically portrayed on several tablets, and clearly not a modern Christian concept.

No, not your nominal Christian fare. In fact, no Christian religious sect in the 1860s (or even now) could have produced this doctrinal statement, either in written or graphic form—that is, if we are, logically, to base the idea of artifact manufacture on the overall doctrines and dogma of their creators. This specific religious doctrine portrayed on the Michigan Tablets is anathema to Christians and Jews alike. It is surely not a "Trinity" doctrine. But Mr. Halsey did not quite notice this fine point of graphic and doctrinal religious detail. All the other, minute details of these tablets can be shown to be biblical stories of creation, the Flood, Adam and Eve, Abraham, Moses, and the Exodus.

Additionally, there is portrayed the life and deeds of the Messiah, Yahushua (commonly called Jesus), and some very readable Egyptian hieroglyphs, in contrast to what Mr. Halsey claims "ersatz Egyptian hieroglyphs," indicating gross "fraud by Mr. Scotford," according to Mr. Halsey, now our linguistic expert. One wonders if Mr. Halsey is truly well-founded in "real" Egyptian hieroglyphs. Mr. Halsey accurately states the stylized cuneiform letters are "a pseudo-cuneiform hieroglyph monogram."

Actually, his is a correct statement. This previously unknown American alphabet is a "pseudo" form of cuneiform when compared to Akkadian-Assyrian or Ras Shamra Syrian styles, but would Mr. Halsey also be an expert in, or be able to read and understand, those "real" cuneiform styles, as well as being an expert in Egyptian hieroglyphs, Norse runic futhark writing, ancient Hebrew (or even modern Hebrew)? He is a truly amazing man, if so. But we digress. Good points all, but off the main one.

It has been reported that a Professor Edwin Worth displayed a collection of the Michigan Tablets, first in Detroit, and later in New York, beginning in the 1860s, many years before the 1874 discoveries of James Scotford that caused so much disbelief among archaeologists, such as Mr. Halsey, a follower of Establishment precedent. So much for John Halsey's stated "belief" that Mr. Scotford fraudulently created all of these Michigan artifacts, and placed them in the ground from Detroit to the upper Peninsula, and elsewhere.

In 1895, the third-century Coptic Gnostic Christian *Pistis Sophia* was translated by a French Egyptologist and Coptic scholar named Amélineau. Its text relates the Gnostic teachings of the transfigured Jesus to the assembled disciples, including his mother Mary, Mary Magdalene, and Martha. The *Pistis Sophia* reveals the complex structures and hierarchies of heaven familiar in Gnostic teachings. For some time previous, about 1851, a German scholar named Schwartze had made a Latin version, but was known only to a few European scholars and not published, per se, save in a limited French-language edition.

In 1891, Adolf von Harnack (1851–1930), Germany's prominent theologian and church historian, pointed out, "...also one or two, other, vague indications, such as a reference to persecution," from which he concluded that it was written at a date when the Christians were "lawfully" persecuted.[4] These considerations led him to assign the most probable date of composition to the second half of the third century. In the arcane, religious doctrine of these early Gnostic Christian Egyptians, called "Copts," spelled out in the *Pistis Sophia,* we see that the doctrine portrayed there, in words, is exactly the same as that which is graphically portrayed on the Michigan tablets. Then, in the *Pistis Sophia*, at a level just beneath the Holy Father, are two, subordinate beings, both sons, both "deities," one good, one bad. One called "lesser YHW," or "little saboath the good" "son of the right hand." And the other deity, "The devil...Sama-el, evil son of the left hand," also a traditional Jewish version of Satan, who was, according to these traditions, Esau's spiritual advisor.[5]

In short, the Michigan artifacts compare to Gnostic Coptic Christianity.

On the basis of this simple, easily understood, consistently graphic doctrinal content, found widely spread throughout the tablets of the Michigan artifacts, compared to the then-unknown Coptic religious doctrine, which is very foreign to nominal Christianity, it may be concluded: These artifacts are real, ancient American documents, created by escaping refugees from the Mediterranean. They were nothing more than Coptic, Egyptian, Gnostic Christians, who had been persecuted by Emperor Constantine's post–Nicean Council, anti-Arianism pogroms. (The Arians belonged to a Gnostic Christian sect deemed criminally heretical by the Established Church) These specific, anti-Arian edicts were codified in 325 AD at the Council of Nicea, with Constantine having the only vote.

Also, it can be concluded a truism, that absolutely no trinitarian-based, American Christian religious person, assumed to be the forger, could have possibly faked this precise, ancient, and long-lost Coptic Christian doctrine out of thin air, particularly based on a work yet to be published anywhere in the world or remotely known at the time the first Michigan Artifact finds were made by post-hole diggers and sewer workers—certainly not by Messrs. Scotford and Soper and Savage, as Mr. Halsey, the authoritative state archaeologist, claims in his fabulous document dismissing these ancient artifacts as "fakes."

If the precise doctrine of those early Egyptian Copts, which was unknown in the modern world before the 1860s, when the Michigan Artifacts began turning up (containing a theology that is anathema to Christianity, as practiced today), and because this doctrine is found accurately portrayed on the majority of them, and this previously long-lost Coptic theology was not published anywhere in the world before 1895 (and then in French only), how could these Michigan artifacts, which predated the first published works on Gnostic Coptic religion (the mirror images of the Michaigan plates), be fakes?

Whoever made these strange and sometimes crude Michigan artifacts was clearly knowledgeable of their own Coptic-based doctrine, which was a *Christian* religion, but not like any known to 19th-century Americans or mainline Christian sects today, although presently revealed sufficiently by a brief perusal of the *Pistis Sophia*. Mr. Halsey condemns these artifacts for their "crudely modeled" nature. But did each and every ancient community harbor a DaVinci or Michaelangelo? The Michigan artifacts are very crude-looking. But they should not be cast off for this reason alone. Having these ancient American artifacts safely in any museum, but in his care is a bit like having one's mother-in-law drive his new Ferarri *Enzo* off a cliff. Mixed emotions, to be sure.

CHAPTER 7

Canada's Viking
"Hammer of Thor"
by Frank Joseph

That Viking settlers established themselves in Newfoundland, at a place called L'Anse aux Meadows, is well-known. But further evidence of the Norse and other foreigners in prehistoric Canada is far less acknowledged, despite some intriguing evidence.

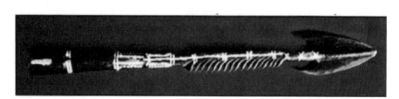

This remarkable object was found during a prolonged drought that swept southeastern North Dakota from 1934 to 1936, when a small buried stone cairn was exposed on the farm of Henry Nathan Madenwaldt, 2.5 miles north from the town of Hakinson, 60 miles south of Fargo, and 200 miles from the Canadian border. Inside the old rock pile, he found a pair of virtually identical iron harpoons, each inscribed with its own different runic characters, probably forming the names of the artifacts' original owners, or those of patron Nordic deities. The specimen photographed here bears the mark of the Hanseatic League, an organization (Hanse) created by North German sailors in defense of their mutual trading interests from the 13th through 15th centuries. As such, the Madenwaldt harpoon is solid evidence for the presence of Northern European mariners in the Upper Midwest during pre-Columbian times.

In August 1972, Dawn French took up residence in the small town of Pushthrough, an outpost 30 miles west of Bay du Nord, on the south coast of the island of Newfoundland. While there, she heard strange tales of the legendary Stone Cross, a structure supposedly venerated by the local Micmac Indians for centuries before the arrival of modern European immigrants.

No one had actually seen it, and its whereabouts were unknown. Curious to learn more, French studied native traditions, which described a sacred precinct, lonely and barren, where people in need of healing would find a large, unusually shaped cross spread out on the ground. It was the site of supposedly miraculous cures, but over time, with the advent of modern medicine, the place was abandoned to myth.

The Micmacs are an interesting people. Their name means "allies," a reference to the confederacy of clans they formed and led, thus becoming the largest and most important native tribe in Canada's eastern Maritime Provinces. A seasonally nomadic people, the Micmacs' Algonquian dialect differs greatly from that of their neighbors and has some suggestion of Scandinavian cognates. Their possible linguistic links to Medieval Europe are underscored by what appear to be Nordic recessive gene traits among the Micmac (recurring blondness) and especially by the discovery at the island's northern extreme of the first professionally authenticated Viking site in the New World, at L'Anse aux Meadows, today a national historic park.

Even more intriguing, the late epigrapher Dr. Barry Fell demonstrated a fascinating parallel between Micmac birch-bark script and ancient Egyptian hieroglyphs. What (if anything) these possible prehistoric themes may have had to do with the lost Stone Cross of southern Newfoundland, French could not be sure, but she was determined to find out. Basing her work primarily on old legends, she compiled a rough map that took her inland from the Bay du Nord and over the high cliffs of Devils Dining Table. On their opposite side, in a barren plain surrounded by hills thick with spruce trees, she eventually found the object of her quest.

It was spread out on the arid ground, the huge outline of a diamond-shaped cross, as though opening itself up from the center. Measuring 30 feet from north to south, it more closely resembled a compass. The design was encircled by a ring of numerous, white stones, some of boulder proportions, others piled into rough heaps, mimicking crude towers or the abstract configuration of statues. From the vantage point of one of these piles, French could make out the faint image of a man upon the cross, not in a crucified position, but as though emerging from the diamond opening. She remembered a Micmac tradition concerning these stones: It was permissible for a visitor to remove one, to keep it for his or her own healing purposes, as long as he or she replaced it with another.

Two stone basins lay near the south end of the structure, one perhaps for ablutions, the other for donations; in the latter she found several old coins, a single example dated 1865. French had discovered (perhaps rediscovered) the Stone Cross, but answers were not forthcoming: How old was it? Who made it and why? Who was the last to see it before us? What illnesses did it supposedly cure? Beyond these questions, she experienced a feeling of profound wonder, a sensation of being in a sacred zone, a sacrosanct area with an emotional character all its own—not frightening, but certainly powerful.

If the Stone Cross of Newfoundland is Norse, its diamond shape renders it a most peculiar Christian design occurring nowhere else. Its compass-like configuration might refer to a kind of "Christ-of-the-Mariners" for Vikings far from home, even if that home were only at L'Anse aux Meadows. It could also pass for an icon of that other people who supposedly impacted the Micmacs, the ancient Egyptians. For them, Ausar (better known by his Greek name, Osiris), the man-god of resurrection, was a proto-Christian concept associated with the Cross of the Four Cardinal Directions.

Despite the presence of a male figure, the Newfoundland Cross is not a crucifix. Whether Christ or Osiris, or someone altogether different, the man received homage in the recent past, judging from the mid-19th-century coins left at the site as apparent offerings. But Micmac traditions indicate a prehistoric origin for the design. It is among the most baffling of all sacred centers, offering determined investigators far too few clues for constructing even the most tenuous explanation.

However, Newfoundland's Stone Cross is not the only object of its kind discovered in Canada. During 1964, archaeologist Thomas E. Lee was scouting near an excavation underway near the village of Imaha, in northern Quebec, when he found a tall, curious monument on the desolate north bank of the Payne Estuary, 15 miles north of the village of Payne Bay, near the west coast of Ungava Bay. The 2-ton stone structure stands 8 feet high and measures 4.5 feet across at its pointed lintel, surmounted by a 14-inch-high capstone. While the pillar was a surprise to Lee and his colleagues, he later learned from native Inuit that they had known of its existence for generations. Yet, they laid no claim to it, insisting that the strange object was already standing long before the first of their ancestors arrived in the area. Moreover, the Inuit never worked in stone on such a large scale.

Lee was struck by its roughly Nordic design and dubbed it "the Hammer of Thor." Possibly a direction indicator, it appears to point toward the remains of a rectangular, stone structure—80 feet long and 30 feet across—not far away. Slanting walls half-buried in the hard ground resemble a Viking long-house from the 10th or 11th century. Greenland is not very far from this point in Quebec, so Norse visitors 1,000 years ago could have sailed the distance in their sturdy dragon-ships and left a memorial to their arrival.

The "Hammer of Thor" in Northern Quebec.

Lee's characterization of the Ungava Bay object as a "Hammer of Thor" does not seem inappropriate. Similar stone structures appeared throughout Viking Age Scandinavia; the Temple of Thor in Sweden dates before 1125 AD. We know that Nordic seafarers voyaged at least as far as Newfoundland, and that they certainly did not lack ships to bring them to Quebec from relatively nearby Greenland. Thor's hammer was the most commonly reproduced religious object of the period. Known as *Mjoellnir*, it was envisioned as the lightning, as it flew from the storm-god's hand. He was the patron deity of fertility, but also of courage and decisive action.

Thor has been portrayed in saga and art as a virile, middle-aged man of great power, with long red hair and beard. He was sometimes shown being carried across the universe in a great chariot drawn by rams. The thousand-year-old Quebec monument was probably set up to call upon his strength of will in a difficult land. Interestingly, a bronze statuette (circa 1000 AD) from northern Iceland (National Museum, Reykjavik) depicting Thor with his hammer portrays him wearing a conical hat virtually identical to the headgear worn by male figures appearing at Ontario's Petroglyph Provincial Park, a collection of native rock art featuring dozens of pre-Columbian illustrations.

Mjoellnir was not merely a symbol for meteorological events, however. The gods of Valhalla proclaimed it the single most valuable object they possessed, and its likeness appears to have been reproduced by Norse shamans for hallowing marriage rites, to bless the recently departed souls of the dead at funerals, and to consecrate newborns into the community. Mjoellnir's image was inscribed on a Swedish tombstone at Stenqvista. It thus resembles a higher symbol of the birth-death duality not unlike the sacred Double-Headed Axe of the Bronze Age, particularly as realized in Minoan Crete. In a particularly revealing myth of Thor and his hammer, he restores the dead to life through the potency of its magic.

As Davidson writes:

> It would seem indeed as though the power of the thunder-god, symbolized by his hammer, extended over all that had to do with the well-being of the community. It covered birth, marriage and death; burial and cremation ceremonies; weapons and feasting; traveling; land-taking and the making of oaths between men. The famous weapon of Thor was not only the symbol of the destructive power of the storm and of fire from heaven, but also a protection against the forces of evil and violence.[1]

Canada's ancient mysteries pre-date the arrival of Vikings 1,000 years ago. More accessible than either the Stone Cross or Thor's Hammer, Serpent Mounds Provincial Park is located south of Highway 7 near the town of Keene, Ontario. Visitors may admire the 194-foot-long effigy of a prehistoric snake winding across a hill among a dark grove of oak trees on the northern shore of Rice Lake. Six feet high, with an average width of 25 feet, the effigy was sculpted from the earth about 2,000 years ago to form a serpentine burial mound.

Eight smaller oval mounds surround the figure. Although unique in Canada, two similar geoglyphs lie in the United States, one in Adams County, Ohio, and the other in Rice County, Kansas. The serpent-egg motif is also found in ancient Mexico, Greece, and Egypt, but the Canadian example is the most northerly of all.

Although Serpent Mounds were excavated as early as 1895, the most thorough investigation was conducted between 1955 and 1960 by the Royal Ontario Museum and Trent University under the direction of Richard B. Johnston. Most of what has been learned about the site stems from his work. He found that the earthworks were built shortly after 200 BC, but never used for permanent settlement. Instead, they represented a ceremonial center occupied only during late spring and summer months for ritual purposes.

Although 3,412 pottery fragments have been uncovered at the site, there is no evidence of permanent habitation. The biomorph was officially identified with the so-called Point Peninsula Culture, a group of hunter-gatherers, who resided in the Rice Lake area, but such a supposition is problematic, because representatives of this culture never built mounds. As minister of Ontario's Natural Resources Vincent G. Kerrio explained, "these mound-builders were not a typical band of Point Peninsula peoples. Skull features in particular show the mound-builders to represent a stock different from, yet related to, their presumed descendants, the Ontario Iroquois."[2]

Also unlike the Point Peninsula residents, the builders of Serpent Mounds were metal smiths working in silver and copper. And their distinctive pottery, wholly superior to anything that came before, shares the same zigzag pattern found at the great ceremonial site of Aztalan, in southern Wisconsin, 3 miles east of Rock Lake (described in Chapter 22). There are other links to Aztalan. Ritually broken clamshells, turtle carapaces, and dogs—all funerary elements typical of the Aztalaners—were found at Serpent Mounds. It seems clear, then, that the builders of Serpent Mounds were not native to Ontario, but came from the south.

As the archaeologist W.A. Kenyon wrote, "Originally, we feel, these serpents must have been conceived in the jungles of Central America or Mexico. As they moved north, their ranks gradually thinned, for the harsh climate of the higher northern latitudes is not suitable for tropical serpents. And so, the last surviving member of that strange breed came to rest in Ontario, on the flank of the Precambrian Shield."[3]

Were the builders of Serpent Mounds the Mayas, who came all the way from Yucatan for the high-grade copper they needed for their ceremonial cities far to the south? Or were they Aztalan miners, who likewise raised a huge snake effigy at the shore of their sacred necropolis, in Rock Lake?

An ancient, eternal symbolism implicit in the altered landscape of Serpent Mounds survives. Though the site is certainly a place of the dead, it is also a temple of rebirth. Interred bodies were found in the flexed or fetal position, as though curled up in the womb, waiting to be born. The individual mounds resemble Earth Mother wombs swollen with new life. Linked together to form a serpent, they reinforce the rebirth concept, because of the snake's ability to slough off its old skin for a new one.

The numerical significance of the mounds is no less telling. Eight egg-shaped earthworks encircle the major figure. Whereas an egg theme underscores the principle of new life, eight is traditionally associated with death: the eight legs of a spider that kills to live, the eight hours we sleep each night, and so forth. Here, the two interact, as separate parts of the same forces for transitional change: life-death-rebirth. Together, the effigies comprise nine mounds. Nine stands for the female powers of rebirth, as exemplified in the nine months of pregnancy.

Serpent Mounds' close proximity to Petroglyph Provincial Park is not coincidental. Both sites are unique in their own right, but undoubtedly shared some sacred relationship. If so, then the incised images do indeed date much earlier than supposed: to 2,000 or more years ago. Perhaps, under the Serpent Mounds of Rice Lake, lie the remains of the artists who carved the mysterious petroglyphs.

CHAPTER 8

Prehistoric Mooring
Stones of Florida
by Archie Eschborn

As a final point of departure for freighters carrying copper from North America, Florida would have offered an accommodating supplies' location used by Bronze Age sailors before setting out on their long, transatlantic return voyages to Europe and the Near East. Accordingly, evidence of ancient docking facilities on the east coast of the Sunshine State tends to confirm the presence of oceanic mariners there more than 3,000 years ago.

The original Garden of Eden was located on the east coast of Florida, according to John Saxer, a longtime resident of Tarpon Springs. His novel conclusion is an ecclectic interpretation of biblical and Classical Greek myth applied to a number of local coral. Some feature unusual holes that, he believes, are evidence of their use in Old Testament times as "sea-anchors" by sailors from the ancient Old World.

If Mr. Saxer's belief in a Floridian Garden of Eden was a bit much, the drilled coral he mentioned seemed to merit investigation. For assistance, I contacted William Donato, a well-known researcher familiar with Atlantic Ocean archaeology. He was unsure about the existence of any "sea-anchors" in Tarpon Springs, but admitted the unusually perforated coral blocks nonetheless bore some affinity with smaller examples he encountered in the Bahamas. A quick Internet search revealed that stone anchors were indeed employed from prehostoric times by a variety of cultures well into the 13th century AD. Saxer was sure his specimens were much older.

Arriving in Tarpon Springs, he was kind enough to show me his "coral anchors." Although at first sight nothing seemed unnatural about them, they were curiously grouped in regular clusters, making it difficult to know with certainty if they had been so arranged sometime in the historic past, or occupied their present position since pre-Columbian times. Driving north on Alternate U.S. 19 to New Port Richey, Saxer took me to several genuinely impressive monoliths that more resembled real sea-anchors. We visited four sites of large standing stones with well-worn holes that had been obviously drilled through. The area is known for its sponge harvesting, fishing, and boat building, but local inquiry into these occupations was unable to connect them in any way to the perforated coral formations.

One of New Port Richey's enigmatic faces carved in stone.

The closer I scrutinized them, however, the more they resembled—not anchors—but mooring stones. As a sailor and boater, I imagined the difficulty in handling these ponderous, uneven stones as anchors. Saxer argued that larger anchors were needed for bigger ships. He then drove us to another site in downtown Port Richey, near a waterfront marina. Enclosed by a wire fence stood a defunct restaurant destined for demolition. Visible from the gate of the fence, about 20 feet away, was a large monolith bearing two carved faces. Their appearnce was a real surprise, because they were by no means modern, suggesting, on the contrary, extreme age. Stylistic execution, weathering, and deposition all strongly implied their pre-Columbian provenance.

To be sure, the immediate vicinity had been the site of prehistoric habitation, providing a suitably ancient cultural context for the two carved countenances. Some months after my first encounter with the engraved monolith, Donato was able visit one of the Florida coral "sea-anchors" himself—a 4-by-5-foot rock, 18 inches thick, featuring a symmetrical hole. "It's possibly a modified rock, an anchor with multiple rope groves," he told Steven Isbitts of *The Tampa Tribune*. Turning to another massive stone with two holes, both 17 inches in diameter, Donato stated, "the size is astounding, far bigger than anything I've seen. The identical diameter and uniformity of either hole argue that they were artificially drilled through the rock. It may have been a mooring stone."[1]

If so, then whose ships were moored to them, and when? Answers may be found among the 5,000 pit mines dug out of Michigan's Upper Peninsula from 5,000 to nearly 3,000 years ago. Archaeologists have known since the late 18th century that some half-a-billion pounds of the world's highest grade copper was excavated by light-skinned foreigners who Native American Menomonie oral tradition describes as "the marine men" arriving from across the Atlantic Ocean. Coincidental with the Upper Great Lakes' massive mining operation and the disappearance of its extracted minerals was the ancient Old World Bronze Age.[2] This epoch would not have been possible without prodigeous amounts of high-grade copper—fused with zinc and tin—insufficiently available in Europe and the Near East.

If Michigan copper was traded on a transatlantic basis, smaller ships coming down the Mississippi River to meet up with larger ocean-going cargo ships could have had a rendezvous point in western Florida. There, they could have taken aboard the last supplies of food and fresh water before their next landfall on Western European shores. Although those vessels, having been constructed of perishable materials, long ago decayed into nothing, the Upper Peninsula's prehistoric pit mines still exist, as do the uniformly drilled holes in coastal Florida's coral formations and their nearby monolith. Perhaps its engraved, human faces were rough portaits of the "Marine Men," sea-faring copper workers, on their way to and from the mines that drove the Bronze Age on the other side of the world.

CHAPTER 9

Ice Mummy of the Andes
by Patrick C. Chouinard

Preserved along with the physical remains of a young girl sacrificed atop a high volcano in the Andes Mountains was her long-kept secret of the Inca people.

Pat Chouinard is editor-in-chief of The New Archaeology Review, former producer of "Archaeology TV," current host of "Conversations with Pat Chouinard" airing weekly on Florida's WTAN 1340 AM Radio, and long-time contributor to Ancient American magazine. He is a contributor to the recent Exposed, Uncovered, and Declassified: Lost Civilizations & Secrets of the Past.

In early autumn 1995, Dr. Johan Reinhard led a team of fellow archaeologists to Peru's Ampato volcano. At its high, barren and remote summit, they made a most unusual discovery. Referred to as the "Inca Ice Maiden," it was the mummy of an apparent sacrificial victim sometime during the mid-15th century AD. In life, she climbed the mountain, perhaps already inebriated from *chica* (Inca beer) and hallucinogens. She stumbled, hardly able to move, with the breath-piercing cold and thin air slowly suffocating her. Yet, she was not alone. A pompous procession of robed priests and crowned nobility marched beside her. They were wrapped in rich, colorful textiles decorated with gold jewelry, and wore sandals strapped with bronze and silver. This girl was much more than a victim of her own feeble constitution, however; she was to be ritually sacrificed to an unknown god.

Inca Ice Maiden from the summit of Peru's Ampato volcano.

The parents of such chosen offerings were given concessions and special gifts by the priesthood, and the children themselves often taken to Cuzco, the Inca capital, to be paraded through the streets in immense celebrations. This was a rare and sacred method of placating the supernatural powers and ensuring the proper irrigation of crops, the well-being of their emperors, the sanctity of a royal marriage, or the guarantee of victory in battle. Indigenous inhabitants of the Andes today believe that the mountains control all aspects of life and death, as did their ancestors half a millennium ago. If the gods were not appeased, then disaster would surely follow. While the priest proclaimed the girl's purity to the gods, she was clothed in a brightly colored death-robe, then placed alive in her tomb.

After having been sufficiently sedated, the Ice Maiden was bludgeoned on the back of the skull with the heavy, lethal blow of a stone axe for the spititual protection of the Land of the Four Quarters, the *Tahuantisuyu*, an empire some 2,500 miles in extent from the Andes in Columbia, southward to the dry, coastal desert of Chile, to the Amazon in the east. In its geographical scope, the Inca imperium was among the history's largest empires, and one of the most advanced. Like the Romans, the Inca were superb road-builders and architects. At its height around the turn of the 16th century, the Inca Empire embraced 10 million subjects, all bound by a communal, theocratic society with a socialist economic system. Its worshippers practiced mountain worship as the primary basis of their theology. From the moment of birth, Inca children were instilled with a dominating sense of duty and a clarity of religious purpose.

An authority on the Incas, William Conklin, writes, "The people of the Andes previous to the Incas did worship mountains, but in a different way. They seemed to have worshiped mountains from a distance, but the Incas are the ones who got the idea of climbing a ladder to heaven, and going up to the top of the mountain, and actually engaging in their ritual practices at that spot, which must have been their concept of heaven."[1]

Related discoveries made by Dr. Reinhard on the slopes of Mount Sara-Sara, not far from the Ampato volcano, revealed additional evidence of child scrifice. "We had waited four days for fierce winds and a snowstorm to abate, while encamped in a snow bowl two-hundred feet below the summit," he told *National Geographic Explorer*.

> This was followed by a day and a half of digging. It seemed only fitting, therefore, that Arcadio was the first to shout the word that caused all of us to stop work instantly: "Mummy!" I put down my notebook, and hurried over to the place where Arcadio was digging. He and his brother, Ignacio, had uncovered a section of a stone-and-gravel platform on the most exposed part of the summit. There, more than five feet down, was a bundle wrapped in textiles: the frozen body of an Inca ritual sacrifice, a boy about eight years old. Beside his left arm lay a sling and two pairs of sandals, objects presumably intended to accompany him on his journey to the afterlife."[2]

The boy and his two slaughtered companions pre-dated the Ice Maiden's time and belonged to an earlier culture, the Wari, from which the Incas would borrow much for their own civilization. CAT scans showed that the organs of the three Wari children were still intact; blood was still frozen inside their veins and hearts. "Human sacrifices are very rare," Reinhard told *National Geographic Explorer,* "and this is one of only about a half dozen ever to be excavated scientifically. No other mountain has yielded four such victims."[3] Their exceptionally well-preserved remains showed that none of them were typically Indian, but evidenced traces of Caucasian features, which were particularly pronounced in the Mount Sara-Sara remains. The Inca Ice Maiden likewise demonstrated racially anomalous traits, although to a lesser degree.

The pre-literate Guarani Indians spoke of the Incas as the "white kings," and a definite physical cleft did indeed exist between the Indian proletariat and the Inca aristocracy. A portrait in Lima's Copacabana Monastery of Huayna Capac, the great Inca emperor who consolidated the conquests of his forefathers during the early 16th century, represents a man with thoroughly European facial features. A profile in Antonio de Herrera's chronicle of the Spanish Conquest, *Historia* (in Madrid's Biblioteca Nacional), shows Huascar with a similarly un-Indian countenance.

A contemporary painting of Huayna Capac's other son, Atahualpa, the last Inca emperor, reveals someone of mixed parentage, suggesting he and Huascar were only half-brothers, a mix of characteristics evident in the Ice Maiden mummy. Pedro Pizzaro, son of the man who conquered the Inca Empire, wrote that "the ruling class of the Kingdom of Peru was fair-skinned with fair hair about the color of ripe wheat. Most of the great lords and ladies looked white like Spaniards. In that country I met an Indian woman with her child, both so fair-skinned that they were hardly distinguishable from fair, white people. Their fellow countrymen called them 'children of the gods'."[4]

The Inca Ice Maiden and her Wari companions were members of this foreign-born elite. Together with their well-preserved remains is mummified the truth of Andean Civilization's vital, forgotten connection to overseas' visitors from the ancient Old World.

CHAPTER 10

Ancient Egyptians Sailed
to America for Corn
by Wayne May

*A*ncient Egyptian temple records document pharaonic expeditions to the "Land of Punt," a distant place of great natural wealth reached only after a three-year voyage. Although the location and precise identity of Punt are unknown, new evidence presented by Dr. Gunnar Thompson strongly suggests it lay in the Americas.

Note that all quotations in this article come from Dr. Gunnar Thompson's findings.

Twenty-one golden corncobs will change everything that has been written about the discovery of America, says anthropologist Gunnar Thompson, PhD. He announced the findings of a February 2011 report on Egyptian maize farming by the New World Discovery Institute in Port Townsend, Washington. The two-year study included Egyptian temples, tombs, and papyrus scrolls, some dating back more than 4,000 years.

"The Egyptian corncobs are actually derived from a New World crop plant," he explains. "They aren't supposed to be in Egypt. This is conclusive evidence that the Egyptians were farming New World corn thousands of years before Columbus was born. All the modern, European historians have claimed that Columbus brought the first Indian corn, or maize, to the Old World. That's a total mistake that needs to be corrected."

A veteran archeologist, Thompson is no rookie when it comes to solving mysteries, and he is no stranger to controversy. He has solved so many puzzles that Hong Kong celebrity Frank Lee dubbed him "the Sherlock Holmes of American history."

Most of his new evidence comes from the Temple of Hatshepsut at Deir el-Bahri, near Thebes. She reigned Egypt as a Queen or "Pharaoh" from 1492 to 1458 BC. Thompson's report includes photographs from reputable sources, including the New York Metropolitan Museum of Art and the National Museum of Scotland. According to their study, ancient Egyptian artists included Indian corncobs, pineapples, and other New World plants in their displays of religious offerings. The Queen's murals coincide with reports that she sent an expedition overseas to a mysterious land called "Punt." Thompson suggests a daring connection: "Punt must have been located someplace in the Americas. The Egyptians had to sail across the Atlantic Ocean in order to obtain all the New World plants."

Egyptian corncobs, circa 1470 BC.

Thompson is elated about his role as a pioneer among the legions of more traditional scholars, but he is not surprised by what he found. Almost 50 years ago, the late Norwegian ethnologist, Dr. Thor Heyerdahl, proposed that the ancient Egyptians had sailed to Mexico and Peru. Most historians scoffed at his theory, but Heyerdahl launched a reed sailboat, *Ra-II*, carefully constructed within the limitations of third millennium BC ship-building parameters, during 1970, as part of a practical experiment. Along with a hardy band of bearded supporters, he sailed across the Atlantic Ocean to prove the feasibility of his unorthodox idea. Thompson says he would have volunteered, but he was not old enough to join the crew at the time. Later, Heyerdahl became his mentor.

"Thor must be laughing from his grave," Thompson said. "My search for clues really heated up in 2006. That was when I noticed an unusual photograph of a mural that was taken inside the Queen's Temple almost a hundred years ago. The mural included a Nubian servant who was carrying a platter of fruits, vegetables, and breads. On the very top was balanced a single corncob. Bingo! I knew they had corn."

The maverick anthropologist has identified similar corncobs at the Temple of Pharaoh Seti I, near Abydos, and at the Tomb of Rekhmire, not far from Thebes. He found more examples on papyrus scrolls dating to the 12th-century-BC reign of Rameses II. "The golden color of the corncobs, the parallel rows of large kernels, the tapered shape, and the green husk leaves all confirm that this grain is the New World maize plant. Indian maize was more resilient than the common Old World staples, such as wheat, barley, and millet. Eventually, maize farming spread throughout the Mediterranean Region, where the foreign grain was affectionately known as 'barbarian corn,' or 'Turkey wheat.' The plant's alien pedigree ultimately led to its exclusion from traditional religious art. However, it was a key ingredient in the growth and survival of Old World civilizations."

CHAPTER 11

A Map of Pre-Columbian America
by Lee Pennington

During spring 1982, an itinerant wood-worker and amateur treasure-hunter in southeastern Illinois allegedly stumbled into a cave containing stones engraved with the likenesses of Roman Era persons, Near Eastern mythological scenes, Egyptian hieroglyphic and North Semitic texts, and Carthaginian ships and symbols, etc. Although these objects seemed too good to be true, their sheer number—at least 1,000—argued on behalf of their ancient authenticity. Here, close examination of a single artifact from the collection sheds light on the entire Burrows Cave controversy.

One of the largest of several Burrows Cave map-stones presents an intricate view of the Mississippi River watershed from the Gulf of Mexico to the Great Lakes—with markings indicating extended exploration along the Tennessee River and the Ohio River and, in one instance, exploration overland to Lake Michigan.

Roughly in the triangle-like shape of Easter Island, the stone measures 7 by 12 inches, and weighs approximately 4.5 pounds. Grooved lines appear to indicate rivers and lakes; a series of dots represent travel routes; panels contain symbols and ancient writing. The outer edges of the stone have been altered, either to change its shape or to express some symbolic information. Seven grooves are cut on the bottom side, and three are cut on the top side. Although the majority of incised information is on the front side of the stone, a few symbols were adroitly carved on the backside.

Burrows Cave map-stone.

Without careful inspection, one can easily miss the human-made marks on the backside, as they subtly merge with the natural marks on the stone. In fact, so blended in are these human-made marks that it appears the map-maker intended them to be camouflaged. Except for two short, parallel grooves on the backside, all the other man-made marks are dots. Because there are no incised lines suggesting landscape or waterways, the dots likely represent star constellations. Three dots in a row close together probably signify the belt of Orion.

From the Gulf area up the Mississippi River, one river is indicated to the west and four rivers indicated to the east. That to the west suggests the Missouri River, and the four rivers to the east, in order from south to north, are the Black River, the Ohio River, the Illinois River, and probably the Wisconsin River. On the north side of the indicated Ohio River, the Wabash River, and either the Scioto River at Portsmouth or the Muskingum River at Marietta are shown—more than likely, the Scioto. South of the Ohio River appear the Tennessee, and Kanawha rivers, with the Monongahela River at the very end.

Two things stand out concerning the Great Lakes region of the map. First, the Great Lakes, along with the St. Lawrence River, are shown as a single body of water. Not to make too much of it, but geologists tell us that Lake Superior, Lake Michigan, and Lake Huron were one body of water until about 100 BC, when isostatic rebound raised the land and separated the lakes. Second, Isle Royale is clearly indicated on the map in the northern section of Lake Superior. The one-body-of-water depiction can certainly be offered as supporting evidence for the age of the map. Likewise, the showing of Isle Royale (a geographic spot not well-known by the general public, but a place highly important in prehistoric America) tilts the scales of debate toward the map's ancient authenticity.

Certain marks suggest that the starting-point of the map, and thus the beginning-point for the explorers, is probably the Gulf of Mexico, rather than that more modernly logical choice, the St. Lawrence Seaway. For example, the dots, which seem to symbolize time-travel measurements, begin at the Gulf and emanate north along what clearly represents the Mississippi River, east along the Ohio River, and south down the Tennessee River. Each dot may refer to the average distance one could expect to travel in one day, or some other designated time period.

Strangely, although there is a clearly marked gulf at the bottom of the map with the Mississippi River emptying into it, there is no indication of Lake Pontchartrain. Perhaps that might be expected, if the base camp of the map-maker explorers were located at the Gulf area rather than in the St. Lawrence area, and cartographers were merely attempting to show distances to and from their camp. For that purpose, just indicating the Gulf would be sufficient. It should, however, be pointed out that Lake Pontchartrain was formed sometime between 2000 BC and 600 BC—again, more supporting evidence for the genuine antiquity of the map-stone.

Clearly, it does not show various landmarks, as is the case on some other Burrows Cave map-stones. Instead, our map-stone under discussion is more concerned with the waterways and approximate distances (via dots measuring units of time) between various points. There are 42 dots from the mouth of the Ohio River to what is apparently the present-day area of Pittsburgh—a distance of 981 miles—indicating average travel of a little more than 23 miles per day. Canoeing enthusiasts believe it is possible to travel 15 miles per day paddling upstream; more than 30 miles per day traveling downstream. Interestingly, an average of traveling both ways, with and against the river current, averages 22.5 miles per day.

Eighteen dots run overland on the map-stone from the north side of the Ohio River at the mouth of the Tennessee River to the west shore of Lake Huron—a distance of roughly 532 miles—averaging out to around 30 miles travel per day. That perhaps sounds excessive, especially for someone walking along primitive trails. It should be remembered, however, that the German army marched approximately 60 miles a day during the first year (1941 to 1942) of their campaign in Russia. Soviet troops trying to keep ahead of the invaders had to travel even farther every day—this while carrying full military gear.

Another map-stone currently in the possession of John White depicts the Great Lakes' area, but also somewhat less detailed is the area to the south. Compared to the 18 dots on the map-stone under discussion, the John White counterpart shows 21 dots. On the White map-stone, the dots start at a point south beside a horseshoe or igloo-like image, and run north to Lake Huron. Lines of dots on both map-stones appear to represent the same overland trail. In addition to the dots on the map-stone, there are seven panels containing script on the front side.

One panel, however, appears to have been scratched in recent times—the depth being much shallower and the patina totally missing. The fresh-looking inscription might be an older inscription recently scratched out, an unlikely assumption, because of the lack of depth on the newer-looking inscription. Perhaps someone, fairly recently, scratched this mark here as a specific test for patina. The fresh inscription appears to have been scratched in with a pin-head. Clearly, all incisions on the stone were wrought with a metal instrument, probably made of iron.

Seven panels contain from three to 11 letters or numbers. The inscriptions, all taken together, appear to include glyphs borrowed from paleo-Hebrew, Phoenician, Etruscan, Greek, old British, and so on. This mixture of letters on Burrows Cave artifacts has caused several researchers to throw up their hands and condemn the entire collection as an obvious fraud perpetrated by amateur forgers who just flung together a hodgepodge of ancient ideograms and symbols from different cultures to form meaningless groupings. If, however, all these alphabets come from a mother tongue, and if the mother tongue (rather than any one of the recognized groups) is what is being used, we should expect nothing less than a mixture—especially if one is not familiar with that mother tongue. Any language derived from a mother tongue would preserve elements from its original source, and, at the same time, develop entirely new elements of its own.

Along these lines, researchers would do well to familiarize themselves with the works of Welsh historians Alan Wilson and Baram Blackett. They argue convincingly that the mother tongue of all those languages mentioned previously is *coelbren*, the alphabet of the ancient Khumry—also known as the Cymry, and ancestors of the Welsh people. Coelbren has been widely discredited as the invention of Edward Williams, who was said to have created the alphabet in the early 19th century. Most scholars still accept that pronouncement, along with the conviction that Williams was a proven forger—all this in spite of manuscripts written in coelbren centuries before Williams's lifetime are extant. Moreover, copies of some of his so-called forged manuscripts pre-date a time before he was even born.

Coelbren possibly forms revealing connections between our Burrows Cave map-stone and other allegedly forged, inscribed stones—specifically, West Virginia's Grave Creek Tablet, the Bat Creek Stone of Tennessee, and New Mexico's Los Lunas Boulder. All these lithic artifacts have something in common, other than their dismissal as frauds by mainstream archaeologists: They share some common, ancient, alphabetical letters.

For example, the map-stone repeats two incised, small, parallel lines, five times on the front side and one time (the set mentioned earlier) on the backside. Although they were overlooked for years as part of the inscription on the Bat Creek Stone, an identical set of parallel lines also occurs there. According to Alan Wilson, these two short lines represent the Khumric word *dwy*, which means "the ruler." The Bat Creek Stone and this map-stone also have at least two other letters in common.

The Burrows Cave map-stone also shares letters with the Grave Creek Stone (at least five) and the Los Lunas Stone (at least seven). The Los Lunas Stone was long condemned by conventional scholars as bearing a contrived alphabet, until the discovery of the Tel Dan Stele between 1993 and 1994 in northern Israel by a team of researchers and workers led by Israeli archaeologist Avraham Biran. The language on the Tel Dan Stele, now confidently dated to around 900 to 800 BC, is virtually identical to that on the Los Lunas Stone. Several letters (at least seven) on the Tel Dan Stele are also identical with those on the Burrows Cave map-stone.

Another inscribed artifact (less regarded as fraudulent than ignored) that shares some common letters with the map-stone is the Brandenburg Stone. Now housed in the Charlestown, Indiana, public library, the Brandenburg Stone was found in Paradise Bottoms near Brandenburg, Kentucky, nearly 100 years ago. Using the coelbren alphabet, Alan Wilson translates the inscription on the Brandenburg Stone as: "towards strength (to promote unity), divide the land; we are spread over purely [justly] between offspring in wisdom."[1]

If the map-stone is genuine, it has much to relate regarding the unknown ancient explorers of our continent during prehistory. Certainly many unresolved questions remain concerning Burrows Cave. Even so, to ignore totally its artifacts and to dismiss them all out of hand without further study does irreparable damage to legitimate scholarship. Even if every single stone of the existing hundreds or thousands of them is a fraud, we need to solve the mystery as to how such a massive hoax, perhaps the greatest of our time, could have been accomplished and by whom. If, however, the stone artifacts are real, what a great tragedy it would be to simply yell "fraud" and lose them to oblivion!

CHAPTER 12

Light on the Aagard Lamp
by Charles F. Herberger

Around 1980, Eugene Aagard, a road crew boss working a stretch of highway between Price and Green River, in central Utah, retrieved a peculiar object from the bottom of a just-excavated barrow pit. The artifact is approximately 5.5 inches long, 1.5 inches wide, and 1.3 inches tall, and weighs about 4 ounces. Although discovered not far from a centuries-old encampment, local Indians affiliated with the Range Creek Fremont Culture never made alabaster lamps. The anomalous find more obviously belongs in an ancient Old World setting, as explained by Dr. Charles Herberger, a retired professor of English at Nasson College in Springvale, Maine, and author of The Thread of Adriane *and* The Riddle of the Sphinx.

The Aagard Lamp described by Steve Shaffer in his article for *Ancient American* in September 2009 (Volume 13, Number 84) has a very significant mark engraved on its side. Composed of a rectangle with crossed diagonals, this symbol is a *quincunx*—an arrangement of five objects with four at the corners of a square or rectangle and the fifth at its center. Its four corners, plus the center point, where the diagonals cross, amount to five points. Today, the quincunx appears in the Five on dice or playing cards.

But it was widely associated by a variety of different cultures throughout both the ancient Old World and pre-Columbian America with the Sun. Gerardo Reichel-Dolmatoff (1912–1994), a renowned anthropologist, known for his holistic approach, in-depth fieldwork among tropical rainforest cultures, and discoverer of a tribal people known as the Kogi, found in their application of the quincunx an expression of their relation to the entire cosmos:

> The concrete form that this symbol takes is a loom used in weaving textiles.... The Kogi conceptualize the Earth as an immense loom on which the sun weaves the Fabric of Life.... The Indians are well

aware of solstices and equinoxes; as a matter of fact, these phenomena are the foundations of their agricultural and ritual calendars, and Kogi priests have considerable astronomical knowledge. The upper bar of this World Loom is formed by the line traced between sunrise and sunset at the summer solstice, whereas the lower bar is drawn at winter solstice. The equinoctial line is the central rod of the loom. Spiraling back and forth, the Sun weaves day and night, on both sides of the cloth, a dayside and a nightside, light and darkness, life and death.[1]

In other words, the quincunx, which the loom forms by its shape, symbolizes the yearly journey of the sun. In the northern hemisphere, the sun rises at summer solstice at Point One and sets at Point Two. At the winter solstice, it rises at Point Three and sets at Point Four. At the equinoxes, it rises in the east and sets in the west. The central point, Five, is aligned with the North Star.

Because the Aagard Lamp was found in Utah, it is pertinent to note that the ancient Maya of nearby Mexico also used the quincunx symbol in their hieroglyphic writing. In their solar calendar, the glyph *Zip* signifies a 365-day year, and it contains the quincunx. So also does another glyph, *Kin*, which means "sun," "day," or "time." Still another glyph, *Uo*, is a day sign. The cross within a rectangle, or the Five corresponding dots, are in all these glyphs.

But this symbol was not limited to the Maya. Historian Norman Totten writes, "The 'suns' or quincunx was used in the American Southwest, Mexico, Central America, Ecuador, Peru, and Bolivia. It conveyed the idea of five ages, five directions (north, east, south, west, center), divisions of a solar year by winter solstice, spring equinox, summer solstice, and fall equinox, as the sun moved through the heavens."[2]

The quincunx symbol, having basically a solar meaning, also occurs at Western European megalithic centers and in Minoan Crete. Its appearance on something found in Utah might suggest diffusion from the Amerindian sources relatively nearby, but no such object has ever been associated with any Mesoamerican or North American tribal culture. Instead, the artifact is typical of an identical household or temple item found in large numbers throughout the ancient Old World, where, again contrary to Amerindian practices, alabaster was commonly worked.[3]

Perhaps most significantly, the Aagard Lamp quincunx appears just below where the wick and flame would be, and the symbol itself means "light"!

CHAPTER 13

Minoan Pendant
Unearthed in Ohio
by Frank Joseph

The Aagard Lamp, described in the previous chapter, is not the only object suggesting Minoan origins found in North America. But few other, similar finds represent a more credible discovery made in the Middle West during the early 21st century.

In October 2006, Daniel Byers was exploring a suburban Cleveland high school practice football field with a White's DFX 300 search apparatus.

"Athletic fields are prime spots for metal detectorists to find dropped coins and jewelry, mostly rings," he explained to *Ancient American* in the March/April 2009 issue (Volume 13, Issue 83). "If the school associated with that field has some age to it—silver coins were last minted in 1964—then the odds of finding silver are good."

Suddenly, the instrument's alarm alerted him to something metallic buried beneath the surface, and he began digging. "My arm was up to the elbow with my Lesche fully down, when I finally got deep enough for my pin-pointer to sound off," he recalled. "A *Lesche* is a popular digging tool used by metal detectorists. A *pin-pointer* is an electronic probe device used to fine-tune the exact position of a metallic object's location down in the earth, once a hole has been opened up."

The football field ground into which he dug was a very compacted, mineralized soil matrix. The soil may not be original to the location. There are indications that it was fill-soil brought in from a riverbed during the 1930s. Even then, I doubt the soil came from somewhere other than Ohio. It appears that a section of this field has fill-dirt probably placed there when the school was built eighty years ago to level the field. The soil is rockier than the surrounding, native soil, as well, so it may be fill-dirt brought from a riverbank, not uncommon.

In view of Mr. Byers's discovery, his observations concerning the soil in which it was found are significant.

After digging down about 18 inches, he found a small, metal, delta-shaped pendant approximately 2.4 inches long by 1.5 inches wide, with a single perforation at the top. At 1.4 ounces, "it is quite heavy for its size," according to Byers, "demonstrating a conductivity reading consistent with bronze." The object "has no casting marks around the edge, and shows clear working marks, so it seems to be carved into the metal, not cast. There are no seams to indicate it was a casting or reproduction, and in fact, if examined closely, there appears to be working marks on the metal surface."

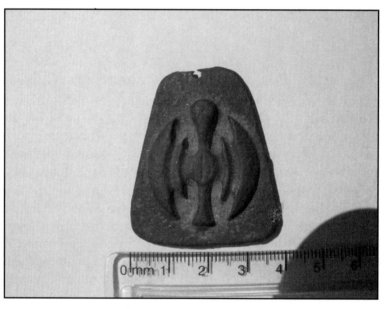

Obverse of the Cleveland-area pendant is emblazoned with a double-headed axe (labrys), the symbol of Minoan Civilization.

An anthropomorphic image on one side depicts a slim-waisted, shirt-less figure striking what appears to be a dancing pose, his hair styled into long locks hanging beneath a headgear of some kind, a belted skirt at his slim waist and pectoral around the shoulders. At the lower right, what appears to be an inverted question-mark shelters inside a semi-circle. The other side of the object is emblazoned with a stylized, double-headed axe.

Everything about the pendant is self-evidently Minoan. The figure resembles the so-called "Prince of Lilles," a painted fresco on the palace walls at Knossos, capital city of the Minoan island of Crete.

The Ohio pendant features a characteristic likeness of Minoan Crete's "Prince of Lilles," at Knossos.

The Minoans raised an exceptionally sophisticated Bronze Age civilization that flourished from 2700 BC to 1450 BC. More of a commercial and cultural than militaristic or imperialist people, they dominated the Aegean Sea as the foremost mariners of their time, sailing beyond the Straits of Gibraltar, out into the Atlantic Ocean at least as far as Britain, where they engraved their emblematic labrys on the flank of one of the great standing megaliths at Stonehenge, where it may still be seen today. Their labrys was the same, double-headed axe found on one side of Mr. Byers's find. It signified the moon-goddess, for whom the "Prince of Lillies" was probably a sacred dancer.

The semi-circle with an inverted question mark on the Ohio pendant is comprised of two, recognizable letters from a written language epigraphers refer to as "Linear A." This was an official script for cult purposes and palace administration current in Minoan Crete. Although Linear A has not yet been entirely deciphered, investigators believe the semi-circle signified "moon," or things lunar, an identification that properly coincides with the moon-goddess imagery of Mr. Byers's discovery. If it is authentically ancient, the appearance of these glyphs on the object dates it from circa 1900 BC to 1700 BC, because Linear A was only current during the Middle Minoan Period.

Byers relates his frustration, however, in having the pendant professionally examined:

> I tried in vain to have it identified by experts, including Sotheby's Auction House and a few others who might be more familiar with a 'period piece' reproduction that would have been done after the Palace at Knossos was discovered—where the Prince of Lilles fresco was first re-built, the same figure that appears on the pendant—and no one was able to find a representative example showing it was modern. One expert—I forgot which museum he was from—wanted me to send the item to him for dating, but I was warned by others not to do that for fear of never seeing it again. I have tried, repeatedly, to have it examined by certified archaeologists, but the "pros" absolutely refuse to even have their names associated with any kind of site that might turn up the "wrong" kind of evidence.

Despite mainstream unwillingness to consider the Ohio find, its bronze composition nevertheless coincides with the pendant's imagery, because the Minoans are univerally credited as great metalsmiths who dominated the Aegean Sea during the Bronze Age, as well as far-ranging mariners.

"I have dug many coins that pre-date 1900," Byers states, "but none appear to be as old as this item in both patina and detail. I have continued to metal-detect this area, but have not found anything even remotely similar there."

Revealingly perhaps, a Numidian coin dating to the first century BC was also unearthed in the regional vicinity, likewise at 18 inches beneath the surface of an athletic field at a middle school in northeast Ohio. If both items are authentically prehistoric, they suggest that the area was important to pre-Columbian visitors from the Mediterranean World.

Nor was the 2006 discovery the only one of its kind. According to archaeologist Gunnar Thompson, PhD:

> Minoan inscriptions have been found in Georgia and in Brazil along the Amazon River. In 1883, antiquarian Herbert Bancroft reported that Pima natives of Arizona showed Spanish explorers

a traditional symbol they used to represent the search for wisdom: it was the Minoan Maze. The symbol's origin dates to the 3rd Millennium BC reign of King Minos. According to Greek legends, Minos demanded the sacrifice of seven Athenian youths and seven maidens as atonement for the murder of his son at the Olympics. Victims were sent into a maze, or labyrinth, which was the domain of a bull-headed demon called the Minotaur. A Greek hero named Theseus discovered the Minotaur's secret and slew the beast. Henceforth, the maze represented the quest for knowledge.[1]

To Arizona Native Americans, a maze identical to its Cretan counterpart belonged to a dart-game they referred to as *Tculikwikut,* the "House of Tcuhu," or *Tcuhiki.* An early-20th-century archaeologist, Harold Sellers Colton, reported that the *Tcuhiki* maze was indistinguishable from a Minoan labyrinth commonly portrayed on Classical Greek coins. It was first noticed by an unknown Spanish traveler in 1761 or 1762, when he observed a Pima Indian drawing the maze "in the form of a whorl arising from a center called *Tcunni Ki*, the council house."[2] Little is known of *Tculikwikut,* which is no longer played, except that its figure, a cultic hero known as Tcuhuki, from whom the game derived its name, was a kind of savior not unlike the Minoan Theseus, who additionally bears a philiological similarity to the Native American character: Tcuhuki-Theseus.

The modern Pima are mixed descendants of the Hohokam, their name for the "Ancient Ones," a highly civilized people who engineered massive, advanced irrigation systems, and built monumental ceremonial structures in Arizona nearly 1,000 years ago. On the ruins of their foremost construction, referred to by admiring Spaniards as Casa Grande, the "Big House," one may still see a Minoan maze inscribed on its adobe walls. Identical mazes appear throughout the fragments of Hohokam pottery, as described by the leading authority on Hohokam Civilization, Emil Haury.[3]

"It is hard to believe," writes Colton, "that such complicated labyrinths similar in every detail could have had separate origins."[4]

Although more than 20 centuries separated Minoan Crete from Hohokam Arizona, the survival of a labyrinthine design at Casa Grande suggests that Bronze Age visitors from the Eastern Mediterranean made an impact, as indelible as it was profound, on native cultures in the American Southwest, so much so, the influence was carried forward over time unto today's Pima Indians.

Dr. Thompson traced other Minoan influences on pre-Columbian construction in Middle and South America: "Monte Alban, Mexico, has stepped terraces and rectangular buildings, which are similar to those in the Minoan palace at Phaistos, Crete. The Castillo at Chavin de Huantar, Peru, was built with a system of air-conditioning ducts which are similar to a system of ducts used in the Creten palace at Knossos."[5] Monte Alban as an imporant urban center for the Maya in the southern Mexican state of Oaxaca from around 100 BC to 900 AD. Located 160 miles north of Lima, Chavin de Huantar was a pre-Inca ceremonial city founded before 1200 BC by an unknown people, subsequently occupied by other culture-bearers until circa 400 BC.

In addition to Byers's discovery, several other Minoan-like objects have been found in North America. During 1975, a representation of the Creten moon-goddess was accidentally unearthed during excavation for the basement of a house on the banks of the Penobscot River, 10 miles north of Bangor, Maine. The 1-inch-by-3.4-inch-wide plate made of a silver-nickel alloy portrays her in iconic, flounced skirt, high, pointed headgear, and large, pectoral necklace, and a serpent in her left hand.

Although lacking unequivocal proof that the Ohio pendant is a Minoan artifact, all available evidence surrounding it argues strongly on behalf of an ancient Old World Bronze Age provenance. Its discovery a foot and a half beneath the surface of a practice field indicates an extended passage of time, and the un-cast nature of its fine workmanship does not suggest any modern reproduction. These considerations are amplified by the obvious integrity of its finder to persuade fair-minded examiners that the little pendant was probably dropped by a visitor from the high civilization of Minoan Crete in northeastern Ohio more than 35 centuries ago. As such, it is the most valuable treasure Mr. Byers's metal detector will probably ever find.

Part II

Sites

CHAPTER 14

An Ancient Semitic Goddess
Leaves Her Mark in New York
by Zena Halpern

After obtaining an MA in history and education at New York University, Zena Halpern took post-graduate courses taught there by the 20th century's greatest Semitic language expert, Professor Cyrus Gordon. His conclusion that overeseas' visitors from the ancient Old World landed in pre-Columbian America prompted her quest for proof supporting their arrival by undertaking personal research in Guatemala, Honduras, Yucatan, Crete, and along the shores of the eastern Mediterranean.

Among her most exciting discoveries was physical evidence linking the ancient city of Dor, on Israel's north coast, with the Maya ceremonial center at Comalcalco, in Mexico. Halpern's articles also appear with The Epigraphic Society (Danvers, Massachusetts), and she has lectured with both the New England Antiquities Research Association (Edgecomb, Maine) and Ancient American Artifact Preservation Foundation (Scandia, Michigan).

In 2000, a New Yorker from Mt. Vernon was hiking through his state's northern Catskill Mountains when he spotted a peculiar carving on a heap of stones off a trail near the Neversink River. Four years later, Don Ruh led me back to the scene of his discovery, where he found the engraved stone face-down on top of the small rock pile. Although most of its surface was severely weathered, I was able to make out the six upward projecting arms of a triangle base and a seventh round upward projection in the center. This first impression suggested the crude representation of a menorah, among the most widely produced articles of Jewish ceremonial art. The seven-branched candelabrum is a traditional symbol of Judaism used in the ancient Temple. When visiting Israel in 1997, I witnessed the excavation of a rare, triangle-base menorah from an archaeological dig, an experience that triggered my interest in this very old symbol. The Catskill Mountain engraving's triangular base is its most significant aspect, leading to connections through the Menorah to the Tree of Life, the goddess Asherah, and her symbol, the triangle.[1]

The Catskill Mountain Stone.

The Tree of Life is further linked with the menorah to sacred trees and the goddess Asherah, in the Hebrew Bible. Ruth Hestrin, curator of the Israel Museum in Jerusalem, has convincingly demonstrated that Asherah is symbolized by a triangle.[2] This deity was worshipped in the Levant as the great mother-goddess, consort of El, the supreme god, in Ugaritic epics. Throughout the Levant, she signified fertility, the cyclical renewal of nature, sexuality, birth, and healing. According to renowned ethnographer, historian, Orientalist, and anthropologist Raphael Patai, she was very popular during the Israelite period from kings Solomon (960 BCE) to Nehemiah (445 BCE), the central figure of the biblical Book of Nehemiah, which describes his work rebuilding Jerusalem and purifying the Jewish community. She was revered for blessing women with fertility and facilitated childbirth, helping mothers in labor.[3]

Don Ruh's discovery is not an isolated artifact. Two other stones inscribed with ancient Hebrew script have been recovered in the vicinity. One was found resting at the base of a tree. It featured a two-inch cutout that another cut stone fit with exact precision, suggesting an infant emerging from the womb. A local Native American historian familiar with the history of the Leni Lenape people informed us that creeks in this area were places for women to give birth. We wondered if the Catskill Mountain engraving might depict the sacred Tree/Menorah/Triangle symbol of Asherah. Its six upward arms with a seventh projection in the center resting on a triangle base appear to represent a very ancient form of the menorah. The antiquity of this famous symbol dates back to its detailed description in Exodus 25:31–40, which relates that a pattern of the candelabrum was shown to Moses on a mountain in the Sinai Desert. He was directed to make a seven-branched lamp-stand out of a solid piece of gold. The resulting menorah became one of the chief sacred objects in the Holy Place of the Tabernacle.[4]

It is important to understand that, despite precise details provided by the biblical account, they do not describe just what kind of base on which the candelabrum stood. Could the original base have been triangular?

Some researchers speculate that an Israeli plant known as the moriah inspired the menorah design. In his third book on *The Antiquities of the Jews*, Josephus, the first-century Romano-Jewish historian, wrote how its seven branches represented the sun, moon, and five planets. Another theory holds that the menorah originated from the Tree of Life found throughout the Bronze Age Levant, a mystical concept alluding to the interconnectedness of all life. The related sacred tree was associated with Asherah, whose symbol was a triangle. This symbolic tree emerged as the menorah in Israelite times during the monarchy period and survived in use even into Judah (circa 1200 BCE to 582 BCE).[5] In Ugarit, Asherah was worshipped as the chief goddess of this major sea-trading city. She was known there as "Lady of the Sea," an apt description for the seafaring Canaanites, who lived on the coast. Asherah was also intimately connected to the seafaring cities of Tyre, revered in Sidon (in modern Lebanon), and the patron deity of harbors. She later fused with the Carthaginian mother-goddess, Tanit, also sometimes depicted with a triangle base.[6]

Asherah was officially worshipped in ancient Israel, where she was deeply connected with sacred trees and "high places." She is mentioned frequently in the Hebrew Scriptures, whereas Asherah adoration was condemned by pre-exilic prophets. She was presumably lost to history in the movement to obliterate her cult sometime between the fifth and fourth centuries BCE. However, she was evidently a popular figure in ancient Israel during Solomonic times (989 to 931 BCE). Patai wrote about her role as the Hebrew people's preeminent goddess figure throughout biblical times.

Asherah worship spread far and wide, across the Mediterranean, into Iberia and beyond. Recent interest in Asherah has risen during the last 15 years, particularly since the discovery in the Sinai Desert of inscriptions with her name linked to Yahweh. This modern concern has been heightened by Tanit figures with triangle bases found in the American Southwest, as documented by Gloria Farley's book, *In Plain Sight*. Hestrin was the first investigator to make a connection between sacred tree and triangle. Based on her observation, I conjecture that the stone Don Ruh found in the Catskill Mountains may be an ancient carving of the Menorah/Tree of Life, with a base in the form of a triangle, Asherah's symbol.[7]

Similar to better-known searches for the Ark of the Covenant, the menorah seized from Solomon's Temple by Nebuchadnezzar II has sparked many quests on its behalf. The fate of these sacred objects remains speculative, and no one was familiar with their physical appearance during First or Second Temple times, because their artistic reproduction was forbidden. After the menorah was constructed and carried with the Ark of the Covenant, its fate became unknown. Nor does the Old Testament tell us about their fate. All we are told is that the Ark and Tablets of the Law were moved into the Holy of Holies in the house and the Tabernacle, and all the other sacred vessels were brought up. Rabbinic tradition states that the menorah and the Showbread Table—loaves of bread on a specially dedicated table in the Temple in Jerusalem as an offering to God—were placed in the central hall of the sanctuary. The Bible states that Solomon made 10 gold menorahs to stand in the First Temple.[8] Patai reveals that a representation of Asherah was placed in the temple by Solomon himself.[9]

The First Temple treasures were looted by Nebuchadnezzar's armies between 603 BCE and 587 BCE, when its treasures were said to be taken to Babylon. There were legends to the effect that the Ark of the Covenant, the Menorah, and the temple treasures of the temple had been previously concealed in secret places. As an indication of ongoing interest in the subject, recent book claims to have traced the 50 tons of gold, silver, and sacred treasure looted from the last Jerusalem Temple in 70 CE.[10]

During Second Temple times, the Maccabees—members of a Jewish rebel army who took control of Judea in 164 BCE—and their descendents, the Hasmonean kings, constructed menorahs for the Temple, but other reproductions were never permitted. The Hasmonean dynasty semi-autonomously ruled Judea and surrounding regions beginning around 140 BCE. However, against all prohibitions, the last Hasmonean king minted coins with a menorah from 40 to 37 BCE.

Not until a 20th-century archaeological discovery in Jerusalem was the precise configuration of the temple menorah understood. Extensive excavations undertaken from 1969 to 1982 conducted beneath the Old City of Jerusalem for the first time revealed the representation of a seven-branched menorah with a triangle base carved. The engraving appeared on the wall of a house buried for 2,000 years under the charred remains of the second destruction of Jerusalem, and was in the Herodian quarter, dating to 70 CE. Inscribed in plaster, it was described by Hebrew University's professor Nahman Avigad, in charge of the excavations, as the most accurate image of the candelabrum that existed in the Second Temple.[11]

In 1997, I was in Jerusalem and visited the underground Upper City and Western Wall Tunnel, where the bedrock of the Temple Mount had been reached. Beneath the Old City was a vast, excavated area of courtyards, villas, and rooms. A posted description there read: "You have descended three meters below the present Jewish Quarter. You have gone back 2,000 years in time to the upper city of Jerusalem in the Herodian Period."

While walking through the remains of homes, I entered an area where a particular house caught my eye, because incised in plaster on its outside wall was a beautifully carved menorah with a triangle base. The official explanation stated that this was the earliest detailed representation of the Temple menorah known so far. The artist who portrayed this menorah, according to Professor Avigad, must have seen it with his own eyes when it stood in the Second Temple, because the house was only 50 yards away. The menorah was exquisitely detailed, its distinctive feature being an unusual, triangle base. Here was the only depiction of the menorah in the last 2,000 years, rendered by an artist in the last days of Jerusalem. Many others who fled the destruction of the city must have also seen this menorah, and they carried its memory far and wide. Some triangle-base menorahs were found in the catacombs of Rome dated to the first century CE.

Three hundred years later, representations of the menorah appeared on lamps constructed to stand on three or four legs, forever supplanting the triangle-base menorah. Perhaps all association of the triangle-base with Asherah was deliberately erased after her cult had been suppressed during the later centuries in Judah. The destruction of the Temple took place in 70 CE when legions under Emperor Titus burned the structure and looted its sacred objects. He carried off the Golden Menorah to Rome, where the object was depicted on his famous Arch. But the Roman sculptor erroneously gave it an octagonal base.

Impressive remains of fortifications, villas, and houses featuring day-to-day utensils in use when Roman legions entered the city have been found. On the floor of one home, charred beams had fallen during the tremendous fires set by enemy soldiers.

Of special interest were the original stone furniture and vessels used by the inhabitants 2,000 years ago, and still in place. The stone vessel industry lasted for only a short time, then disappeared within a century. Such vessels were considered ritually pure. Interestingly, a stone cup on display with pre-Columbian artifacts from Newark, Ohio, artifacts at the Coshocton Museum resembles first-century Jewish examples. In an underground maze of ancient rooms still showing evidence of the Roman destruction of Jerusalem and the Western Wall Tunnel, a numismatic exhibit on one of the walls presents coins minted during the first century BCE by the last Jewish king of Judah. His name was Mattathias Antigonus II, a direct descendant of the Maccabees, and the great-great-grandson of Simon Maccabee, a heroic figure in Jewish history (143 to 135 BCE).

Antigonus II was engaged in a bitter struggle with Herod and the Roman army for control of Jerusalem. He minted the displayed coins emblazoned with the menorah as a powerful device to rally the citizens of Jerusalem. The minting of these coins with the sacred candelabrum was a daring act, for, by using it as a symbol, he broke with a very ancient proscription forbidding the depiction of any holy objects that stood in the Temple. The preserved coins bear a triangle-based menorah with his name inscribed in Greek: "Of King Antigonus." Inscribed in ancient Hebrew letters on the obverse are the words, "Mattathias the High Priest and the Community of Jews"[12]. Paleo-Hebrew was used exclusively in special circumstances and for coins or seals well into the Bar Kochba period (130 to 133 CE). The centuries-old proscription against depicting any sacred object that formerly stood in the Temple was broken by Antigonus during the first century BCE. The ancient artist who depicted the triangle Menorah on the wall of a house in the last, desperate days of the war with Rome likewise broke with the prohibition about 100 years later.

Could the triangle-base menorah have been one of the last vestiges of Asherah's triangle symbol from the First Temple period? Because no menorahs were allowed to be depicted, the one remaining in Herod's Temple must have had the triangle symbol, as established by the 20th-century find. After all, Asherah worship was a powerful force in ancient Israel and Judah. According to Patai, it lasted well after the return from Babylonian Exile (536 BCE). Small, clay figurines of the goddess were found throughout Palestine dating to the Israelite period.[13] But it was not until the third or fourth century CE that the menorah came into use as a ubiquitous symbol, and no examples stood upon a triangle base; they were all depicted on three or four legs. I propose that the association of the triangle base and the menorah was obliterated because of its association with Asherah. Later menorahs spread throughout Jewish communities in Mediterranean lands to synagogues, additionally appearing on graves, lamps seals, and amulets. All had three or four legs as a base.

Menorahs spread throughout the Diaspora to Jewish communities located at key harbors along the Mediterranean, to Catalonia, Aragon, the Iberian Peninsula, to distant lands, including North America. Ancient carvings of menorahs have been found on canyon walls in Arizona, in Michigan, and in New York State. The symbol was carried across the Atlantic Ocean from ancient harbors such as Caesarea, Dor, Jaffa, Carthage, or Iberian ports. None of these menorahs have a triangle base except Don Ruh's discovery. The menorah with a triangle base carved on a stone found in the Catskill Mountains could only have been carved by someone who had seen or known of a very ancient association of the sacred tree/Asherah with her symbol of the triangle. I suggest that this engraving is a rare relic from the ancient Israelite period, dating to the Early Iron Age.

A supporting rock art menorah was found carved on a canyon wall in Arizona. The renowned epigrapher, Barry Fell, connected it to an Arizona community of early medieval Jews who named their city "Calalus." A pair of worshipping figures appear together with two paleo-Hebrew glyphs Fell translated in an August 25, 1977 letter to Dr. Cyclone Covey, professor of history at North Carolina's Wake Forest University: "After 9 months of uncertainty, a solution can now be offered of the puzzling Central Arizona petroglyph...Using your and my combined results, we now have indicated the 1200 AD record of the looting of Calalus by the Apaches—a) 'menorah' (of the temple of Calalus, presumably.); b) figures, in typical Navajo Apache style, of warriors; c) illiterate Iberic Hebrew sh-l, sholl = 'The Looting'."

Fell connected this rock art menorah to Arizona's early medieval Jewish community. Its founders had sailed from one of the Mediterranean ports in the south of France, sometime during the eighth century CE to the American Southwest. Decades of controversy surround this discovery, but early medieval history confirms a large Jewish community in the south of France. Jewish shipping was active at the time, and ships were capable of crossing to North America. Ships from Mediterranean ports had already completed transatlantic voyages, as evidenced by a Roman pottery head found by Mexican archaeologists in the pyramid floor—"in situ"—of Calixtlahuaca. Thermoluminescence testing dated it to the second century CE.

Comparison of Arizona's rock art menorah to the first-century-BCE counterpart from a synagogue at the great harbor of Caesarea on the Mediterranean coast of Israel establishes an undeniable relationship. Other examples appear on inscribed stones from a far more controversial collection from southern Illinois. Among their most significant features is depiction of the triangle base menorah along with the same paleo-Hebrew letters carved on the triangle base or beneath the base. Three letters are clearly *Yod, Hey,* and *Daled* in differing arrangements (perhaps the Aramaic spelling, "Yehud," for *Judah*). An accompanying circle with a line through it may be a monogram from the Persian period (538 BCE to 400 BCE). The significance of the triangle, Asherah's symbol, the Tree of Life, and the Menorah is documented from recent discoveries and their reports.[14] Originally the goddess was connected to tree worship and later suppressed, but did her powerful and ancient belief go underground?

Was the triangle a coded symbol for recognition of her secret identity?

We have barely skimmed the surface of a very intriguing and complex discovery that appears to have made its way across the ocean, a relic from a lost time, when Asherah was worshipped, not only during Israelite times, but among the Canaanites, in Ugarit, Crete, and Sumer. The same deity was revered in all these places, only under different names. She took many forms and had several titles, but essentially she was the mother goddess over a vast time period. The Catskill Mountain carving of a tree with six upward branches and a round projection in the center with a triangle base certainly resembles a menorah. If this impression is correct, then it may well represent a primitive origin for the menorah beginning with Asherah, whose cult was worshipped in pre-exilic Israel from the 10th to the sixth centuries BCE, perhaps earlier. An artifact from Lachish, an ancient Israeli town, dated to circa 1220 BCE, shows a tree and triangles with what appears to be a menorah.

The menorah may have originated from a period when the ancient Israelites worshipped the goddess Asherah, as evidenced by her presence in the First Temple for some 230 years. Her cult was deeply rooted in the Iron Age, well after 536 BCE, despite strenuous objections and efforts to obliterate her by prophets and reforming kings. Depiction of the typical sacred tree—not always with a central pole, but with six branches—has a striking resemblance to the menorah as it is described in Exodus 25:31–40, minus information concerning configuration of its base. If the Exodus menorah had a triangle base, as do the Jerusalem and Hasmonean menorahs, then the Asherah cult must have been prevalent during the time of the Exodus.

The triangle is connected with the pubic triangle depicted on an ewer from Lachish dated 1220 BCE, a time when the Israelites were in Canaan. Hestrin connected the tree and triangle, as stated in "Understanding Asherah—Exploring Semitic Iconography,"[15]. In it, she told of the "The Lachish Ewer and the Asherah" in the *Israel Exploration Journal*[16], which depicts a tree/menorah and triangle. The Catskill Mountain menorah implies that the goddess, "Lady of the Sea" and foremost fertility, was transported across the sea by northern Israelites or Phoenicians from key harbors along the coast of the Near East. Asherah, the sacred tree, and the triangle belonged to this ancient, female Semitic deity commonly worshipped by coastal and inland peoples in the Levant. She may have originated as a megalithic goddess.

Don Ruh's discovery should be regarded within the context of other, ancient Israelite incursions into America during the Iron Age. New Mexico's "Decalogue Stone," the Bat Creek Stone from Tennessee, related Ohio artifacts, and Iberian inscriptions in various states all attest to voyagers from Mediterranean lands to our continent from harbors in ancient Israel and Judah, from Carthage and Iberian ports, well into the early medieval period.

CHAPTER 15

Great Serpents From
Kansas to Scotland
by Frank Joseph

Something happened on our planet that induced men to raise colossal earthworks in the form of an egg-spitting snake from Western Europe to the Central Plains of North America. Could these massive effigies commemorate a natural catastrophe witnessed by its survivors on two continents, 3,000 or more years ago?

Some Americans might imagine that the middle of Kansas is synonymous with the Middle of Nowhere. Accounts of a splendid and ancient civilization with a mystical site in the Great Plains State may seem too far-fetched for belief. The first modern Europeans to hear these stories were the Spanish Conquistadors, who defeated the Aztec Empire during the early 16th century.

The story of the Seven Cities of Gold, sometimes collectively referred to as Quivira or Cíbola, predated the Spanish Conquest by 350 years. It began in 1150 AD, as seven bishops and their congregations fled Spain by ship, carrying away certain religious relics before the Moors could seize the city of Mérida. Although the refugees were never heard from again, rumor had it that they crossed the Atlantic Ocean to land on another continent, where they set up seven cities, one for each bishop, soon growing very rich in gold and precious stones. The legend persisted over the centuries and abruptly swelled to hysterical proportions with the Spanish Conquest of Mexico.

The legend was reinforced in 1519, when Emperor Moctezuma II told Hernán Cortés that the Aztec, previous to their occupation of Tenochtitlan, dwelled north of the imperial capital at a place called Chicomoztoc. With its translation as "the Place of the Seven Caves," the

104 ·

Spanish concluded that the Aztecs' former residence could have been none other than Cíbola's Seven Cities of Gold. In reality, Chicomoztoc was either Rock Lake in far-away Wisconsin, or a large, if relatively humble settlement built around a height near the present-day town of San Isidro Culhuacán, 60 miles northeast of the Valley of Mexico. In either case, there was no gold to be found in Rock Lake or San Isidro Culhuacan.

Spurred on by inflated traditions of Chicomoztoc and other local tales describing far-off cities overflowing with riches, Viceroy Antonio de Mendoza dispatched an expedition led by Marcos de Niza, a Franciscan monk, in search of Cíbola and Quivira. After 10 months, de Niza returned to claim he had visited a populous urban center where its residents ate from dishes of gold and silver, decorated their houses with turquoise, and adorned themselves with enormous pearls, emeralds, and other stunning gems.

Sure that the Seven Cities of Gold were to be had for the taking, de Mendoza ordered a large military contingent to conquer the famous Cíbola and Quivira. The expedition was led by Francisco Vásquez de Coronado, who set out at the head of the Viceroy's well-equipped army from Culiacán on April 22, 1540. After crossing the Rio Grande, he was encouraged by various tribes and pueblo peoples, who knew at least something of Cibola-Quivira, and urged the foreigners ever northward—perhaps to be rid of the avaricious strangers.

Finally, Coronado and his 40 men reached what is now central Kansas, the first modern Europeans to visit that part of North America. The Aztec guides had followed their instructions faithfully, and the landscape matched descriptions provided by their superiors back in Mexico. But there were no Seven Cities of Gold, not even their ruins. All that the Spaniards found were scattered, underpopulated villages of dried-grass shanties inhabited by primitive buffalo-hunters. Marcos de Niza had lied to Coronado, whose disappointment was keenly felt. "I arrived at the province they call 'Quivira,' to which the guides were conducting me, and where they had described to me the house of stone with many stories, and not only are they not of stone, but of straw, but the people in them are as barbarous as all those whom I have ever seen and passed before this."[1]

For the next 430 years, Cíbola was universally regarded as a baseless myth. But in the 1960s, Waldo R. Wedel of the Smithsonian Institution excavated the first of five unusual structures in Rice and McPherson counties in Kansas. Referred to for want of a better name as "council circles," the ruins belonged to circular earthworks 60 to 90 feet across and averaging about 3 feet high. They were surrounded by shallow ditches and showed evidence of intense burning covered over by numerous sandstone boulders.

Pits contained the bones of children and adult skulls. The resident Witchita Indians knew nothing of the "council circles." The compound symbol of egg and serpent appears in the tribal culture of no Plains Indian nation, although several tribes in the Southwest, such as the Hopi, practiced ophiolatreia, or snake idolatry. But after more than a four-century lapse, stories of Cíbola began to circulate again.

Nothing more conclusive was obtained until 1982, when archaeologist R. Clark Mallam identified a far more dramatic feature nearby: the image of a colossal snake cut into the ground like a reverse cameo known as an intaglio. From its gaping jaws emerged a huge egg. Subsequent tests of the 160-foot-long effigy revealed that it was oriented not only to the three Rice County council circles, but, more significantly, to the winter and summer solstices. Fires that long ago burned in the pitted mounds were lit when the Sun's position was opposite to the tail of the serpent.

The terraglyph's discoverer described a propitious sunrise in words that convey what must have been at least an approximation of the aboriginal experience afforded by the serpent intaglio:

The morning of December 21st dawned lambent and clear. A crowd of thirty-five people gathered in the Higgins prairie to watch the beginning of the solstice day. As the eastern sky brightened, bringing warmth to the frost-tinged landscape, a blanket of fog formed in the low areas of the headwaters. Moving slowly, it soon spread to the uplands emerging as a narrow band on the horizon. At that point, the Sun appeared—a small, dull-red disc rising languorously through the mist. Perhaps in the distant past this was the time when religious leaders struck the fires in the centers of the council circles, a signal that "new time" had begun again.

Within the space of only a few moments though, this halcyon scene transformed into a dialectical struggle between natural forces. The Sky and the Earth are at odds, and God shudders. As the fog intensified, the Sun alternately disappeared and reappeared. Finally, after what seemed an interminable period, it broke free from the constricting mist, and once more dominated the landscape. From that point on until June 21st, it would progressively gain in strength. What we witnessed that morning was an event common to native peoples throughout the western hemisphere.

The manner in which it was experienced, however, differs considerably between ourselves and them. To us, the rising of the Sun on December 21st constitutes little more than a calendar notion. For native peoples though, it represents an event of momentous social and religious significance. It is the recreation, the regeneration of the life cycle, a point in time when humans attempt, through ritual means, to call back the Sun from its southwestern house. Practically foreign to us, this human involvement in the recreation of the universe essentially functions as a world renewal ceremony.[2]

These solar alignments suggest that the lost Cíbola does indeed lie below the plains of Kansas. The gold of which the Aztecs spoke, however, may not have had anything to do with metallic wealth sought for by the Spaniards. Rather, the gold of this vanished capital was far more precious: It was sunlight. This interpretation is underscored by the Aztec description of the Seven Cities of Gold. Seven, separate and distinct "cities"—urban population centers—certainly never existed in pre-Columbian Kansas.

Far beyond the Plains State, snake-egg imagery was indicative of healing, regeneration, and rebirth, attributes connected with the Sun, and made all the more cogent in the case of the Kansas serpent by the abundance of natural springs in its immediate vicinity. In such disparate places as Classical Greece, Pharaonic Egypt, and Maya Yucatan, the snake-egg theme was emblematic of Asclepius, the divine founder of medicine; Knepf, the demiurge of the universe entwined about the staff of Thaut, the god of healing; and emblazoned on the façade of Uxmal's so-called Nunnery.

"Seven" should be understood as a sacred numeral defining the esoteric principle of Cíbola. In Mesoamerican cosmology, number seven signified the completion of cycles. It was associated with the movement of the Sun and an earmark of serpent symbolism. All three esoteric characteristics perfectly describe the Rice County intaglio and its solar orientation. As though affirming the metaphysical qualities of that alignment, its relationship with the council circles may extend to the local environment, thereby comprising an organic whole. As Mallam noticed during aerial reconnaisance of the site, "the 'council circles,' demarcated by dark, green patches, seemed to be located virtually in the center of this hydrologic network. It was as if we were seeing an architectural order."[3]

He was inspired enough by the feature to state:

I believe that in this cosmological conviction the serpent intaglio functioned as a "life metaphor." It signified and expressed, through its placement and orientation, the natural and cyclical process of death, rebirth, and the regenerative power of life. Inherent in this theme are certain basic Native American concepts. Cross-culturally, the serpent represents "primal chaos, disruption, disharmony, and dissolution," and continued renewal througfh annual shedding of its skin, and hibernation. The themes of cyclical order and centerality became visibly evident at least twice each year as hierophanies. During the solstices, the sacredness of the headwaters was defined, reaffirmed and intensified the arrangement of cultural symbols. Cosmos emerges from chaos, summer out of winter, and life from death.[4]

With Mallam's credible interpretation of the Rice County effigy, the real mystery still remains: Who were the sophisticated astronomer-engineers who created the snake effigy and its council circles in the middle of Kansas, during prehistory? And why did they choose such a remote part of the world, hundreds of miles from the nearest civilization in Olmec-dominated Mexico, to fashion their solar observatory? The riddle is made all the more curious when we learn that there are only two other snake images of this kind in the world: one atop a high hill on the lip of a meteor crater in the Ohio Valley, the other near an idyllic lake in Scotland. Ohio's Great Serpent Mound has its only material counterpart in, of all places, Scotland. The recurrence of snake-egg imagery as far afield as Ancient Greece, Dynastic Egypt, and the Maya ceremonial city of Uxmal has already been cited. But the only geoglyphs executed in this theme occur in Kansas, Ohio, and Scotland.

Similarly disgorging an egg from its gaping jaws, the Great Serpent Mound is the 1,254-foot-long image of a monstrous snake writhing in seven humps across a high, wooded ridge located near Locust Grove, in the Ohio Valley. At 5 feet high and averaging 20 feet wide, the effigy's tail terminates in a large, perfectly engineered spiral. A 40-foot-tall observation tower provided by the local museum allows its bioglyph to be seen in better perspective than circumambulating it via the foot-path. Even so, only from an aerial outlook of 200 or 300 feet does the effigy appear in all its perfect proportions. No sufficiently high prominence exists in its immediate vicinity. Why the prehistoric artists would have gone to the immense difficulty of sculpting such a magnificent work of landscape art they could never see properly evokes questions beyond the purview of this article.

Its physical construction is better understood. Its builders chose flat river stones for uniform size, combining them with lumps of clay carefully laid out on the ground in a serpentine pattern. Basketfulls of soil were then piled over the design and sculpted into shape. Before the close of the 20th century, archaeo-astronomers determined that the biomorph's humps had been deliberately oriented to a constellation known as *Draco*, or the Dragon, in the West. Thus was discovered the first of additional cultural connections between Ohio's Great Serepent Mound and the ancient Old World. More revelations were soon forthcoming. Of especially dramatic interest is the effigy's position within a 4-mile-wide circular area of layered bedrock that was long ago shattered into enormous cracks by some incredibly powerful phenomenon that forced some blocks steeply downward, and others sharply upward.

The cause was massive impact generated by an object approximately 200 feet in diameter traveling at some 45,000 miles per hour when it struck the Ohio Valley, between 5,000 and 4,000 years ago, according to some researchers. Although no consensus opinion has been reached concerning a precise time frame for this event, its celestial origins are not in doubt. It seems self-evident, however, that the effigy was meant to memorialize this cataclysm, landscaped as it was on the lip of an astrobleme four times wider than Arizona's Meteor Crater. Numerous cultures employed snake imagery to signify cometary or meteoric appearances for thousands of years. A comet's sinuous motion across the sky finds an obvious likeness in the reptile. Such sky symbolism is especially pronounced in the Great Serpent Mound, spewing an obate object—the meteor—from its distended jaws.

That the same natural catastrophe may have been simultaneously witnessed and identically memorialized on the other side of the world seems borne out at the shore of Loch Nell, an afternoon hike from the coastal town of Oban, in Scotland. There, a 100-foot long effigy in three humps unwinds from a perfect spiral to disgorge an egg-shaped cairn, or ceremonial rock pile, from its gaping mouth. Like its Ohio counterpart, "a small circular elevation of large stones much burned once existed in its centre, but they have been thrown down and scattered by some ignorant visitor under the pervading impression probably that gold was hidden beneath them."[5] The cairn was apparently used as an altar for burnt offerings, judging from the remains of charred nutshells and scorched bones dating to the third millennium BC.

The Scottish serpent mound is located in the west part of the country, perhaps 5 miles from the Hebridean Sea, at Glen Feochan, near the hamlet of Dalnaneun, or "Place of Birds," in Gaelic, a few hundred feet from Loch Nell, on a low hill within sight of the triple-cone of Mount Ben Cruachan. "Why lies the mighty serpent here, let him who knoweth tell, with its head to the land and its huge tail near the shore of fair Loch Nell," sang 19th-century poet George Blackie.[6] Dalnaneun was an active ceremonial center from early Neolithic times into the Late Bronze Age, according to findings preserved at Oban's Archaeological Museum, and renowned throughout Argyllshire for its cultic significance. So too, celestial alignments incorporated into the Locust Grove hill-figure date it to around 2000 BC, time frames for both the Loch Nell terraglyph and Ohio's meteor impact. Did members of the same culture on both sides of the Atlantic dedicate shared, serpentine imagery to a world-shattering event they both experienced?

The Scottish snake effigy does not appear to possess astronomical orientations of any kind, but its strong, physical resemblance and shared period (in at least one instance) with its two, North American cousins suggest a connection of some kind. Like the Great Serpent Mound's close relationship with the astrobleme, the Dalnaneun biomorph implies its surrounding region, still scarred by prodigious lava flows that anciently swept in great waves of molton rock for miles around Oban. Clearly, geologic activity of extreme, widespread violence once blasted much of the Hebridean area.

Who laid out the Scottish or Kansas geoglyphs is uncertain. But the Mandan Indians at least preserved an oral tradition of who built Ohio's Great Serpent Mound. It was there, in the effigy's immediate vicinity, that they allegedly originated, and the earthwork was constructed at the behest of an alien race that came up from the south following a terrible deluge commemorated by the Mandan themselves in their *O-kee-pa,* or "Bull Dance." After some inter-marriage with the newcomers, the Mandan were expelled from the region to resetlle along the banks of the Missouri River and two of its tributaries—the Heart and Knife Rivers—in present-day North and South Dakota, where their last pure-blood tribal member died during 1971.

Although presently residing in the American Southwest, far from Ohio, the Hopi Indians still preserve a complimentary, though more detailed folk memory of the Great Serpent Mound people. They tell how *Pahana*, the "White Brother," commanded fleets of large reed boats filled with family members and friends to escape the Great Flood. After landing on the eastern shores of Turtle Island—that is, North America—he led them into the Ohio Valley, where they built the Great Serpent Mound, naming it *Tokchii,* the "Guardian of the East," to commemorate the direction from which they fled the Deluge. Today, Hopi Snake Clan members adorn themselves with seashells in memory of their transoceanic origins in the east.

No *Tokchii*–like effigies are known to exist in Europe. But the ancient Greeks, like the Hopi Indians, claimed descent from deluge-survivors remembered as the *Ophites*.[7] The totem of this ancestral "Snake People" was none other than a snake with an egg emerging from its mouth.

CHAPTER 16

Stone Fangs of the
Great Serpent
by Ross Hamilton

*M*onumental standing stones are diagnostic features of Neolithic sites across Western Europe. Their unexpected discovery in North America—and at our continent's most important effigy mound, to boot—represents a major find reported for the first time by Ancient American magazine.

Ross Hamilton is a tour guide at Ohio's Great Serpent Mound, where he is a leading authority on this spectacular effigy earthwork. His published books include The Mystery of the Serpent Mound, A Tradition of Giants, Wonders, and Mysteries of the Great Serpent Mound, Star Mounds: Atlas of an American Mystery.

Nestled in a cozy margin between the western cliffs and a special path fit for those with strong legs and good balance is one of the most interesting landmarks in the entire Serpent Mound Park acreage. What appears to be a megalithic-type standing stone has lay on its side, partially buried beneath the Stone Serpent Head, for an untold number of years, perhaps many centuries. It is 9 feet, 4 inches long, and about 24 inches wide and deep with some consistency, tapering to a narrow, thin end with what appears to be cut marks in the lower part. The opposite end is a square formed by a large notch out of the right side. A core of what is identified as "calcite crystal" runs through the center of the stone. On a hunch, we tapped softly on one end with a dime while someone touching his ear to the monolith listened on the other. The result was that the outwardly imperceptible tapping was quite audible through the entire length of the stone.

The long rock is tentatively recognized by local geologist and fossil expert Tom Johnson of nearby Locust Grove as a very hard form of Greenfield dolomite (limestone in combination with conductive magnesium), apparently differing from the brittle surface rock called "Peebles dolomite" found atop the isthmus on which the serpent effigy rests. The Peebles dolomite has been subject to millennia of rains percolating through it and has become brittle. This corruption of the surface layer is due to the creation of sulfuric acid through water interaction with minute amounts of iron found in the dolomite's chemical composition, explaining the presence of large sinkholes and caves right in the park area itself. Because this long stone may be identified with the harder Greenfield variety of dolomite, the stone could possibly have been brought from a distance away.

Artist's rendition of the Great Serpent Mound.

In 1995, the science team of John Burke and Kaj Halberg discovered a high degree of telluric (silica-based) current activity at the Serpent Mound. The park is well-known to have both gravitational and magnetic anomalies, as hand compasses at the site give unusually incorrect readings. The magnetically charged positive energies are believed piezoelectric in origin, due mainly to the highly faulted rock extending an estimated 2 to 2.5 miles beneath the surface. Serpent Mound Park is on the western margins of a 240-million-year-old meteor impact-crater more than 3 miles across. It is to the margins having cliff faces that much of the generated current finds its way by any evidence. Burke and Halberg describe a controlled growth experiment using seeds exposed upon the coils of the Serpent Mound during the overhead passage of a thunderstorm. The results were rather dramatic, as the ionized atmosphere produced an internal change in the seeds that showed a nearly three-fold improvement in growth and disease resistance over identical seeds left in their car.[1]

The Serpent Mound peninsula also attracts an extraordinary number of lightning strikes, and many trees on the hillsides surrounding the mound are dead or in a stage of dying from the perceived overload of thunderbolt hits. So, the idea of a strategically placed, long stone to be used as a gathering point of positive electrical forces from the body of the effigy and the outcropping in general has received much attention.

A stone megalith found at the base of the Great Serpent Mound.

The gentlemen explorers, Squire and Davis, wrote in 1847 of the oval feature at the head end of Serpent Mound: "A small, circular, elevation of large stones, much burned, once existed in its center, but they have been thrown down and scattered by some ignorant visitor.... The point of the hill within which this egg-shaped figure rests seems to have been artificially cut to conform to its outline, leaving a smooth platform, ten feet wide...."[2] This 10-foot-wide "platform" becomes a sharp cliff from where such large stones could have been thrown. The lower end of the long stone shows what appears to be cut marks, the action of which may explain the narrowing of the stone to a relatively thin blade-like end about 4 inches or less thick from a 24-inch-thick center.

The main problem with any effort to identify this stone as being of the same function or purpose as the British *menhir*, or standing stone, is a dearth of supporting evidence throughout the Ohio Valley or, for that matter, the entire North American continent. The Megalithic Period featuring *menhirs* in the Insular Celtic region (3500 to 1500 BC) precedes by at least 300 years the commonly accepted dates (1200 to 1000 BC, C-14) for the earliest mound-building society in Ohio, the Adena People. However, the famous Serpent Mound's design may now be reasonably fixed to about 3000 BC by a method of star dating, among other proofs, lending us the tantalizing prospect of this stone having been used as either a celestial marker of some type, a special sort of earth current capacitor, or both.

CHAPTER 17

Colossal Earthworks
of the Middle West
by Frank Joseph

The world's largest astronomical cumputer was built in Ohio by an unknown people 2,000 or more years ago. The overall elegance and vast scale of its advanced construction boggle the mind.

To explore Ohio's Newark earthworks is to experience one of the grandest miracles of ancient engineering. The entire vast complex of walls, mounds, and apertures is, according to archaeo-astronomers, our planet's largest observatory, in addition to being the greatest earthwork in the world. Its titanic scale and precise celestial alignments are on a par with Egypt's Great Pyramid or Britain's Stonehenge. The two sacred centers of Newark enfold more than 200 square acres, including a parallel wall running more than 6 miles long.

The Great Circle, with its 14-foot-high embankment, is 1,200 feet in diameter. But the Octagon enclosure to which it is connected is 11 times larger. Archaeologists refer to prehistoric inhabitants of the Newark area as members of the Hopewell Culture, but little is known of their actual identity. They allegedly built the Octagon and related structures between 200 BC and 400 AD. Thus, a civilized people with advanced knowledge of public works construction on a grand-scale flourished in the Ohio Valley when Rome ruled the Mediterranean World.

The Octagon Mound is joined by a corridor to another circular wall, the south end of which features a 170-foot-long mound 8 feet higher than the embankment, and perfectly oriented to the most northerly rising of the Moon. The main structure is actually composed of line segments separated by regular, measured gaps. Behind each one stands a uniform mound just off center. The purpose of this peculiar arrangement was to provide accurate fixes for the risings and settings of significant astronomi-cal events: solar and lunar eclipses, solstices, the position of Venus, the appearance of significant constellations, such as the Pleiades, and numer-ous other sky data—some of which archaeo-astronomers are only just beginning to discover.

Ohio's Mound City.

No one, they believe, resided behind the far-flung earthworks. Nor, supposedly, did these impressive ramparts comprise a cemetery or fort. The vast complex was strictly a ceremonial center, the largest outdoor church on earth, where tens of thousands of people gathered for all the mass-rituals of a religion dedicated to the movement of the heavenly bodies.

While the Newark Mounds display many astral alignments, their chief orientation is lunar. They form a gargantuan calendar, in which some 16 generations regulated their existence according to the celestial mechanism perpetually moving above them. They were worshippers not of the earth's satellite, but of time, of all it brought forth and everything it destroyed. Every living specimen materialized, prospered, declined, expired, and returned in various related forms through the supreme power of time. If this interpretation is correct, then acting as they did in accordance with the cycles of time, the Ancient Americans felt they were living in harmony with the will of the gods, as expressed in the observeable laws of nature. That same sacred calendar may have originally told them when to come to Ohio—from where, no one knows—and when to leave, because long before arriving in the American Middle West, the people who created the Octagon colossus some 3,200 years ago already possessed their technology and knowledge of astronomy. Their mysterious evacuation of the site, which involved such great labor to erect, may have occurred also at the behest of their astral clock.

But Wayne May, *Ancient American* publisher, reveals the weaknesses of mainstream theories about the Newark earthworks in his book, *This Land.*[1] He points out that the berms and mounds do not comprise a very clumsy, if not altogether unworkable "observatory," but rather represent a highly efficient military installation. Particularly obvious, May believes, is a deep trench surrounding many of the formations, a feature with no astronomical value, but identifiable as a moat protecting the outer defenses of a fort. Conical mounds off center behind each one of the eight gaps are apparent redoubts commonly featured in breast-works throughout history and around the world to allow easy access during peace-time, but serve as "crowd control" measures against massed assaults by an invading enemy.

Because astronomy became all the rage among archaeologists after Stonehenge's mostly lunar correspondence was re-discovered 40 years ago, they have been seeing heavenly alignments—real, coincidental, or imagined—at every prehistoric site. Although the Newark Mounds unquestionably incorporate at least some celestial information, these orientations may have only been used in originally surveying the out-sized earthworks. In any case, the main thrust of their design is clearly military.

Even so, the ancient center has not survived in its entirety. A major square embankment, many mounds and large sections of the parallel walls were obliterated during 19th-century expansion of the modern town. But the Great Circle and some of its walls are still preserved as part of a state memorial park. The Octagon has likewise been saved from destruction—although under less dignified circumstances—as a golf course. Both sites are open to the public year-round, from 10 a.m. to dusk.

The most splendid rituals and military spectacles at the Newark earthworks must have been on a level of theater comparable to the grandeur of the site itself. They involved thousands of people at a time, beginning in one of the enclosures, passing through others via miles of ceremonial double walls, and climaxing in the Great Circle or the giant Octagon. Thirty-two centuries later, the emotional imprint of millions of celebrants and warriors has bequeathed the site a terrific spiritual resonance, a lingering magic that has not been completely subsumed by the banality of a golf course trying to take its place.

More than five centuries after ancient Newark was abandoned, a truncated pyramid boldly dominated Kentucky's heavily forested region on a strategic rise overlooking the Mississippi and Ohio rivers. At its broad base, a moderately sized village of wood and adobe houses was inhabited by a people skilled in the uses of copper and social organization. They buried their dead in family groups, often joining husband, wife, and children in a common interment, and orienting their bodies to the southeast—perhaps in alignment with the rising of the "Morning Star," the planet Venus.

The prehistoric planners at Wickliffe erected their impressive pyramidal mound of soil and clay in six stages, beginning sometime after 900 AD. Throughout the next 400 years, they rose in prosperity and regional influence as part of the Mississippian Culture that spread from Florida to Wisconsin. Then, as suddenly as they had come, they vanished for reasons still sought after by researchers. Today, Wickliffe Mounds Archaeolgical Park is surrounded by buildings displaying hundreds of skeletons laid out on elevated platforms. They are the remains of the people who built the settlement more than 1,000 years ago.

But the site's leading feature is its well-made mound. It stood proudly among the collection of sturdy houses on a steeply sloping ridge that gave the structure the noble facade of a river citadel. Upon its flat top perched a high-gabled, ceremonial temple of wood and dried grass covered with white lime. From this elevated position, the leaders of Wickliffe society surveyed their abundantly fruitful land for many miles around. The stately temple is gone and the vicinity is somewhat overgrown, but the massive earthen pyramid remains almost as impressive as it must have appeared in its heyday. Immediately behind the large mound sprawled a spacious plaza, where markets, public ceremonies, and sporting events were held. The most popular game, *Chunkey*, was a cross between shuffleboard, bowling, and Scottish hurling.

Other mounds—low, elongated structures—once fronted the plaza, but these features disappeared during scientific excavations of the 1930s. Infant burials at Wickliffe are common finds, although they appear to be the results of a relatively high, early mortality rate, rather than evidence of ritual sacrifice. Retrieved artifacts stored in the Lifeways Building, which occupies the former site of the plaza, include beautifully crafted copper items (particularly fish hooks), decorated pottery with imaginative, geometric patterns, and less-identifiable ceremonial items. The pyramid is accompanied by another platform mound, which, while not as prodigious, sets off the larger structure in a wonderful perspective.

No burials were included in its construction, nor was it aligned to any celestial orientation. Yet researchers speculate the long-vanished temple building at its summit may have featured some alignment with the setting sun. There is no indication of war, social upheaval, or epidemic. The orderliness of the excavated graves in apparent family groups suggests a peaceful passage through life. Naturally, the site's sacred center is the pyramid itself, especially its summit. From its flat top, visitors may look west, where the ground slopes dramatically away from the sturdy pyramid and down toward the Mississippi River among vast forests of oak, pine, and cedar.

An entirely different archaeological site is met with at Wisconsin's Lizard Mounds. The peculiar location is approached by car, on roads crossing peaceful Wisconsin farm country, and stands out with a discernible boldness—a small, lone forest of tall trees among green fields spreading to the horizon. From the parking lot, a marked trail winds through the woods to each of the 31 large effigy mounds masterfully sculpted from the earth into vibrant images of birds, reptiles, panthers, buffalo, and unidentifiable mythical creatures.

There are also elegant linear structures, ritual embankments, and conical pyramids. About 10,000 such effigies once spread over Wisconsin. Only a small handful survive, and Lizard Mounds is the greatest remaining collection in North America. No other group is so well-preserved, nor so diversified in form, and none exhibits such outstanding examples of prehistoric native art on such a large scale.

The figures are expressionistic, though stylized. Nothing about them speaks of the crude, the savage, or the primitive. They are proportional, refined, and graceful, reflecting the ordered minds that conceived, molded, and appreciated them, to say nothing of the skillfully organized system of labor and level of surveying technology responsible for their creation. Who their creators and worshippers were, not even the resident Menomonie Indians can tell. The place is, therefore, a prehistoric enigma. All that seems certain is Lizard Mounds' abrupt abandonment about 1310 AD.

Even the dates of its construction and occupation are doubtful. It would appear, however, to have been part of the Aztalan Civilization that flourished about 75 miles to the southwest, because identically styled earthworks once surrounded the ancient capital. If so, the structures date to the 12th or 13th century, although their origin could be earlier by 1,000 years.

A few of the effigies served as tombs. The deceased were placed in pits beneath the mounds with decorated clay pots, bone harpoons, pipes, copper implements, and religious crystals. The precinct was used exclusively for spiritual purposes. No one ever resided within the sacred area. The settlements were in surrounding villages. The largest effigy of the group is 300 feet long, but the site derives its modern name from a 238-foot-long figure thought to represent a lizard.

The figures are not so large that they cannot be identified and discerned at ground level. Seen at high altitude, however, they assume a startling perspective, implying they may only be fully appreciated from the sky. More than 90 percent of North America's earth effigies existed in the Wisconsin area. Exceptions, such as Ohio's Great Serpent Mound, are cultural anomalies. Large-scale geoglyphs were rare in the Ancient World, with the only other groups appearing in Britain and among pre-Inca peoples along the Peruvian and Chilean coasts. The very existence of these widely separated effigies invites comparison, and, in fact, they do share some important points in common.

As mentioned, the Lizard Mound collection is best seen from altitude, as are the British and South American versions. The celestial orientation of many of the figures has been established: Lizard Mound's own winter solstice configuration, and Cerne-Abbas Giant's relationship with the Constellation of Hercules outside Dorchester, in the south of England. Whether these and other parallels suggest cultural coincidence on a grand scale, or some forgotten contact in antiquity between the ancient Old World and pre-Columbian America are points for inquiry.

CHAPTER 18

A Templar Tower
in Rhode Island
by Scott Wolter

A stone structure in Rhode Island has been an unsolved mystery since Colonial times. In February 2008, Ancient American (Volume 12, Number 77) broke the story of geologist Scott Wolter, who established that the Newport Tower's construction was completed long before Christopher Columbus set sail from Sapin in search of a New World.

After months of speculating about the possibility of astronomical alignment features with the planet Venus originally built into the Newport Tower, I decided, in December 2007, to investigate it myself. The question first came up following three years of research into the history of the ideology of certain medieval monks and their kindred, military brotherhood, commonly known as the Knights Templar, which the Cistercians created in 1128 AD. The planet Venus became my focus upon learning that the origin of matriarchal, goddess-based religions began with ancient man's reverence of the brightest star in the sky as a female deity. The Cistercians and Templars also revered the Sacred Feminine, using the Virgin Mary as a metaphor for the ancient goddess. Members of these faith-based military orders understood the sacred, historical connection with Venus and used astronomical cycles of the planet in conjunction with geometry and mathematics in a variety of both practical and religious ways.

The capturing of astronomical alignments of the Sun, Moon, and Venus in Western European standing stone sites and churches allowed the builders to use these structures as clocks and calendars, and for determining longitude (using solar and lunar eclipses) and latitude. The religious aspect of alignments was primarily associated with the winter and summer solstices, and spring and fall equinoxes. Much of the solar and lunar alignments in the Newport Tower have been documented by professor emeritus Dr. William Penhallow.[1] His research effectively proved that the numerous windows and niches inside the Tower were intentionally made to capture various astronomical alignments. But he was apparently unaware of Venus alignments and did not study them.

This paper proposes that Venus alignments are captured in the Tower, providing evidence consistent with medieval Cistercian/Templar construction practices that reflect, in part, their religious ideology.

On December 19, 2007, I traveled to Newport, Rhode Island, to investigate this theory with fellow researcher and friend David Brody. We selected three mornings (December 20th, 21st, and 22nd) that bracket the winter solstice. After making arrangements to gain access to the Tower with the City of Newport Parks officials, Susan Cooper and Scott Wheeler, who were most accommodating, we arrived each morning at 4 a.m., just as Venus was rising in the southeastern sky. To our great frustration and disappointment, never once were we able to actually see the planet, due to heavy cloud cover. However, we were able to make some important observations.

Scott Wolter at Rhode Island's Newport Tower.

The first observation showed that there is a horizontally oriented, rectangular opening in window W-6, allowing light from Venus to enter the Tower and hit niche N-4, as predicted. However, we did not observe an opening in window W-7 that would allow light from Venus to hit niche N-1 or N-2 (likely N-2). Future research into Venus alignments by qualified researchers will hopefully provide validation of their existence.

The first alignment involves the four-year period in the eight-year cycle when Venus is a morning star in the southeastern sky. Its altitude is approximately 22 degrees, which is the same angle of a line drawn from the square niche (N-4) on the west inside wall up through the small square window near the top of the Tower on the southeastern side.

The second alignment involves the four-year period in the eight-year cycle when Venus is an evening star in the west-northwestern sky. Its altitude is again approximately 22 degrees, which is the same angle of a line drawn from the square niche (N-2) on the east southeast inside wall up through the small square window near the top of the Tower on the western side.

When we checked the W-7 to N-2 alignment, there was not a visible opening to allow Venus to be seen. It is unclear why this is so. However, it is possible that an opening did exist at one time, but has since been altered due to repairs of the upper walls. Former Rhode Island governor William C. Gibbs reportedly told historian Benson John Lossing, who was visiting Newport in 1848, "...roughly between 1775 and 1780, the British [occupying Newport] used the tower for an ammunition magazine. When they had to evacuate Newport, they tried to destroy the old building by igniting a keg of powder in it. The masonry did not collapse, however, and the only result was the loss of the roof and two or three feet of the upper stonework of the wall."[2]

It is unclear if two or three feet were lost above the present height of the Tower, or if the present top two or three feet were lost, and then repaired.

On December 22, 2007, the rays of the rising Sun on the winter equinox cast a vertical rectangle that hit directly on the egg-shaped keystone in the west archway between columns P-7 and P-8. In spite of the heavy overcast weather and our failure to see the planet Venus, the other important objective of our trip was successfully accomplished on that same morning. At 8:15 a.m., we arrived at the Tower to record the precession of the rectangular box of sunlight through window W-2. Researcher Jim Egan was the first to document this event in 2001, and presented the information at the first-ever Newport Tower Symposium on October 27, 2007. He did not however, offer an interpretation as to what the illumination might represent.

The light of the rising sun on the winter solstice shines through the southern window (W-2) and casts a rectangular box of sunlight that first shines through the west-facing window (W-3) at approximately 7:45 a.m. As the sun sontinues rising at an increasing angle to window W-2, the rectangular box becomes wider and moves downward in a northerly direction from W-3 along the west-northwestern wall inside the Tower. At approximately 9 a.m., the box of sunlight hits squarely on and brightly illuminates the light, tan-colored, egg-shaped keystone in the west-northwest archway. When personally witnessed, intentional incorporation into the structure by the original builders seems abundantly clear.

Following is my interpretation of an explanation for this feature that is consistent with the religious beliefs of the Cistercians/Templars:

The round Tower was considered a church nave that represented the womb of the sacred feminine (goddess). The egg-shaped keystone on the inside was constructed as the Orphic egg within the womb. When the light of the Sun, considered a male deity, struck the egg on the winter solstice, it was metaphorically inseminated. The allegorically fertilized embryo inside the womb underwent gestation until it hatched with the "birth" of the new ideology (goddess-worship), along with new life (spring), in the New Jerusalem.

Beginning at 8:15 a.m., on December 22, 2007, a rectangular box of sunlight passing through window W-2 moved progressively with the rising sun, downward and north along the west-northwest inner wall of the Tower. At roughly 9 a.m., I was able to photograph the rising sun's rays illuminating the egg-shaped keystone on the west-northwest archway of the Newport Tower.

That these celestial orientations were deliberately built into the Rhode Island structure seems certain. If so, they continue to identify its Templar/Cistercian architects, who incorporated the astronomical symbolism of their heretical spirituality in the Newport Tower decades before Chistopher Columbus sailed for the New World.

<CHAPTER 19>

Indiana's 12th-Century
Welsh Fortress
by Rick Osmon

When early 19th-century portrait painter George Catlin lived with the Mandan Indians of North Dakota for eight months, he was struck by a number of Welsh words in their spoken language. Ever since, independent investigators have speculated about possibilities for the arrival of Medieval Welsh sea-rovers in North America, a hypothesis given new support by analysis of an intriguing stone ruin in the Middle West.

A lifelong resident of southwestern Indiana, Rick Osmon holds an associate of science degree from Vincennes University and has traveled extensively throughout North America, Western Europe, and Scandinavia. He established The Oopa Loopa Café on-line talk show in 2007, specifically to investigate out-of-place artifacts, hidden history, and lost civilizations. Osmon conducts his research through the Ancient Artifact Preservation Society (Marquette, Michigan), Midwestern Epigraphic Society (Columbus, Ohio), and Ancient Kentucky Historical Association.

The year 1968 was a banner year for the recurrent story of Prince Madoc, who supposedly brought or sent Welsh colonists to North America, three centuries before Christopher Columbus landed in the Americas. As local southern Indiana rumors go, this one, also from that year, is a die-hard.

Dr. Barry Fell was lecturing at Indiana University regarding his research into epigraphic evidence of ancient Old World visitation and habitation in the New World. His audience consisted primarily of faculty and staff, with only one or two students, or other interested parties. Only about a dozen people in all attended. After the lecture, senior members of the audience asked Dr. Fell if he would consider making a side trip to examine an inscription on a cliff side written in a language that none of the Hoosier State academics had been able to identify. That inscription was at Clifty Falls and the mouth of Clifty Creek, where it joins the Ohio River, near Madison, Indiana. The gist of what Dr. Fell claimed to have found at that location read: "I, Owan ap Zurinch, in the year of our Lord 1170, did bring to this place...."[1] The text goes on to list a number of persons, cows, pigs, arms, tools, and ships.

The year 1968 also saw the re-publication, at private expense, of a local history of the Falls of the Ohio, first compiled in 1882. The following passages are excerpted from that compilation:

> But this tradition of the Delaware does not stand alone. That the prehistoric inhabitants of Kentucky were at some intermediate period overwhelmed by a tide of savage invasion from the North, is a point upon which Indian tradition, as far as it goes, is strong and explicit. It is related, in a posthumous fragment on Western antiquities, by Rev. John P. Campbell, M.D., which was published in the early part of the present century, that Colonel James Moore, of Kentucky, was told by an old Indian that the primitive inhabitants of this State had perished in a war of extermination waged against them by the Indian; and that the last great battle was fought at the Falls of the Ohio; and that the Indians succeeded in driving the aborigines into a small island below the rapids, 'where the whole lot of them were cut to pieces.' The Indian further said that this was an undoubted fact handed down by tradition, and that the Colonel would have proofs of it under his eyes as soon as the waters of the Ohio became low. When the waters of the river had fallen, an examination of Sandy island was made, and 'a multitude of human bones were discovered.[2]

Having been born and raised in southern Indiana, where I have resided all my life, I was familiar with variations of this story repeated many times. *History of the Ohio Falls Cities and Their Counties* was the first time I encountered the story in print. But I had always heard more to the tale, and, sure enough, it followed immediately in a flea market treasure:

There is similar confirmation of this tradition in the statement of General George Rogers Clark, that there was a great burying ground on the northern side of the river, but a short distance below the Falls. According to the tradition, imparted to the same gentleman by the Indian chief Tobacco, the battle of Sandy Island decided finally the fall of Kentucky with its ancient inhabitants. When Colonel McKee commanded the Kanawha (says Dr. Campbell), he was told by the Indian chief Cornstalk, with whom he had frequent conversations, that Ohio and Kentucky (and Tennessee is also associated with Kentucky in the pre-historic ethnography of Rafinesque) had once been settled by a white people who were familiar with arts of which the Indians knew nothing; that these whites, after a series of bloody contests with the Indians, had been exterminated, that the old burial-places were the graves of an unknown people; and that the old forts had not been built by Indians, but had come down from 'a very long time ago' people, who were of a white complexion, and skilled in the arts.[3]

Historical investigators from both Washington, D.C.'s Smithsonian Institution and Chicago's Field Museum of Natural History dated this steel helmet with chain-mail accidentally discovered by John Brady in 1898, near Clarksville, Indiana, from 310 to 379 AD.

The history has one further reiteration of the story, but no significant differences appear except this: a differentiation between "white Indians" and "black Indians" (as told by an Indian). And that the burial site, a short distance down river from Clarksville, was then (circa 1780) "covered with an alluvial deposition of earth six or seven feet deep."[4]

We have at least three accounts of the genocide of a racially separate people that inhabited an area below the river. But the burial ground is either in the river on an island, or is north of the river. And we have documentation of the Indians' great leaders (Tobacco and Cornstalk) telling the same story, with the account ending in at least three different locations: Sandy Island, Corn Island, and a field down river from Clarksville. There are pioneer accounts of bone fields being found in each of two of those locations. All we can conclude from the various differences is that the story was very old at the time it was re-told to white settlers.

Who might have been these "white Indians"? The history also contains a clue; namely, that Mr. Thomas S. Hinde, an old citizen of Kentucky, neighbor and companion of Daniel Boone and Simon Kenton, wrote a letter in his old age from his home in Mount Carmel, Illinois, dated May 30, 1842, to the editor of the *American Pioneer*, in which is related the following startling bit of information:

It is a fact that the Welsh, under Owen ap Zurich, in the 12th Century, found their way to the Mississippi and as far up the Ohio as the falls of that river at Louisville, where they were cut off by the Indians; others ascended the Mississippi, were either captured or settled with and sunk into Indian habits. Proof: In 1799, the skeletal remains of six soldiers were dug up near Jeffersonville; each skeleton had a breast-plate of brass, cast, with the Welsh coat of arms, the mermaid and harp, with a Latin inscription, in substance, "virtuous deeds meet their just reward". One of these plates was left by Captain Jonathan Taylor with the late Mr. Hubbard Taylor, of Clark County, Kentucky, and when called upon by me, in 1814, for the late Dr. John P. Campbell, of Chillicothe, Ohio, who was preparing notes of the antiquities of the West, by a letter from Hubbard Taylor, Jr. (a relation of mine), now living, I was informed that the breast-plate had been taken to Virginia by a gentleman of that State, I supposed as a matter of curiosity.[5]

Mr. Hinde continued, "The Mohawk Indians had a tradition among them, respecting the Welsh and of their being cut off by the Indians at the

Falls of the Ohio. The late Colonel Joseph Hamilton Daviess, who had for many years sought for information on this subject, mentions this fact, and of the Welshmen's bones being found buried on Corn Island; so that Southy, the king's laureate, had some foundation for his Welsh poem."[6]

The editor closed this passage by stating, "The story of the Jeffersonville skeletons, we hardly need add, is purely mythical. It is not probable that any pre-Columbian Welshman was ever at the Falls of the Ohio." [7]

The rest of the tradition I have heard throughout the past 40 years or so includes the existence of 12 cut-stone fortresses spaced one day's march apart, and stretching all the way across Indiana from Clifty Creek on the Ohio to Merom Bluff on the Wabash. The compilation book only once includes the one phrase *old forts*, offering no further details.

There we have the bulk of the known evidence on this side of the Atlantic for the Welsh having emigrated to what later became Indiana, and most of that evidence is documentation of oral tradition. And that, sadly, is not much to take to any university's history or archeology department. I knew of several "old fort" locations before reading the history, including Clifty Creek, a bluff overlooking the Ohio River on the Indiana side, now part of Clifty Creek State Park. According to the local lore, all the stones of this fortress were used in the late 19th century to build a railroad trestle over the Ohio.

Then there was Merom Bluff overlooking the Wabash River, but in an area of controlled access owned by a power utility. A few of the flooring stones of this site are supposed to be still in place, but because I can't access the site easily, I am unable to verify that they do, in fact, exist. The site of another ancient fort is located at Five Points Trail, aka Saddle Creek Trail, in the Charles C. Deam Wilderness Area (National Park Service–managed property). All the flooring stones and about half the stones of two walls remain intact at this site, according to a reliable witness.

All these locations have some governmental or other factor restricting on-the-ground research. Consequently, I set out to find one or more of the 12 that might be on real estate I could more easily access. I examined topographic maps and waterway maps, and used the idea that a "one-day march" between the sites meant that all of them had been chosen using a defensive mind-set. Such a mentality would include, as evidenced at the previously known places, that the military planners originally wanted at least one side that could not be assaulted, and that they therefore would not have to defend. They would also require easy access to water.

As such, I needed to find high, steep bluffs overlooking free-flowing rivers or tributaries. One meeting these criteria occurs in Lawrence County, very near Fishing Creek, and within a half mile of the East Fork of White River. From here, the 12th-century Welshman surveyed a wild landscape they dreamed of incorporating in their royal realm. But it was not to be. Like others before and after them, they and their ambitions were swallowed by the immensity and native hostility of prehistoric America.

CHAPTER 20

Prehistoric Forts or Observatories?
by Victor Kachur

That massive military operations were carried out across the American Middle West appears confirmed by a series of stone hill-forts with close parallels to virtually identical constructions raised by the Kelts throughout Central and Western Europe, more than two millennia ago.

Before his death in 2009, Victor Kachur was a lifetime member and researcher of Columbus, Ohio's Midwestern Epigraphic Society. His articles published in the Society's quarterly Journal continue to serve as rich sources of invaluable information for fellow investigators of the deep past.

When the first pioneers began crossing our continent 200 years ago, they encountered a number of large, abandoned "castles" local Indians claimed were built by a non-native people exterminated in a long series of wars in the ancient past. These unusual locations, comprising stone walls of prodigious extent, were found perched atop high hills with commanding vistas in all directions. To early Americans, fresh from their experiences in the War for Independence, the impressive structures were obviously designed as military fortifications—hence, their designation as "forts."

Much later, during the second half of the 20th century, archaeologists were convinced almost everything pre-Columbian was astronomically oriented somehow, and therefore insisted that the ramparts actually comprised celestial observatories built by the members of a family or two in their spare time. Salaried academics insisted a military interpretation was no longer fashionable, because they were promoting their notion of an idyllic pre-Columbian North America, where the peaceful arts of astronomy flourished in contradistinction to politically incorrect portrayals of the natives as wagers of war.

In examining two surviving hill-top sites, readers are invited to determine for themselves the truth about their purpose for construction.

Recreation of the Newark Earthworks.

Our first example is located in the Ohio Valley. Sprawling across a bluff 235 feet above the Little Miami River is a colossal network of stone ramparts covered with earth. Running 3.5 miles in circumference and varying in height from 4 to 20 feet, the walls enclose 100 acres studded with conical mounds and crescent-shaped gateways. To level the top of the hill-top, raise its walls, and build their interior mounds, the prehistoric American engineers moved an estimated 480,000 cubic yards of earth. That was enough material to fill a line of modern dump-trucks stretching for more than 200 miles! Clearly, such an immense public works project could only have been undertaken by a populous community whose members rated its massive construction at the utmost priority.

Fort Ancient is part of a state park comprising 764 acres of plant and animal life, and featuring 2 miles of trails through enchanting woodlands. The 4 miles of walls left by an obviously gifted people define a gigantic precinct capable of enclosing perhaps 12,000 persons at a time. It is not known if such numbers were ever assembled behind the enduring walls,

· 133

but great multitudes certainly gathered there for special occasions. Only a few burials took place within the enclosure, and these apparently contain the remains of dedicated sacrifices made when the site was first opened.

It comprises two main areas joined by a middle section connecting both with an ancient limestone processional way. Extending for a quarter of a mile from the enclosure are parallel earth-works, which lead to a single large mound. Across the river, in a clearing, are limestone slabs arranged in the 35-foot-long configuration of a snake. A large pole stands at its head to cast a shadow along the length of the effigy on the morning of every summer solstice. An identical serpent image oriented to the winter solstice sunrise lies a short distance from the river bank. Both effigies are on private property belonging to the YMCA, but access to them is normally possible through the local museum. According to official archaeological opinion, the impressive walls of Fort Ancient do not belong to a "fort," as the first pioneer discoverers assumed, even though its modern name is still in use. The site, they argue, is a ceremonial sacred center never used for habitation or defense. Its master builders belonged to the Hopewell Culture that began around 200 BC, but came to an end 600 years later for reasons which still elude most investigators.

There are no known celestial alignments behind the walls, however, so the crescent-shaped gateways there are all the more intriguing. The precinct contrasts with the solar-oriented serpent effigies outside, across the river. The moon universally signifies inner-quests, psychological states, and subconscious conditions, paralleling the interior of the site. As such, its walls enclosed the internal, deepest spiritual life of its creators. The discovery of a pavement near one of the walls in the narrowing middle section of the site, a feature found nowhere else in pre-Columbian North America, suggests a ritual path perhaps corresponding to the irregular gaps appearing in the enclosure.

Trees within the precinct were not cleared, so the preserved stands of forest were perhaps regarded as sacred groves. There is a kind of plaza or open area near the south overlook, where general assemblies took place. But the groves themselves are set apart by the walls, the purpose of which seems to have defined their sacred character. It is this hallowing aspect that was alone responsible for the construction of Fort Ancient.

In other words, the groves determined its creation. The ramparts are really like garden walls enclosing naturally sacrosanct ground. It is possible that the shaman, whose bones and a large quartz crystal were found in one of the area's few graves, was the same person who originally determined the site as a *sanctum sanctorum*. The walls, mounds, gateways, and paved pathways are only adjuncts to the sacred grove, the real spiritual focus of the place. The walls would enshrine the center, pay homage to it, define it, and focus it.

Fort Ancient actually represents one link in a stupendous chain of stone enclosures spanning almost 500 miles from the Mississippi and Ohio rivers. At least 15 similar, though smaller stone structures, all dating to a common era, circa 1 AD, are known in southern Illinois, and Fort Hill, nearly 50 miles east of Fort Ancient, is practically as large. No one knows how many of these prehistoric ramparts, all located atop high bluffs overlooking rivers in thickly wooded areas, originally stood across the three-state region, although they appear to have been the work of a single race, judging from their uniformity of style and shared dates. Of their surviving number, Fort Ancient is the largest and most easily accessible. The site is professionally maintained, and visitors should begin their self-conducted tour at the main entrance, where a small but highly interesting museum displays treasured artifacts excavated from the area.

Fort Ancient's Tennessee counterpart is Old Stone Fort. High on a remote and deeply wooded bluff, on a site overlooking two swiftly flowing rivers, an unknown people arrived to create a sacred center that would last for the next 2,000 years. While Rome ruled the other side of the world, they erected an enclosure more than a mile long, skillfully raising a line of stone walls across the edge of the steepest slopes. The lofty ramparts surrounded 40 acres of hallowed ground, which had been set aside strictly for ceremonial purposes. During the next four centuries, the walls were built, repaired, and reconstructed, as unguessed thousands of celebrants conducted their lost rites of empowerment within the holy clearing. Then, just as suddenly as they appeared, the inhabitants abandoned their ritual precinct in the early years of the fifth century AD, and vanished into North America's pre-Columbian past. The reason for their abrupt departure remains as mysterious as their identity.

When early, white settlers stumbled upon the overgrown site in the late 18th century, they presumed it originally constituted a military complex. Archaeologists later assigned the Fort's construction to the Middle Woodland Tradition, a period in which highly organized societies flourished throughout the Ohio Valley and down through Tennessee. They subsequently determined its function as a religious center.

The enclosure is approached through a complex arrangement of walls, mounds, ditches, and embankments. A pair of conical mounds adjoining the walls stood on either side of the entrance. Just beyond lay an 8-foot-deep ditch, giving the site a roughly rectangular outline. Little of the original configuration remains. The prodigious ditch, once as much as three-quarters of a mile long, is now a 4-foot dip, but its position on the site's high ground affords the best panorama of the sacred clearing. It was formerly entirely surrounded by water, a condition afforded by the ditch connecting the Big Duck and Little Duck rivers.

The average height of Old Stone Fort's walls is 4 feet. They were constructed in an unusual manner. First, stones were piled in parallel rows to form a trench, which was floored in between with small shale slabs, then filled with rubble. The ramparts were finally covered with earth to make a smooth cap. They begin where the cliff ridges end, presenting the appearance of having grown from the bluff itself.

The Big Duck and Little Duck rivers run on either side of the sacred site, dropping 100 feet to create a dramatic waterfall with numerous deep pools at the northwest overlook. A small, but important and informative museum (imaginatively constructed in a building style of the ancient architects who built Old Stone Fort) stands a few paces before the original entrance to the enclosure. Wonderful views of the Big Duck River are visible from the museum roof.

The official guidebook to Old Stone Fort states that the site "was probably a special and mystical place even before the enclosure was built. Its location in the forks of a river may have given it special significance. The cliffs and the waterfalls were certainly as remarkable as they are now."[1] The eastern walls of the site run above the banks of the Little Duck River, stopping parallel just before a small island, at which the rampart suddenly turns due west.

Here, the sacred center demonstrates its response to the hallowed landscape. The little island in the stream was a consecrated spot that compelled the construction of the walls to execute the turn. At this point, as perhaps no other part of the enclosure, the site reveals mystical interdependence on the special environment.

The park guidebook also mentions the "processions which may have passed through the entrance alley-way and the ritual significance the entrance-way may have had as you passed from the outside world to the sacred ground enclosed beyond."[2] Rites associated with the sun were probably carried out at Old Stone Fort, because "the ritual significance of the entrance way" was determined by archaeo-astronomers in 1989, when they discovered that it was oriented to sunrise of the winter solstice.[3]

Examination of the walls showed that their ridges had been "worn down from traffic on top," where mass-processions took place during hundreds of years.[4]

Although ceremonial and even ritual elements may be found at some of the ancient American hill-top sites, these spiritual features are ancillary, even incidental to each such location's fundamentally military character. In this, they are all identical to contemporaneous hill-forts found across Western Europe. These are the so-called *oppida*, fortified settlements atop strategically located hills, built by the Kelts to defend their settlements against expansion by Roman imperialism, 2,000 years ago. The European and American hill-forts not only came into existence at the same time, but examples on both continents shared identical construction techniques of inter-mixing stone and wood with earth.

The *oppida*'s outer bulwark of stone slabs and timbers filled with an earth-gravel mixture cited by Julius Caesar in his *Bello Gallico* as a *murus Gallicus,* or "Gallic wall," exactly describes Fort Hill, in Ohio.[5] Tennessee's Old Stone Fort bordered on either side by the Big Duck and Little Duck rivers is a mirror image of the layout and even configuration of Germany's Heuneburg hill-fort, situated between two tributaries of the Danube. Keltic *oppida* at Zavist in Bohemia, Ireland's Dun Ailinne, Mont Beuvray in France, Portugal's Citania de Sanfins, and Numantia in northeastern Spain could all pass for hill-forts in the Ohio Valley.

The close, physical resemblance of these Western European hill-forts with their Adena American counterparts, and their common time frame and construction methods, undoubtedly define the impact made on the prehistory of our country by Keltic culture-bearers, who arrived in the Western Hemisphere and raised the impressive bulwarks that still stand today, after the passage of two millennia.

CHAPTER 21

Libyans' 3rd-Century
Eclipse in Kentucky
by David Feldman

In 1938, Isidor Feldman purchased a small tract of land on Buckeye Road in Lancaster, Kentucky. Fifty years later, he handed over the business to his gandson, David, who occasionally stumbled upon ancient rock art at the family property. One petroglyph in particular attracted his special attention, and he was encouraged to pursue the enigma by Dr. Myron Paine, professor of agricultural engineering and nominated for Who's Who in Engineering (1977). In 2002, Ancient American (Volume 7, Number 46) broke David's story of a third-century astronomical alignment uncovered in the Midwest. The significance of this find cannot be over-valued, because it confirms the arrival of overseas' visitors to the Bluegrass State during pre-Columbian times.

Dramatic evidence for the arrival of prehistoric seafarers on our continent has been found near Drip Rock, Kentucky. Although the discovery took place eight years ago, it is published in 2004 for the first time in an *Ancient American* exclusive.

The find was made in early March 1994, across the road from my cattle farm in the Estill-Jackson County area of the South Fork of the Kentucky River. I was led by his neighbor, Anthony Smith, to a 25-foot-high sandstone cliff, located near or on the so-called "Warriors Trail" (the east fork) that enters Jackson from Clay County, proceeding north to Ohio. At a small opening between a pair of rocks, we examined a strange set of petroglyphs, unlike anything with which we were familiar. The images seemed more like part of an inscription than rock art, so I sent my photograph of the markings to Harvard professor Barry Fell (San Diego California), president of the Epigraphic Society, an organization dedicated to the study of ancient inscriptions.

Dr. Fell was impressed with the Kentucky find, and set to work at once on a translation. He believed it was indeed an inscription, written in the language of ancient Libya. More than 2,000 years ago, the Libyans of North Africa were racially different from present-day

The Drip Rock inscription.

Libyans. They were ruddy-complected, fair-haired seafarers, noted for the sometimes-extensive voyages they undertook. Their *tarchana*, or "reckoner," was a navigational device, perhaps a kind of magnetic compass, they either invented or inherited from their Phoenician ancestors, and it enabled them to sail great distances through open water. These are the people Dr. Fell concluded were responsible for engraving the Kentucky inscription.

After a few weeks' work, he was satisfied with the translation and planned to publish his findings in the next issue of his "Official Papers," and he considered the Smith-Feldman discovery important enough to include in an upcoming, revised edition of his popular book, *America, B.C.*[1] The glyphs, he declared, commemorated a prehistoric solar eclipse. In my April 5, 1998, letter to Fell, I narrowed the date specified on the inscription with the assistance of Dr. Fell's close Texas friend, Bill Rudersdorf. "I re-ran the eclipse data for the period 499 BC to 1000 AD," Fell responded in a June 6, 1998, letter, "and I'm confident that the only total solar eclipse visible at the Drip Rock, Kentucky site you specified is the one on April 23, 255 AD, at 16:34 (middle of totality). The sun was well up in the evening sky, about 180 degrees above the horizon, at the middle of totality, and almost exactly due west."

Later that month, however, Fell passed away, just two days exactly before the 1,739th anniversary of the solar eclipse he translated from the Libyan original. Dr. Fell's translation is published here for the first time in *Ancient American* magazine.

< CHAPTER 22 >

A Dragon in Rock Lake
by Archie Eschborn

Founder of the Rock Lake Research Society in 1997, Archie Eschborn dedicated the last 10 years of his life to finding Wisconsin's sunken City of the Dead. But only after his untimely death due to pancreatic cancer at 56 years of age in 2008, the same Establishment archaeologists who consistently snubbed or deprecated his tireless efforts admitted to the existence of some 1,100 prehistoric, man-made structures on the lake bottom. Eschborn's words are, therefore, not only those of a visionary explorer, but describe a lost world he went far to resurrect.

My real reason for coming to Rock Lake was practically forgotten. I had been running from boat to boat, setting up electronics and video equipment for most of the morning of July 17, 1998. Ever since our first, unsuccessful underwater video expedition the previous May, our goal was the same: namely, to somehow photograph the sunken pyramidal structures in Rock Lake.

The site for this ongoing enigma is located in southern Wisconsin, just south of Highway I-94 between Milwaukee and Madison. Situated in the charming town of Lake Mills, pear-shaped Rock Lake is 2.5 miles long from north to south, 1.7 miles at its widest extent, with an average depth of 40 feet. The deepest point lies in the middle of the north end, going down to 90 feet. Just 3 miles due east is an archaeological park, Aztalan, a 21-acre ceremonial center of walls and earthen temple-mounds occupied until the early 14th century. Gouged out by a retreating glacier 12,000 years ago, Rock Lake got its name from stories told by resident Winnebago (Ho

Chunk) to pioneers around 1830 about "rock tepees" concealing the dead of "an alien people" at the bottom of the lake.

These ancient foreigners were said to have given the lake its original name, Tyranena, although the Indians no longer remembered what it meant. Dismissed as a fairy tale by the practical newcomers, this native tradition was virtually forgotten 70 years later, when a pair of duck hunters peered over the side of their boat during a severe drought that lowered lake levels and greatly improved water clarity. They were shocked to behold a massive pyramidal mound of black stone sitting on the bottom. For the rest of the 20th century, Rock Lake attracted numerous pyramid-hunters, clashing with Establishment archaeologists, who laughed off the "pyramids" as nothing more than glacial debris.

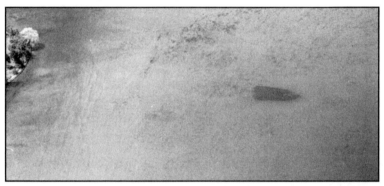

Aerial photograph of pyramidal stone mound under the surface of Rock Lake.

I knew that without any type of photographic or digital image there could be no meaningful, scientific debate. There were credible authorities on both sides of the controversy. But I chose to team up with experts who actually had done real fieldwork; they were not armchair archaeologists. These foremost included James Scherz, professor of surveying and civil engineering at the University of Wisconsin (Madison), and glacial geologist Lloyd Hornbostel. Both had already performed decades-long research before my arrival at Rock Lake. I also sought out Frank Joseph, who published several magazine articles and two books on the subject, the result of some 100 expeditions—above, on, and under the lake—beginning in 1983. Our July attempt was armed not only with the latest in sonar equipment, but included a multi-disciplined team of divers, researchers, and underwater photographers, along with qualified support people.

We budgeted two days for side-scan sonar work, but were already four hours behind schedule due to motor malfunctions aboard our boats.

We were also dealing with power supply problems for both the side-scan sonar boat and the 3-D SLS sonar equipment on our research vessel, R.V. *Tyranena*. I notified the captain of the dive-boat via cell phone that we would be heading out shortly, and he should proceed toward "Diving Target One," as we earlier discussed in our morning briefing. Lloyd Hornbostel would guide our divers to the spot. "Hard Target One" received its name—"Bass Rock Bar One"—years earlier from a local fisherman. BRB-1 ("Bass Rock Bar One") was mapped via sonar previously by Scherz and Hornbostel, albeit not with the sophisticated instruments we were about to use, but their equipment was nonetheless effective enough to demonstrate its apparent geometry.

Hornbostel dove on this structure numerous times in the past. His observations confirmed sonar readings of this interesting formation. In short, BRB-1 displayed definite elements that tended to confirm its man-made identity. I focused our research on BRB-1 primarily because producers at the Arts & Entertainment Channel required more Rock Lake footage to include in their "Pyramids Episode" for an "Unsolved Mysteries" series they planned to air in early 1999 (telecast February 11th). Through my conversations with Hornbostel and the data he presented, BRB-1 displayed on its southern terminus an undeniable delta shape. It looked like the side of a pyramid. Additionally, BRB-1's compass orientation from a geological perspective would preclude it from being a glacial remnant.

I learned from our dive the previous May that conventional underwater photography would probably be very problematical during this time of year, due to reduced water clarity. However, given the shallower depth of BRB-1, an underwater video attempt here would stand a better chance of rendering useful images than among other pyramid targets, such as the "Kennedy" or "Limnatis," because of their deeper locations and subsequent lack of available, natural light. Besides, I was confident that our new side-scan sonar would capture these structures in their true form, and thereby end the controversy surrounding their existence.

We decided that BBR-1 offered the best potential for successful underwater video footage, simultaneously satisfying A&E's needs concerning their proposed special about Rock Lake. Of course, our original and more important mission involved a sweep of the lake with the same kind of side-scan sonar Dr. Robert Ballard used to find R.M.S. *Titanic* in 1982. Our own R.V. *Tyranena* headed south, while Professor Scherz and I studied the monitor. Computer-generated imagery of the lake bottom began to appear on the screen, as the vessel glided at a steady two to three knots, towing the side-scan array. Our sonar operator, Captain Clark Willick, had one hand on the wheel and the other on the "mouse," ready to digitally capture any image we wanted to preserve.

"Ah, Zeke's Wall!" Professor Scherz exclaimed, as we passed over the legendary structure named after a Lake Mills resident who claimed to have seen a standing wall in this quadrant of Rock Lake about 50 years before. I judged from our course that we would encounter our next target based on aerial photos made by assistant team leader Jack Letourneau. The shots were taken during his fly-over the year before. These extraordinary photos allowed us to corroborate both location and size of the structures we would encounter through sonar and the visual sightings made by our divers.

I held one of Jack's aerial photos over the computer monitor and told the professor, "I can tell you what's coming next. A large pyramid structure, plus the so-called 'Seven Sisters'."

"Who are *they?*" he asked, just as the undeniable image of pyramidal structure drifted across the screen. It was massive, about 150 feet long and 12 feet across, with right-angle geometry and dead-straight, sloping walls—a colossal sight, thrilling confirmation that man-made structures do indeed lie on the lake floor. I then predicted that the next formation would be the "Seven Sisters." Their name was based on several astronomical and mythological references (namely, the Pleiades), which seemed appropriate after seeing them for the first time in Jack's aerial shots. When they appeared on cue across the computer screen, Professor Scherz realized that nearly a century of sub-surface exploration had just entered a new era.

Our voyage proceeded on a south-by-southwesterly heading, the instruments capturing on hard-drive uncertain feedback from the bottom that needed further analysis. I was continually checking my video recording equipment; it was making a live, running record of the sonar imagery coming up from the bottom of the lake.

Suddenly and quite unexpectedly, something came across the viewfinder that made my jaw drop. In a scene out of a movie, I called to Scherz: "Do you see *that?!*" He seemed mesmerized and said not a word, as his eyes were glued to the computer monitor. What stretched out before us on the screen was unbelievable. My memory flashed back to old Indian legends of a monster in Rock Lake, because directly below us was a stylized, but discernable image apparently made of solid material configured into the shape of a dragon!

I remembered reading about local reports of a serpentine creature in Frank Joseph's *The Lost Pyramids of Rock Lake*:

> The antiquity of Rock Lake's monster was suggested by a gargantuan effigy mound that skirted the south shore until its destruction in the 1920s. Dating back at least to the time that Aztalan flourished 900 years ago, and described by T*he Wisconsin Archaeologist Magazine* as a "water spirit," the 84-foot-long earthwork portrayed some monstrous being dwelling in the lake. It was reported that this monster effigy was obliterated when a railroad trestle was put in at the south end of the lake at the turn of the Century.[1]

Joseph went on to state that sightings of an actual creature based on anecdotal accounts of the late 1800s described the monster as having a serpentine torso, and sprouting a long neck and a horse-like head—similar to the sub-surface figure moving across our computer screen. Was the dragonish monster really the effigy that early observers had reported as having been destroyed? Or was it a different one that had become inundated, as water levels rose with the construction of local mills in the mid-19th century? Could it be that our dragon was the same, mystical animal or "water spirit" that the destroyed earth effigy was supposed to warn native inhabitants about, since or before the time of nearby Aztalan? These questions raced through my mind, while we drifted slowly over and passed the tail.

Almost immediately, another enigmatic surprise burst on the screen. What appeared to be a set of artificial steps next to the dragon commanded my attention. They seemed to lead directly to the creature's head. Was this a natural formation or man-made? But if natural, what a splendid coincidence! As much as we would have preferred to linger over this dramatic image, we were determined to comply with our schedule for sonar-sweeping the rest of the lake. In any case, images of the dragon, pyramid, and Seven Sisters had been recorded on video. Moreover, there would be no difficulty finding their locations again within 5 feet of precise longitude and latitude, based on our DGPS (differential global positioning satellite) coordinates.

But more discoveries were soon to follow, and other revealing pieces of the puzzle were to fall into place, as we got under way. A photograph taken by Jack LeTourneau showed a large formation in the southern vicinity of the lake. I refused earlier to speculate on its significance with other team members, because I wanted sonar verification first. The controversial target was publicized as far back as 1967, when a professional diver, John Kennedy, was searching for the fabled pyramids in Rock Lake. He did indeed find a colossal, tent-shaped building and felt sure it was not a natural formation. After concluding a visual inspection and running low on air, Kennedy surfaced, and tried to pin-point his position and notify his dive buddies. Unfortunately, neither he nor they were able to locate the structure again. Rock Lake investigators always assumed he had actually discovered Bass Rock Bar-1.

Joseph speculated in *The Lost Pyramids of Rock Lake* that Kennedy may have dived on one of the structures in the northern end of the lake. In honor of this supposed find, he dubbed it the "Kennedy Pyramid."[2] But these explanations of the Kennedy dive always troubled me. I had been to Rock Lake several times previous to our expedition, scouting the area and trying to get a feel for it. By Kennedy's own account, it would have been almost impossible to swim that far north to Bass Rock Bar-I and survey it. Further, being a diver myself, it seemed obvious to me that Kennedy could not have started on the south end of the lake, swum north almost 3 miles, and hit the northern pyramids without being half-fish, or at least having some self-propelled underwater sled. I was able to eventually interview John Kennedy and can attest he did not exhibit any gills or fish-like appendages, nor did his account of the 1967 dive disclose any type of underwater conveyance, other than his flippers. When we discussed the structures that Kennedy was supposed to have dived on, he, too, was uncomfortable with their recollected location.

A month later, I met with Jack LeTourneau and felt certain that one of the underwater objects appearing in his aerial imagery of Rock Lake could possibly be the actual structure Kennedy saw. It was within underwater swimming range, related to his starting point, and matched his description. It seemed necessary to verify the image in the photo. It was a high-altitude shot of a sub-surface target that appeared to exhibit regular, geometric proportions. Jack and I decided to digitally scan the photo and manipulated it in such a way as to enhance the image using state-of-the-art software. Once we had processed it and improved the resolution, we were both convinced that we were looking at a pyramidal structure.

Another aspect of the Rock Lake story that did not set well with the existing data was the story of the Wilson brothers and their discovery of an underwater pyramid shortly after the turn of the 20th century. Various accounts all read the same. They were duck hunting in the midst of a prolonged drought, so lake levels were very low and the water unusually clear. They sailed above shallow depths, when one of the brothers looked over the side to behold a building sitting on the bottom of the lake. They claimed to have been able to touch the top of it with their oars. The excited men rowed back into town and notified local townsfolk, and a flotilla of citizenry descended on the lake in all manner of vessels led by the Wilsons, who guided them back to the mysterious, underwater structure. Arriving at the spot, they were awed by the drowned spectacle.

Young boys dove into the water and swam around the top of it. Others touched the apex with their oars, as the Wilson brothers had done, and now no one could doubt the veracity of the old Indian tales. A week or so later, a reporter from *The Milwaukee Herald* entrained for Lake Mills to investigate the story of the sensational, sunken pyramid. The man was rowed out to the same position on the lake by the Wilson brothers. But when he looked over the side of the boat into the cloudy, dark waters, he saw nothing. Claude [Wilson] explained that lake levels had risen again since the sighting, and recent rainstorms stirred up silt and algae so much that visibility had badly deteriorated. The visiting reporter's published article lampooned Lake Mills residents for engaging in a hoax or some sort of hucksterism on behalf of profit. The townspeople took this hard, and mention of the pyramids was generally avoided for the next several decades.

Now, long after these events, the digitally enhanced photo I held in my hand clearly showed what could only be the pyramid found by Claude and Lee Wilson, nearly 100 years before. And I had good reasons for this supposition. Their account put them at the south end of the lake and in relatively shallow water. Their described position was nowhere near the locations of currently known structures. And the drop in lake levels caused by the 1901 drought would have had to have been of biblical proportions for anyone to touch the tops of the monuments discovered at the depths recorded by Frank Joseph's expeditions in 1989. Those targets were farther to the north at 60-foot depths. Other physical descriptions of the area of the lake gleaned from published accounts correlate the Wilson brothers' find. The structure they saw in 1901 appears to have been the same pyramidal mound Kennedy found independently in 1967. To confirm this conclusion, we needed to verify the presence of a real, physical object in Jack's photo. Any possibility that the apparent structure in the lake might be something natural or modern had to be eliminated.

After the mid-point of our July expedition, we approached an area of the lake, where the Wilson/Kennedy pyramid would be most likely found. I noted several landmarks that I had committed to memory from the aerial photo and guided Captain Willick in what seemed the proper direction for our first sweep. At first, the sonar revealed nothing unusual on the lake bottom. But just as we were coming around for another pass, what appeared to be the edge of something man-made flitted across the monitor. The roughly made structure was reminiscent of Kennedy's description of the "fist-sized" rocks that he said comprised the pyramid he saw in 1967. Now the figure we observed seemed as though it, too, was composed of many thousands of similarly fist-sized stones.

A sudden course change was ordered, because the vessel was entering shallow water. The sonar's torpedo-like tow-fish needed to be reeled in before it collided with the bottom. At least enough of the sunken target had been documented by the side-scan for us to establish that it was real, and probably the same monument seen by both the Wilsons and Kennedy. We also had its DGPS location, enabling us to revisit it without further search. Following our July voyage, I shared my deductions about a common identity for the shallow water pyramid with Frank Joseph. It seemed to him an enlightening discovery. Doubtless, this was the same monument encountered in 1901 and again in 1967. And it meant that the structure his expedition located at 60 feet 10 years earlier was actually a completely new find, never seen before.

Joseph seconded my proposal that the shallow-water structure we discovered be henceforward known as the Wilson-Kennedy Pyramid. I reminded him that we would need to rename the current pyramidal structure still associated with John Kennedy. He suggested it be re-christened the Taylor Pyramid, in memory of Victor Taylor, a Lake Mills scholar, who was the major force behind Rock Lake exploration during the pre–World War II period. Taylor suffered persecution for his quest, and died prematurely as a consequence. He lies buried in the cemetery behind Lake Mills "Pyramid Motel," less than a mile from Rock Lake. It seems only fitting that this important predecessor of all subsequent efforts there be memorialized by one of the structures he researched.

On day two of the July expedition, I met up with our team aboard the R.V. *Tyranena* to direct dive activities. Professor Scherz and Lloyd Hornbostel rejoined Captain Willick aboard the sonar vessel. We were doing final filming at Bass Rock Bar-I, and planned to cruise over the giant triangle Jack LeTourneau photographed from the air. This massive delta shape had been the subject of much discussion and speculation among Rock Lake investigators since its discovery in the early 1930s. Its existence as an unnatural formation was beyond question. But what was it? Jack's aerial reconnaissance firmly established the three-sided figure's precise position, but how to find it by boat, now that the feature had disappeared under Rock Lake's dark, green waters and abundant weeds? Moreover, its low profile would make the triangle almost indistinguishable to the sonar, compared to the other smaller structures, with their steep flanks. Lloyd wanted to measure its sides and determine the structure's overall size.

When our research boat arrived at the delta's location, we could see that the weed-bed would not allow our divers visual definition of its perimeter. Our sonar did reveal, however, that the feature showed some height. This information was later verified by running its image through a video-wave-form monitor. We are still analyzing its data, and trying to calculate the great triangle's exact dimensions and size. From an aerial perspective, it approximates 300 feet on each side.

We may be the first investigators to use the wave-form monitor as an archeological research tool. Results of its work at the delta are slow in forthcoming, because the rules, formulas, and protocol of the device are still being written. Meanwhile, that elusive formation remains undisclosed, until we return for our spring expedition.[3] The forest of weeds that cloak it should be gone by then, leaving an opportunity for our divers to make their observations and photographs.

Coincidentally, the Great Triangle in Rock Lake points due north, an important parallel with nearby Aztalan, with its own northerly oriented delta formation. Data we are collecting about the man-made structures at the bottom of Rock Lake continue to confirm earlier descriptions of the site. So much valid evidence must eventually move authorities at the State of Wisconsin to validate the existence of these features, thereby assuring their protection. That, in fact, is our chief goal: to preserve these remnants of a lost civilization within its sunken, 3,000-year-old time capsule.

CHAPTER 23

The Walls of Poseidon
by William Donato

Although Bimini in the Bahama Islands is not part of the Americas, it does lie just 55 miles outside Miami, and, therefore must have played a significant role as a final port-of-call for Bronze Age ships, laden with copper, returning to the ancient Old World.

William Donato is a leading authority on Atlantis in the Bahamas, where he participated in and led dozens of expeditions—from spotter aircraft scuba dives to submarines—for more than 20 years. He is also president of the Atlantis Organization, headquartered in Buena Vista, California.

Is it possible that the most specific and critical part of Plato's account of Atlantis has already been discovered right under our noses? Many researchers believe that the Empire of Atlantis was far-flung, with outposts in distant places, as would be expected of a maritime culture actively involved with many trading partners. Yet, it is also believed that one, or several, main centers operated simultaneously. After all, even Plato's account implies that a number of countries, or kingdoms, made up the heart of the Atlantean imperium.

If we look for Atlantis in the Atlantic Ocean, the best candidates include the Canary Islands, the Madeiras, Azores, Bermuda, and Bahamas. Anomalous features have been reported at most of them, though by far the greatest number of photographed, videotaped, measured, and explored occur in the Bahamas. This is probably for a good reason. Even though all of the others may have been part of Atlantis, the only location with the least amount of geological activity is in the Bahamas.

As it turns out, they comprise, in effect, a "mini-continent." Its geological basement is believed to be granitic (acidic continental rock) covered by thousands of feet of carbonate material. The National Geographic Society's Dr. Maurice Ewing and American geologist Bruce Charles Heezen discovered granite in the Caribbean, and speculated that it was either from a continent in formation, or an ancient continent; they favored an ancient hypothesis. The Azores, on the other hand, lay in one of the most geologically active and unstable parts of the planet, the Mid-Atlantic Ridge, which is actually creating new material.

The Bahamas are near a subduction zone, where material slides under the crust for "recycling," a feature that really could cause things to disappear "in a day and a night," such as Port Royal, the Jamaican city that literally fell into the sea, Atlantis-like, on June 7, 1692, with its 3,000 residents.

Reflecting this geologic potential for violent change, the Bahamas' native Lucayan Indians believed that their islands were once far greater in extant than today, because long ago they were "engulfed by the arms of the sea."[1] Their oral tradition compliments folk memories of another tribal people—the Yuchi—in the eastern Tennessee River valley. They claim that two of their "gens" (the Cat and the Fish) originated in the Bahamas—specifically, Andros. They recall this island as an almost "legendary" place in the deep past. The Cherokee—also of Tennessee, but also Georgia, Oklahoma, and the Carolinas—recall the former existence of five islands in the Atlantic Ocean. Their *Elohi Mona* resembled the Old Testament's *Elohim*, the "gods." Similar to Plato's account, the Atlantic islands described by the Cherokee were allegedly destroyed for the immorality of their human inhabitants.

Whereas most investigators in search of possibilities for ancient civilizers near the Americas have focused on Bimini and Andros, a new and highly promising site has appeared on the opposite side of these locations known as the "Out Islands"—specifically, Cat Island. It is the highest point in all the Bahamas, topping out at a little more than 200 feet. When researcher Ron Smith examined maps of the western Atlantic, he noticed a significant number of unusually shaped "coral heads" and three concentric arcs between Cat Island and Little San Salvador. I had speculated in the early 1990s that it was possible, and even likely, that any architectural remains in shallow water would have probably become overgrown with coral, and human artifacts might be disguised by such accretion.

In fact, coral growing over artificial objects could even help date them. Some suspicious formations have been observed not far from Cat Cay, south of Bimini, including a vertical structure near Moxon Rocks. Smith noted that the part of Cat Island currently above sea level resembles the likeness of a dolphin. Dolphin imagery crops up significantly in Plato's account of Atlantis, such as the 100 Nerieds, or sea nymphs, riding on dolphins in the Temple of Poseidon. While sharing Ron's "Map Quest" findings with me, he indicated what appeared to be two parallel arcs that seemed man-made. "That's it," he declared, "the Temple of Poseidon." Looking closer, I could discern three parallel arcs suggesting the southern parts of as many concentric circles. He then had me measure the common center and project the rest of the outer circle: exactly 3.2 miles, which is precisely the size Plato gave for the innermost island of Atlantis after converting Greek stadia into miles.

Other features Ron pointed out began taking on new significance. The "coral heads" distribution and shapes seemed atypical. When viewed with respect to the concentric arcs, they took on a more architectural appearance, especially some u-shaped corals close to the arcs, as if they could have been remnants of bridges or tunnels that had collapsed. The long lines of "coral heads," sometimes parallel, evoked canals. One, again echoing Plato's account, was 6 or 7 miles in length (just as long as the Grand Canal in his account), leading to the west and what would have been a huge bay prior to the melting of the Pleistocene glaciers at the close of the last ice age, some 10,000 years ago.

Ron also indicated what would have been a huge rectangular plain to the south of the canals. In all significant respects, the Bahamas fit more of the criteria for part of Atlantis than any other proposed site: It and the surrounding ancient land-masses (such as Cay Sal Bank) encompass the same land area (thousands of square miles), as presented in Plato's report, including provision for magnificent harbors and enormous bays conducive to the formation of a maritime culture. These features resemble the famed triple, concentric, ringed canals of the indicated sizes, numerous, sunken, geometric figures photographed consistently since the 1970s. Their artifactual nature is underscored by petroglyphs under water at Andros, a huge triangular depression (like an ancient reservoir, miles in length), and legitimately identified artifacts from the Bimini area itself.

By any definition, the Bahamas deserve the most careful scrutiny. The islands' Atlantean parallels match the only land area large enough to have possessed those details described by Plato. They encompass the Bahamian land mass of virtually thousands of square miles of surface land area. Before worldwide sea levels rose more than 320 feet following Pleistocene flooding, one could quite literally have walked from the mountains of the Bahamas across a vast plain to the plateau of Andros with the Tongue of the Ocean forming one of the best harbors on the planet: 6,000 feet deep and well-protected on all sides, almost in the center of this ancient landmass. In fact, this area was surrounded by several large bays that would have provided excellent harborage. It would have been most unusual if a maritime culture had not developed here.

The ancient extent and richness of this land is not derived solely from geological data, but from the remains of large animals and birds that could not possibly have existed on the resources of today's small islands. Large predatory birds, as well as the remains of big quadruped mammals, have been found. Three miles off the Georgia coast, the remains of ancient elephants have been recovered, suggesting the possibility of these pachyderms in the Bahamas, as well. They would not have needed a land-bridge to cross into the Bahamas, as they are excellent swimmers.

One of the ancient anchor-stones found at the Bimini Wall.

The Grand Bahama Bank might even have had its own source of precious metals. A few miles northwest of Bimini, the Bank bulges out more than it should for the current geological model. Several geologists have hypothesized that there may have been some deep volcanic activity in the geologic past that burst through thousands of feet of carbonate material (limestone) bringing metals, possibly even gold, closer to the surface. Gold, silver, and copper are frequently found together. Accordingly, there actually could be deposits of some of these metals, as described by Plato, in the Bahamas. Of course any maritime society could also trade for such things: The gold and copper in the Maya area waeres obtained through extensive trade networks, as were many other valued items.

In 2002, our nonprofit corporation, APEX ("Advanced Planetary Explorations") Institute, undertook an expedition to the Bahamas for investigating Bimini and Cat Island. We contracted with Ocean Technologies, L.L.C. to operate the side-scan sonar part of our project, thereby verifying targets obtained four years earlier. All of the underwater features measured proportional to human architecture. They included two post-lintel systems, multiple rectangular features with corresponding shadows of what seemed to be a structure, and a large feature with apparently multiple tiers and a staircase. It looked very much like a Mesoamerican temple. After bad weather terminated any further efforts, I flew to Cat Island to examine the triple concentric arcs 5 to 7 miles from shore toward Little San Salvador. One of the circles was just inside the outer arc, the only one that breaks the top of the water. On its inward side, I saw flat, exposed surfaces of limestone. If this was indeed the outer wall of Plato's Atlantis, one would expect it to be higher than the inner ramparts, because it would be the primary, defensive wall. I next examined what appeared to be a line intersecting the second, inward arc, 6 feet beneath the surface.

Atlantis has been searched for in every quarter of the globe, without success. Perhaps all that remains to be done is following the clues to Plato's lost civilization among the islands not far from our own shores.

<CHAPTER 24>

Bolivia's Atlantean Canals
by J.M. Allen

A former air-photo interpreter for Britain's Royal Air Force, J.M. Allen proposes that South America is Plato's lost continent of Atlantis. The results of Allen's extensive research have been published in Atlantis: The Andes Solution,[1] Atlantis: Lost Kingdom of the Andes, and The Atlantis Trail. His Website is available at www.atlantisbolivia.org/theatlantistrail.htm.

Aerial photograph of ancient canal system on the Bolivian Altiplano.

High-resolution satellite imagery reveals the remains of an ancient canal system in South America similar to that described by Plato in the dialogues *Timaeus* and *Kritias*, his fourth-century BC account of Atlantis. Are these canals proof of the lost civilization's former existence? I have long held that it originally flourished in a region of Bolivia known as the Altiplano, the "High Plain." My conclusion was based upon a number of geographic factors from Plato's report, which corresponded to the Altiplano and to nowhere else in the world.

To begin, Plato's Atlantis was a large continent opposite the Straits of Gibraltar. He stated that in the center of this continent, midway along its longest side, there existed a smooth and level plain surrounded by mountains. These were rich with gold, silver, copper, tin, and a mysterious alloy called *orichalcum*, the second-most valuable metal. In the center of the plain and 5 miles from the sea stood a mountain forming a central island surrounded by concentric rings of land and water. The plain itself was of rectangular configuration and criss-crossed by a system of irrigation-drainage canals, sometimes represented in popular drawings in a checkerboard pattern, or, as Plato said, "channels were cut in straight lines across the plain, and they transported also on boats the seasons' products by cutting transverse passages from one channel to the next."[2]

He went on to state that the civilization of Atlantis disappeared during the course of a single day and night of terrible earthquakes and floods. Since then, scholars have been unable to determine whether the whole story was invented by Plato, or had at least some basis in geographical and historical fact.

Contrary to standard arguments for and against Atlantis, I conclude that the entire continent on which it perched did not sink into the sea, but only the region surrounding the capital city, which was built on a volcanic island in the center of the plain. This continent could have only been South America. Plato's level, rectangular plain is the Altiplano, which, in fact, exists exactly where he assigned it: in the center of the whole continent and midway at its longest side. All the metals Plato mentioned are found here, including *orichalcum*, a natural native alloy known as *tumbaga*, a mixture of copper and gold. When the copper is dissolved from its surface, tumbaga has the appearance of pure gold.

After a series of five expeditions to the region, an island volcano was indeed found in the center of the plain, 5 miles from the sea. This island has two concentric rings of land. Its canal-like depressions could have contained water when the level of the nearby inland sea—Lake Poopo—was higher. The island also features red, white, and black stone—the same colored construction materials Plato wrote were used to build Atlantis. Furthermore, the Bolivian island has been inundated by earthquake-generated flooding. Parts of it are covered with coral-like deposits called *katawi*. These are fossilized sediments from a period when the area was totally submerged beneath great lakes geologists know once covered the area.

A local native myth known as "the Legend of the Desaguadero" tells how a great city was punished by the gods and sank beneath the sea, closely paralleling Plato's version. The name "Atlantis" consists of two native American words, *atl,* which means "water" in Tenoche—the language spoken by Aztecs in the Valley of Mexico—and *antis,* or "copper" in Quechua, as spoken by the Incas. Plato also mentions that the god of the sea, known to his fellow Athenians as Poseidon, had five pairs of twin sons. According to Spanish historian Sarmiento de Gamboa, the Andean god of the sea, Viracocha, also had five pairs of twin sons. Gamboa clearly identified South America as Atlantis in the beginning of his work, and relates that it was variously named "the Atlantic Island" (Atlanticus), "New Castile," or "America."[3]

Plato provided a date of 9,000 years before Solon for the end of Atlantis, but in fact says this period coincided with a war between the people of Atlantis, Greece, and Egypt. If lunar years, which were used by the same temple-priests who related the story of Atlantis, are substituted for solar years, then this would bring the date of its destruction to around 1200 BC, coinciding with the Trojan War and the contemporaneous attack on Egypt by invaders known as "the Sea Peoples." In any case, the precise time-parameters of Atlantis are unclear.

A key factor in Plato's description was the system of irrigation canals said to cross the plain at regular intervals. In the beginning of my research, I sought to identify these canals in Bolivia using Landsat surveys of the area. However, at that time (1983), the images were so small in scale that, although possible canals might be discerned, their positive identification was inconclusive. I later obtained high-resolution satellite images of the region, which clearly show a system of straight and parallel canals crossing the plain, with transverse canals at regular intervals. Another system of channels appears to connect a system of wells for drawing water from underground resources. Originally, these canals would have fed a system of parallel waterworks, making the whole undertaking an immense and sophisticated system of engineering, and representing a large population in an area presently consisting mainly of sparsely populated salt desert.

It now remains to precisely locate these ancient channels on the ground, to measure them and establish the extent to which they may have covered the whole area during prehistory. Further investigation of these features might just reveal the capital city of Atlantis lies, not beneath the sea, but under the sands of Bolivia.

CHAPTER 25

American and Japanese Dragons:
Related or Coincidence?
by Professor Nobuhiro Yoshida

Professor of languages Nobuhiro Yoshida is president of the Japan Petrograph Society and editor of its Newsletter, in Kitakyushu. The author of 30 books about his country's prehistory, he is the best-known scientist in Japan, where he lectures widely and appears on numerous television programs concerning the ancient past.

During the summer of 1983, I was involved in the research and preservation of public artworks for a project known as "Paintings of the Latticed Ceilings in Old Shrines," sponsored by the Ministry of Education. We found no less than 5,000 paintings in the course of our restoration endeavors.

It was then that I chanced to discover a strange painting among the 80 illustrated panels long ago installed in the compartmentalized ceiling of a small shrine at Yukuhashi, Fukuoka Prefecture. The building was named *Hachi-Rai,* or "Eight Thunders," after a powerful dragon believed to have lived about 3 miles north of the village on a sacred hill, in a cave approximately 3,336 feet above sea level. The painting shows a winged dragon flying in stormy weather over agitated water. It was created by none other than Seikoh Kano, father of the more famous *Hohgai Kano* (1828–1888), the most famous artist family and school of the Edo Period. Fifteen years after my association with the art restoration project, I received a letter from Mr. J. Hahn, in the United States. He wrote of a large pictoglyph, or painting on stone, that formerly existed near his home in East Alton, Illinois. This was the mysterious *Piasu,* and, having learned of my work with the Japan Petrograph Society, Mr. Hahn wondered if I observed any parallels it may have shown with other ancient rock art encountered during my travels throughout the world. He was kind enough to include a description of the image, together with an illustration of the Piasu from an old newspaper.

The Japanese dragon.

The Piasu of Alton, Illinois.

I was unfamiliar with the North American pictoglyph, but was immediately struck by its resemblance to the dragon depicted by Seikoh Kano in his painting for the ceiling of the Hachi-Rai shrine. Both the American Piasu and the Japanese dragon have talons, are winged, bearded, horned, and multi-colored—too many diverse elements in common, it might seem, for mere coincidence. Moreover, I was aware of legends similar to those associated with the Piasu around Yukuhashi. They tell of a blue dragon, which dwelled in a high cave (again like the Piasu) near the eastern summit of Mount Nuki. Below the cave runs the River Nagao, which means "Long Tail," probably a reference to the dragon's tail, which he used to violently stir up the waters, just as the Piasu was said to have done. In fact, the Nagao connects with Mount Nuki's dragon cave and its Hachi-Rai shrine.

Unlike the murderous Piasu, however, dragons were the objects of Japanese prayers and rituals, because the creatures were personifications of drought-ending thunderstorms. Where people survived on the successful harvesting of rice and vegetables, rain was fundamental to life. Hence, the dragon as the bringer of welcome rains was equally revered in ancient China. Perhaps these concepts traveled with early peoples migrating out of Mongolia, across the Bering Land-Bridge, and throughout the Americas. Over time, the dragon degenerated from a helpful water-deity into a monster. The origins of the Japanese dragon, in any case, are suggested by a recent find made by Mr. Tadahiko Ueno. On the side of Mount Ryugatoh, in Amakusa (Kumamoto Prefecture), he discovered the large fossilized remains of a flying dinosaur, a species of *Pteranodon* or *Pterodactylus*, a genus of extinct flying reptiles found as fossils in Late Cretaceous deposits in both North America and Asia that existed more than 70 million years ago. Prehistoric myth-makers may have stumbled upon fossils such as the one located by Mr. Ueno, and found inspiration for their happy dragon from its suggestive contours.

August 1, 1673: Father Jacques Marquette was on a mission—not from God, but from Louis, Comte de Frontenac, the Governor of New France (today's Quebec, Ontario), to find the direction and mouth of the Mississippi River. The famous Jesuit missionary commanded a provisioned group of canoes carrying fellow explorers around a large curve in the river between what much later became the states of Missouri and Illinois, when a most amazing sight hove into view.

"As we were descending the river," he recorded later in his diary:

we saw high rocks with hideous monsters painted on them and upon which the bravest Indian dare not look. They are as large as a calf, with head and horns like a goat, their eyes are red, beard like a tiger's and face like a man's. Their tails are so long that they pass over their bodies, ending like a fish's tail. They are painted red, green and black and so well drawn that I could not believe they were drawn by the Indians and for what purpose they were drawn seems to me a mystery.[1]

Other 17th-century explorers, including the renowned Jean Nicolet (who saw the Illinois rock art 40 years before Marquette) and Louis Hennepin, also visited the site. Both illustrations measured some 30 feet long to 12 feet high, the largest pictoglyphs ever documented in aboriginal America. Their location about 80 feet above the river was unique, as well. "How could the carving have been made on the sheer face of the cliff?" asked investigator Norbert Hildebrand. "Perhaps it wasn't a cliff then. Perhaps the Indians built scaffolds, or let themselves down from the top by leather thongs. Or perhaps they built a huge mound of earth before the face of the rock."[2] But according to Father Hennepin, "The Illinois told us likewise that the rock on which these dreadful monsters stood was so steep that no man could climb up to it." If not the Indians, who then? "Nowhere else in North America has anything similar been recorded."[3]

They were singular for yet another reason: "Indian petroglyphs (sic) usually were drawn from nature, from actual sight and experience."[4] The Mississippi River pictoglyphs are nightmarish fantasy-figures, different from representational forms found in Native American art. The large paintings portrayed a mythical beast known among many Middle Western tribes as the Piasu, or "the bird that devoured men." They believed it dwelt in a cave high up the cliff face above the Mississippi River, where it runs west to east for 20 miles from Grafton to Alton, Illinois, where the large pictoglyphs were found. The cave was washed away by rising flood-waters after the turn of the 20th century. But in 1840, Professor John Russell, from Jersey County, Illinois, explored its interior to find "innumerable bones littering the stone floor. The roof of the cavern was vaulted, the top of which was hardly less than 20 feet high. The shape of the cave was irregular, but so far as I could judge, the bottom would range between 20 and 30 feet. The floor of the cave throughout the whole extent was one mass of human bones. Skulls and other bones were mingled together in the utmost confusion. To what depth they extended, I am unable to decide, but we dug to a depth of 3 or 4 feet in every quarter of the cavern and still found only bones. The remains of thousands must have been deposited there."[5]

Who were these numerous dead? Human sacrifices to a cultic deity represented by the Piasu? Or were they victims of a natural disaster it personified? Native tradition recounts that one monster made the Earth violently tremble when it beat its tail on the ground, while its partner thrashed the mighty Mississippi into huge waves, over-spilling its banks and drowning all living things on shore. Such descriptions suggest cataclysmic geologic upheaval in an area infamous for deadly earthquakes. Alton is perched between two active fault lines, the Wabash and New Madrid, which, in 1810, triggered the biggest earthquake in United States history. It was powerful enough to ring church bells as far away as Philadelphia, and make the Father of Waters momentarily reverse its course, recalling Illini stories of the Piasu catastrophically agitating the Mississippi River.

Researcher P.A. Armstrong learned from questioning Indian sources that "the time when the Piasu existed in this country, according to the Illini tradition, was 'many thousands of moons before the arrival of the pale faces,' while that of the Miami says, 'several thousand winters before the pale faces came.' Though indefinite as to the exact period, both indicate a very long period of time ago—many centuries."[6] However old, the giant pictoglyph was so hated by Indians floating past in their canoes that they invariably took pot-shots at it as soon as they acquired firearms from their "pale face" dealers. Even so, the Alton Piasu was still in at least a recognizable state of preservation, when it was utterly destroyed in 1865 by prison laborers quarrying the cliff on which it had been painted. Writing 22 years after its loss, Armstrong concluded, "The combination and blending together of the monster specific to the Earth, sea and air, so as to present the leading and most terrific characteristics of the various species thus graphically arranged, is an absolute wonder and seems to show a vastly superior knowledge of animal, fowl, reptile and fish nature than has been accorded to the Indian."[7] Long before Armstrong, Father Marquette and others came to the same conclusion. Consequently, are overseas origins for the Piasu worth considering?

Hildebrand writes, "In medieval France an effigy of the devil that bears some resemblance to these monsters was marched through the streets and ritually destroyed"[8]—echoes of the Illini and Miami Indians who blasted away at the Alton pictoglyph whenever the opportunity arose. Indeed, the Drache, or "dragon," familiar in Teutonic Northern Europe from the Dark to High Middle Ages, was a similar figure appearing as a griffin or protective beast throughout funeral and other Nordic art. Although these Old World comparisons with the Illinois rock art should not be completely dismissed, the dragon portrayed at Yukuhashi's Hachi-Rai shrine is a far closer match to the Piasu. The Japanese beast was said to have occupied a cave on the side of a mountain overlooking a river, just as the Piasu dwelled inside a bone-littered cave above the Mississippi. Seikoh Kano's painting (which doubtless carried on a descriptive tradition predating by centuries, at least, his time in the early 1800s) represents the Hachi-Rai dragon flying through a storm over tumultuous waters.

It recalls one of the Piasus, which lathered the Mississippi to violence. The elements they share in common, though not total, are nevertheless remarkable. Both have wings, talons, scales, beards, open mouths, long teeth, and horns. Missing only from the Japanese version are the serpent and fish themes of its Illinois counterpart. Yukuhashi is very near the coast. Did its sea-faring culture-bearers sometime in the unknown past embark on a great expedition to the other side of the Pacific Ocean? In view of persuasive physical evidence for Japanese seafarers in pre-Columbian America from Ryukyu metal tools at the Ozette site, in Washington State, to Jomon pottery shards in Valdivia, Ecuador, such voyages certainly took place. Sailing up the Mississippi River to the cliffs at Alton, Illinois, they may have familiarized the natives with an anti-drought cult symbolized by an abundance-giving dragon representing the elemental forces of nature. Over time, to propitiate the god (perhaps following a killer earthquake), human sacrifices were offered, accounting for the hecatomb of human skulls and bones in the Piasu's cave, and the creature's evil reputation among subsequent generations of Illini and Miami Indians.

Half a century ago, Hildebrand wrote, "Men have sought the answer to this mystery for hundreds of years, but it still eludes them. Only the Mississippi, Father of Waters, could tell—if it could speak."[9]

CHAPTER 26

Ecuador, Point of Contact
by Bruce Scofield, PhD

Bruce Scofield, PhD, is a faculty member at both Kepler College and the University of Massachusetts, where he researches solar influences on climate and life. A teacher and lecturer at many regional and national conferences during the last 20 years, his published work includes Aztec Circle of Destiny: Astrology and Divination from the Ancient Aztec World (with Angela Cordova; Llewellyn Publications, 1989) and Signs of Time: An Introduction to Mesoamerican Astrology (One Reed Publications, 1997).

There are two locations in the Americas where the archaeological evidence for cultural diffusionism is so convincing that discussions of ancient transoceanic voyages actually appear in school textbooks. One of these is the Atlantic coast of Canada, where there is concrete evidence of Norse occupation. The site called L'Anse aux Meadows, in northern Newfoundland, is now a government-operated historical location with a visitor center and costumed guides. Archaeologists say it was probably occupied for about 30 years sometime during the 10th century, long before the time of Columbus. The other major location that supports the diffusionist perspective, and has also been taken seriously by at least some in the academic Establishment, is on the Pacific coast of Ecuador in South America.

Named for the fact that it lies astride the equator, Ecuador has many interesting geographic features. It is a land of many climates, including those of the tropical Pacific coast, the temperate highlands, and the humid

Amazon basin. On its Pacific coast, the Guayas River, the largest river on South America's west coast, has created an immense gulf and estuary, where the country's largest urban center, Guayaquil, is located. This major harbor-city was founded by the Spanish on the site of earlier native towns. The distinctive opening of this river's mouth on an otherwise-featureless west coast of South America is suggestive of its importance as a port or landmark. The general region, known as the Guayas Basin, is also blessed with a long shoreline and an abundance of vegetation, including balsa trees. In pre-Colombian times, the region was dotted with villages, the first major signs of civilization that Pizarro encountered on his trip south from Panama.

At the southern end of the Gulf of Guayaquil, right on the border, is the old Peruvian port of Tumbez (Tumbes), the gateway to the realm of the Incas and the place where Pizarro landed and began his conquest of that civilization. Traveling east from the Pacific coastal plain, the land in Ecuador rises quickly and reaches a highland area dotted with volcanoes, some active. In this mountainous region, snowcapped, volcanic peaks occur in two parallel bands running roughly north and south, a feature called the "Avenue of the Volcanoes." The land between these high peaks is quite fertile and the climate temperate, strikingly attractive when you consider that this territory lies on the equator. The highlands have been inhabited since ancient times, and the natural corridor formed by the volcanoes has long served as a transportation route between Peru and Columbia.

Civilization existed in Ecuador many centuries before the arrival of the Incas. The pre-Colombian kingdom of Quito and the fierce Canari of Tomebamba in the southern highlands were highly sophisticated, purely Ecuadorian cultural centers that resisted Peruvian expansion for years. Although a majority of surviving Incan ruins are located in Peru, and most people associate the Incas with that country, Quito was the northern Incan capital, and the last two Inca rulers were born in Ecuador. To the east of the Ecuadorian highlands are the rivers that feed the Amazon and a vast rain forest, a region called El Oriente. Rainfall on the highlands drains into several major tributaries of the Amazon, including the huge Rio Napo. In 1542, just a few years into the Spanish Conquest of Andean civilization, explorer Francisco de Orellana descended from Quito to the Ecuadorian rainforest. He followed the rivers eastward, and seven months later reached the Atlantic Ocean. Orellana gave the Amazon its name.

What we find in Ecuador is a major Pacific port surrounded by forests that approach the coast, a major north-south land route, and a water route east to the Atlantic. Such a unique location invites human culture in two ways: as a permanent feature, but also as place on the way to somewhere else. It is therefore not surprising that some evidence for contact with a distant culture has been discovered there and has become part of the typical (albeit somewhat controversial) curriculum for the student of South American archaeology. This particular evidence is the Valdivia pottery.

Just to the north of Guayaquil, on the Pacific coast of Ecuador, is the small town of Valdivia. There, in 1956, a distinctive type of pottery was found that excited archaeologists for several reasons. First, this pottery was dated as early as 3000 BC, making it, at the time of discovery, the oldest known pottery in all of the Americas.[1] Second, the archaeologists who discovered it believed that this pottery appeared abruptly in the archaeological record in a fully developed form. Third, a close resemblance to Japanese pottery of the same era led these archaeologists to speculate about contact with the ancient Japanese Jomon culture.[2] So serious were these speculations that they were published in the Smithsonian Institution's *Contributions to Archaeology, Volume I* (1965) and included in an exhibit at the Smithsonian Institution in Washington, D.C.[3]

A few years after the discovery of the Valdivia pottery, a large-scale dig took place where thousands of pottery shards and other artifacts were sorted and classified. Valdivia pottery is characterized by deeply incised designs and decorations on jars and bowls. Another type of artifact found at the excavation included distinctive female (Venus) figurines with emphasized hair treatments. The supervising archaeologists of the dig, and authors of the scientific paper reporting the finds were Betty J. Meggers, Clifford Evans, and Emilio Estrada. As they sorted through the artifacts, they established a chronology of Valdivia phase periods lettered A through D. The earliest, phase A, is dated from about 3000 to 2200 BC. Period B is 2300 to 2000 BC; Period C 2000 to 1400 BC; and Period D 1400 to 1000 BC. Interestingly, other early pottery sites in South or Central America that share traits with Valdivia pottery were dated to Period C or D. In their report, these archaeologists noted that Valdivia A pottery shared the most common traits with pottery from ancient Japan, where the oldest known pottery in the world is found.

The diffusionist hypothesis described by Meggers, Evans, and Estrada in their first reports suggests that Japanese fishermen of the Middle Jomon Period drifted out to sea and were caught by the Japanese Current. Months later, having been swept along by ocean currents for some 9,000 miles, they landed in Ecuador. Once ashore, they mixed with the native populations, taught them to make pottery, and also established some burial customs (which the two cultures appear to have shared). In other words, their view was that it was only by chance that contact between ancient Japan and ancient Ecuador occurred, and it was probably a one-time occurrence.

Later discoveries at the Valdivia site showed that the chronology proposed by Meggers, Evans, and Estrada may have been incorrect. Estrada thought that similarities with Jomon pottery are more characteristic of the Valdivia B period. Also, a pre-Valdivia pottery was discovered and a new chronology has since been established (Valdivia I–VIII) that puts Valdivia A in a category called Valdivia II. Valdivia I refers to a previously undescribed occupation with early ceramics. The situation has become more complex, and thinking about the Japan-Ecuador connection has changed during recent years. The discovery of possible Japanese artifacts dated to about 500 BC at another site in Ecuador was reported by Estrada that suggests a more complex linkage between Japan and Ecuador than was previously imagined. Also, some artifacts similar to those of the Han Dynasty China (about 200 BC) were also found in this small country.

Records show that the ancient Chinese did know of a land to the east, and they even had a name for it: Fu-Sang. Chinese voyages in this direction are believed to have occurred in 219, 210, and 100 BC, and 500 AD. A fleet of boats carrying some 3,000 people, funded by the emperor and led by a man called Hsu Fu, was known to have sailed to Fu-Sang in 219 BC. They never returned (Needham, 1971, p. 533[4]). Another interesting piece of information supportive of an Ecuador-Japan connection is biological. The human T-cell leukemia virus HTLV-1 has its highest occurrence in Japan; in South America, its existence is restricted to the Andes (Meggers, 2010[5]). This fact, the lack of decisive data, and the complexities of establishing pottery horizons have not been enough to change the trend in mainstream archaeology to seek indigenous causes for cultural development.

There is no doubt that coastal Ecuador and the Guayas Basin have been occupied since very early times. The Formative Period in Ecuador, which includes the Valdivia Culture, was centered in this region. The Machalilla and Chorreara style of pottery (1500 to 1000 BC), produced just to the north of this region, had a tremendous influence on distant cultures, including those in Mexico, Guatemala, and Peru. More recently, between 500 BC and 500 AD, the urban Bahia culture flourished. The earliest metalwork in the New World began about this time in Ecuador. Later, the

Mateno culture-bearers, who were said to be excellent sailors, inhabited the region. Ecuador was not a backwater to Peru in ancient times; it was a thriving center of human activity and, apparently, an exporter of culture.

The Gulf of Guayaquil itself may have been an important feature for ancient navigators. It has been suggested by Gunnar Thompson that this geographical feature is actually noted on a number of European pre-Colombian maps.[6] If this is so, it implies that ancient voyagers from the West were able to reach this part of South America. Thompson also suggests that the ancient Incan city of Cajamarca, just south of the Gulf of Guayaquil, may have been the "Cattigara" on ancient Roman maps that was located in the biblical land of Ophir. There is certainly something of a match between the Ecuadorian coastline and a mysterious body of land shown on the DeVirga map of 1414, though it could likewise be said that this body of land may refer to the northern portion of Australia. As already mentioned, it is also possible that ancient voyagers from China or Southeast Asia reached the South American coast, perhaps as recently as the 15th century (see Menzies, 2002[7]). Until recent times, these peoples were ahead of the West in the development of watercraft and navigational techniques, including the use of the compass.

As Thor Heyerdahl long ago demonstrated, navigating the Pacific is most easily done by using the powerful Japanese and Humboldt currents.[8] Ocean travelers coming from China or Japan would utilize the Japanese Current, which would take them to the North American west coast by a route that runs north of Hawaii and south of Alaska. Though this may seem like a round-about way to reach America, it is actually shorter than sailing due east from China or Japan. The curvature of the globe is such that real distances are difficult to grasp on a two-dimensional map, particularly a Mercator projection. On reaching the American coast, navigation further south would be more difficult, but possible. Near the equator, in particular, the currents and winds are more complex and subject to changes. Ocean travelers leaving South America and heading west would utilize the Humboldt Current, which is easily reached from Peru and Ecuador. As Heyerdahl himself proved, it is possible to sail from South America to the Polynesian Islands and beyond.

Aside from the Valdivia pottery and possible transpacific contacts, Ecuador has other surprises and a long history, much covered by Colonial and modern construction. Cuenca, one of Ecuador's largest cities, is just the latest settlement in an area that had a very long history. It was built over an Incan city called Tomebamba, which was completely destroyed. In its heyday it was said to have rivaled Cuzco in grandeur. Tomebamba itself was built over a major Canari city; the Canari being the native Ecuadorian Indians who held back the expansionistic Incas for decades. Architectural remnants of these ancient native cultures exist in the region, though they not very visible, and Spanish clergymen, bent on Christian conversion, made the natives outsiders in their own land. Once exception was Father Crespi of Cuenca. He was a friend to the local Indians, who repaid his kindness and concern for them with gifts of archaeological artifacts that they reportedly found in deserted cities and deep tunnels (described and fantastically interpreted by Von Daniken, 1972[9]) to the east of Cuenca.

Throughout the years, Father Crespi's collection came to include large pieces of hammered sheet metal with highly sophisticated engravings, sculptures that are clearly reminiscent of the ancient Near East, and curious objects that are difficult to place in the context of ordinary archae-

ology. He was presented with artifacts with images of llamas, bronze Phoenician calendars, pyramids, enigmatic inscriptions, and even the engraving of a dinosaur! There were also metal and stone mechanical devices, bronze air pipes, and woven, copper, radiator-like objects. Author Richard Wingate photographed a portion of Crespi's extraordinary collection and published some of the photos in his book, *Lost Outpost of Atlantis*.[10]

Father Crespi was known to have accepted these gifts, many of which were obvious fakes, from hungry Indians, whom he fed. His mission was one of compassion, not science. Unfortunately, this approach, combined with his eccentricities (he collected Charlie Chaplin movies) worked against the credibility of his collection. No professional archaeologist would get involved with

This silver statuette from the Crespi Collection depicts a mythical guardian of Babylonian kings from the 18th century BC.

analyzing these clearly contaminated and untraceable artifacts. Even worse, in 1962, his museum was partially destroyed in an arsonist's fire. The remains of his collection are now owned by the Central Bank of Ecuador.

In conversation with a private collector at Cuenca, I learned that Crespi was locally regarded as someone duped by the Indians. He wanted to believe that the artifacts they gave him were proof that Ecuador's earliest cultures were in contact with the others from the Ancient Mediterranean world. He believed that the Amazon was a transportation route between these two worlds, and that the artifacts came from an undiscovered, prehistoric city on the eastern side of the Andes. Aside from his own collection, Crespi would point to the resemblance between Valdivia Venus figurines and ancient Egyptian figures known as shabaktis. It is true that these two categories of artifact share similar hair treatments.

Despite the questionable nature of many of Crespi's artifacts, they at least raise the question of travel from the Atlantic to the Pacific. Movement from the Amazon basin over the Andes to the Pacific via mostly waterways was possible at several places in the north of South America. One is up the huge Amazon River to one of several rivers that drain the highlands. From these rivers (the Napo, Pastaza, and Santiago), it is only about 100 miles up and over the highlands to the Guayaquil region. A combination of waterway and land crossings through Ecuador to the Pacific is also possible from the Caribbean. Near the city of Cartegena, the rivers Cauca and Magdalena (where the oldest pottery in Colombia is found) can be followed south almost to the Ecuadorian border. From there, one can follow the Avenue of the Volcanoes down to the Pacific near present-day Guayaquil. This was a well-traveled route in ancient times.

There are other intriguing speculations about Ecuador and cultural diffusionism. A recent book on Mesoamerican calendrics (Malmstrom, 1971[11]) presents a case for the origins of Mesoamerican culture on the Pacific coast near the ancient city of Izapa. This region, called Soconusco (today's coastal Chiapas and in the general vicinity of the Mexican/ Guatemalan border) is characterized by abundant wildlife, fertile soils, and an extreme diversity of habitat within a small area. Vincent Malmstrom, the author, argues that this is the only comfortably habitable stretch of land along the Pacific coast north of Ecuador. In between are inhospitable mangrove forests.

Archaeological evidence dates the earliest significant cultural developments in Soconusco to about 1800 BC. Around this time, the people living there were farming, building large houses on raised mounds, and making elaborate pottery. About 1500 BC, it appears that newcomers arrived in the Soconusco region by sea, and the native pottery styles began to change and evolve rapidly. Eventually, the Soconusco culture moved north and east across the Tehuantepec gap between the Oaxaca and Chiapas highlands to establish the early Mesoamerican sites identified as Olmec. Malmstrom argues that the most significant innovations of the Soconusco culture are to be found in their astronomy and calendrics. According to him, Soconusco is the place of origin for the 260-day astrological calendar, a key component of the Mayan calendar.

A Babylonian priest (center) receives benediction from a jiin.
The significance of the figure at right is unknown.
Solid silver cast, circa 18th century BC.

Malmstrom and others have suggested that voyagers from Ecuador may have significantly influenced Mesoamerican civilization in their explorations up and down the Pacific coast around 1500 BC. Similarities in ceramics, burials, clothing, metallurgy, and the distribution of dogs and jays have been cited as evidence for possible links between Ecuador and Mexico (Anawalt, 1997[12]). Geography, Malmstrom's field, is also an important argument for him. He points out that it is only north of the western point of the Ecuadorian coast that the Equatorial Countercurrent sweeps northward along the coast of Central America, reaching as far as Soconusco.

He also notes that balsa trees for making rafts were far more available from the huge Guayas River estuary than from the banks of the small desert rivers that empty into the Pacific along the shoreline of Peru. In his view, it may have been Ecuadorians, as carriers of the earliest Andean cultures, who stimulated the development of high civilization to Mesoamerica. A single carving on a wall of the ball-court at the ruins of Izapa, a major site in Soconusco, holds an interesting image that suggests that the area's contact with seafarers was an important part of their heritage. This enigmatic image suggests that outside contacts may not have been limited to Ecuadorians on rafts. It represents a bearded man in a sea-boat with outstretched arms holding a cross of some sort.

There is no question that ancient South Americans set out into the Pacific Ocean on rafts. These rafts, called "balsas," were made of huge balsa logs arranged so that the central log was longest, with the others flanking it laid in decreasing length, creating the effect of a prow. A wooden cabin and a bipod mast for a sail sat atop the main logs. Boards shoved between the logs served as small keels, allowing the raft to sail at an angle to the winds. Bartolomew Ruiz, one of Pizarro's pilots on a reconnaissance voyage south of Panama to the equator, reported sighting a native raft 100 miles off the coast in 1526.[13] The raft, about as big as his ship, was carrying 20 well-dressed natives and about 30 tons of cargo. The raft was also sailing against the current. Ruiz had 11 natives thrown overboard, took three women to be trained as translators, and let the rest go free.

Long-distance balsa raft navigation was an Ecuadorian tradition. Spanish historians recorded an interesting story about a voyage led by the Inca Tupac Yupanqui. He was, at the time, engaged in conquering Ecuador—specifically, the regions along the Gulf of Guayaquil—and had heard stories from seafaring merchants of lands to the west, lands that he wanted to add to the Inca Empire. Tupac Yupanqui apparently set sail with 20,000 men on a flotilla of rafts in search of two distant populated islands supposedly rich in gold. His expedition was gone for perhaps a year, but the Inca did return with some metal and prisoners. Some think his voyage took him to the Galapagos (Means, 1931: 270–272), others suggest he had reached Easter Island (Heyerdahl, 1979: 190 ff).[14]

Thor Heyerdahl challenged academic resistance to the idea of the feasibility of ancient voyages by doing them himself, and went to Ecuador for logs to build his raft, *Kon-Tiki*. After felling huge balsa trees on a tributary of the Guayas, he floated them downstream to Guayaquil and then had them shipped to Peru, where they were assembled. Heyerdahl modeled *Kon-Tiki* after rafts constructed by the Mateno, a coastal Ecuadorian people known as excellent seafarers. The tradition of balsa raft navigation in Ecuador was made possible by both the abundance of balsa trees in the region, and the nearby, powerful ocean currents.

Heyerdahl himself believed that the Guayas region of Ecuador and northern Peru was the mid-point of ancient American maritime activity. It was certainly a center for commerce, as observed by the first Spaniards who sailed into the region. They found huge rafts loaded with tons of products sailing (not drifting) miles offshore. Reports of "distant traders" who came to the port of Zacatula in West Mexico, were sent to the king in 1525. (Interestingly, this harbor is at the mouth of the Rio Balsas.) These distant traders apparently remained at the port for months at a time before they attempted a return voyage (Anawalt, 1997[15]). There is evidence, in the form of pre-Colombian ceramic remains, of routine 600-mile voyages to the Galapagos Islands.

It is certainly possible to sail great distances on seaworthy balsa rafts. Since Heyerdahl's famous *Kon-Tiki* voyage in 1947, many other researchers have successfully sailed the Pacific Ocean on balsa rafts. In 1969 and 1973, Vital Alsar led voyages that began in Ecuador and reached Australia.[16] In spite of all this, Western archaeologists, historians, and alleged experts on the peopling of Polynesia have emphatically resisted accepting any suggestion that ancient South Americans were capable of such voyages. Some responded to Heyerdahl's voyage by saying he only proved that Norwegians are good sailors.

The more one studies the ancient history of Ecuador, the more one realizes its importance as both a long-distance sailing center and a point of cultural diffusion. Ecuadorian pottery alone suggests that, in very early times, the region may have been a major origin-point in the New World from which culture spread. If so, it was probably diffused more by sea than by land. Some mainstream archaeologists are at least beginning to consider the possibility that the Olmec culture, the earliest civilization in Mesoamerica, was "jump-started" by ancient Ecuadorian trading voyages, and that later Mesoamerican cultures benefited from repeated contact with "distant traders."

Whether or not voyagers from other continents reached Ecuador regularly in ancient times is still open to question, though evidence suggests that there may have been at least some contacts with ancient Japan, and possibly also Han Dynasty China. Whether or not ancient Mediterranean travelers sailed up the Amazon to trade with the early cultures of Ecuador and Peru is more questionable. But where did at least some of Father Crespi's collection originate? Heyerdahl has shown that Polynesia was visited and settled (along with immigrants from other places) by ancient South Americans who most likely sailed from northern Peru and Ecuador. This is still disputed by experts on Polynesia, who, as Heyerdahl repeatedly pointed out, are not experts on South America.

One thing for certain is that Ecuador was where the Conquest of Peru began. When Pizarro sailed into the Gulf of Guayaquil, he encountered civilization in South America. At the southern end of the Gulf he found Tumbez, the gateway to the kingdom of the Incas and the point from which the conquest of the Inca Empire began. Strangely enough, this may have been the same place where an earlier, and probably more benign, influence on Andean civilization began as well. A Peruvian legend recalled that, long ago, bearded gods had arrived on these shores (Heyerdahl, 1979, p.104 ff[17]). In these two instances, one history and the other legend, coastal Ecuador was indeed a "point of contact." As mainstream archaeologists continue their efforts to reconstruct South American prehistory, they will no doubt find that Ecuador's cultural role in pre-Columbian times was wider and more complex than previously assumed.

The Stone Towers of Japan and Easter Island
by Professor Nobuhiro Yoshida

According to a report received by the national headquarters of the Japan Petroglyph Society in Kitakyushu, an ancient stone tower discovered on an off-shore island suggests cultural links from Japan to the other side of the Pacific Ocean, 1,400 years ago. And it may explain the unique civilization that arose on Easter Island.

On December 10, 2000, Mr. Hiroaki Hayashi (chapter president, Tokushima Prefecture, Shikoku) was joined by five Japan Petroglyph Society (J.P.S.) members at Shodoshima, located between the cities of Takamatsu and Himeji. About 13 miles long and 10 miles across, it is the second largest island in the Harima Sea. Following local traditions of ancient ruins atop Mount Hoshigajo, Hayashi and his colleagues began their ascent. At its summit, 2,680 meters above sea level, they found two magnificent stone domes, one approximately 18 feet high and 12 feet wide at its base; the other about 30 feet high and 15 feet wide. Sado-jima legend assigns their construction to some 2,600 years ago, when the first Japanese emperor, Jimmu, built them as astronomical observatories, an identification suggested by the very name of Mt. *Hoshigajo*: "Star Castle Mountain."

Not far from the domes, on the island's western peak, the J.P.S. researchers found stones arranged into a square approximately 30 feet in diameter and 3-feet-high. It is oriented to sunrise so perfectly that dawn light appears through a gateway on the eastern wall of the sanctuary. Although constructed many centuries ago, the location is still venerated by local pilgrims as a sacred site. The enclosure is dedicated to the deity of fertility, the so-called *Guardian of Red Beans*. In not only Japan, but China, Burma, Thailand, Tibet, and Korea, red beans have been the traditional components of sacred feasts. Together with boiled rice, they are consumed in memorial day ceremonies. Cakes, or *mochi,* presented as offerings to the gods include red beans mixed with rice and honey or sugar. Interestingly, the very name *Shodoshima* means "Island of the Red Beans." Perhaps it was among the most important religious centers in Asia, a suggestion underscored by traditional associations with Japan's first emperor.

The tower Hiroaki Hayashi and his Japan Petroglyph Society colleagues investigated at Shodoshima, an island in Hiroshima Bay.

When I saw Mr. Hayashi's photograph of the Mt. Hoshigajo dome, I was struck by its resemblance to a structure on Easter Island sketched in a 19th-century lithograph reproduced by *Ancient American*.[1] In the foreground, a human figure emerges from an open enclosure not unlike the stone square on Shodoshima. This apparent structural parallel between Japan and Easter Island is supported by contemporary traditions found at both locations. For example, Easter Island was supposed to have been discovered and settled by a sea-faring king, Hotu Matua, along with his royal family and followers. They arrived from a faraway land known only as Hiva. "Easter Island" derives from its discovery made by Dutch captain Jakob Rogeveen on Easter Sunday 1772.

The Azumi were a powerful sea-people who controlled much of Japan until banished by the Kinki Dynasty, around 600 AD. They sailed away to the west, never to return. Were the Azumi Hotu Matua's people who landed on the shores of Easter Island? A comparison of time frames implies as much, because archaeological dating of the earliest human settlement at Easter Island begins around 400 AD, followed by successive waves of immigration for the next several centuries. Moreover, the summit of Japan's Mount Hiva (yes, the same name of Hotu Matua's lost homeland!) features an immense boulder, locally revered as the tomb of the god, Izanagi, who created the Japanese islands. It appears as several important place-names throughout Japan, such as Hiroshima Prefecture's Hiva, the site of a very old shrine.

These correspondences are supplemented by racial evidence for trans-pacific connections. Isolated populations in the northeast prefectures of Japan, unlike the Polynesian inhabitants themselves, strongly resemble the persons portrayed in the giant statues for which Easter Island is best known. Did the sixth-century Japanese sea-people, remembered as the Azumi, who possibly sailed to Easter Island, range farther beyond to South America? Mr. Hiroaki Hayashi's discovery during late 2000 of an ancient domed tower on the island of Shodoshima compares with a similar structure uncovered about 30 years earlier in Ecuador. Referred to as *La Olla* (the "oven"), the prehistoric dome is perched atop a hill 600 feet above the capital city, Quito.

Conventional archaeologists have erroneously designated the structure as a "temple of the Incas," because its existence even pre-dated the Quiteno Indians, who were conquered by the Incas some 1,200 years ago. The Quiteno themselves spoke of the alien "magicians," builders of a much older civilization that included *La Olla*. In any case, its obvious similarity to Japan's mountain-top dome of Shodoshima is compelling. In support of such transpacific comparisons was the discovery made in the mid-1960s of Japanese ceramic fragments at the coastal Ecuadoran site of Valdivia. Dating the ceramics placed them as early as 3800 BC, when the Jomon Culture was flourishing throughout much of Japan.

Ecuador's pre-Inca La Olla. *Compare with Japan's Shodoshima site. The representation of a solar figure is featured above* La Olla's *entrance. Shodoshima's tower is likewise associated with celestial orientations.*

Combined with new evidence from Shodoshima, they indicate that prehistoric Japanese sailors were familiar with Ecuador from deeply ancient times, and throughout the course of many centuries.

CHAPTER 28

Peru's Lost City of the "Cloud People"
by Beverley H. Moseley, Jr.

Until his death at 85 years of age in 2011, Beverley H. Moseley, Jr., was an activist in the Midwestern Epigraphic Society (Columbus, Ohio), which he headed from 1989 until 2005. His outstanding contribution to the cause of cultural diffusionism was a pronounced artistic talent, which he applied to rendering artifactual images otherwise too eroded or faded to be properly and fully examined.

On August 15, 2008, after a month of hacking their way through the rainforests of northern Peru, a team of American and Peruvian explorers finally stood before the mighty ramparts of their quest. Earlier, all they had to go on were years of preliminary research into legends and rumors of an otherwise-forgotten metropolis deep in the Amazon jungle.

"It's a tremendous city," exclaimed Sean Savoy, the team leader, "containing areas with etchings and ten-meter (33-foot) high walls." Sean is the son of Gene Savoy, who accompanied the expedition, and whose earlier discoveries, such as the sacred city of Peru's Gran Pajaten, have been featured in past issues of *Ancient American*. He christened their new find "Gran Saposoa," after the nearby village of Saposoa.

Although the area had been mapped out with preliminary drawings, the explorers were surprised by the vast extent of the ruined city, located 9,186 feet above sea-level. Its 39 square acres enfold five citadels standing among waterfalls and lakes, all surrounded by massive walls hung with thick vegetation. Matted jungle growth covers their numerous carvings and figure paintings, Sean Savoy reported. He went on to say that his team also found well-preserved cemeteries containing the mummified bodies of Gran Saposoa's original inhabitants "in almost perfect condition."

Study of the remains may help to confirm 16th-century accounts of the Chachapoyas, a fair-complected people renowned for their prowess as outstanding warriors and encountered by early Spanish explorers. The Chachapoyas were already virtually extinct when Francisco Pizarro and his Conquistadors overthrew the Inca Empire, which had absorbed the earlier civilization and established its own settlement—perhaps a garrison—within the walls of Gran Saposoa.

Until its discovery, little of the Chachapoyas was known, save for a number of oversized burial caskets, attesting to their reputed tall stature, found in Peru's northern jungle region. Like Egyptian sarcophagi, the coffin lids had been sculpted into representations of the deceased. The Chachapoyas appear to have been the white-skinned "giants" described throughout Andean legend and allegedly responsible for building the pre-Inca city of Tiahuanaco in remote antiquity. Ten thousand of them flourished in Gran Saposoa around 700 AD, when its farming terraces were watered by an ingenious system of stone canals. Their application during the eighth century proves the Incas, who rose some 600 years later, inherited rather than invented, as historians assumed, these sophisticated agricultural and irrigation techniques.

Discovery of the lost city is an important achievement in Peruvian archaeology, because it promises to shed new light on the development of Andean Civilization.

CHAPTER 29

Pennsylvania's Stone
Sepulchers
by Wayne May

The Cherokee are an untypical Native American people, because they evidence a variety of different racial types too broad for a single tribe. Remarkably, their variation is not entirely the result of modern inter-marriage with modern non-Amerindians. When the earliest settlers from Europe arrived in Tennessee, they compared some Cherokee to Moroccans and Sicilians. This unresolved heritage may be part of the same, no less anomalous structures examined by the publisher of Ancient American magazine.

In January 2006, I visited a small town just north of Philadelphia, Pennsylvania, where I met Danawa Buchanan. As an "elder" among the Eastern Band Cherokee, she could tell me about their oral traditions. Her knowledge of Native American history is prodigious, and I was anxious to learn her reaction to several artifacts I brought along from my personal collection. These included a number of ceremonial pipes and portrait stones with recurring symbols. In return, she escorted me to several ancient sites, scattered and remote, but surprisingly familiar.

I immediately recognized them, thanks to a back issue of my own magazine with is cover story by Irvin N. Shirk about "Pennsylvania's Burial Cairns."[1] He described massive stone burial structures atop large granite, boulders deep somewhere in a southeastern Pennsylvania woodland. To protect the pristine sight from possible vandalism, Shirk requested we refrain from publishing the site's exact location.

Now, to my astonishment, Danawa led through Pennsylvania's heavily wooded forest to a large cairn burial-ground on private land. Granite boulders were everywhere. Not just one or two, but more than a dozen, as far as I could see. A fence ran through the property, but the collection of cairns extended beyond my line of sight to another privately owned estate. According to Danawa, the people there were not particularly cooperative, and we could not go any further.

To appease the "spirits of place," Danawa sang a beautiful melody in her native tongue. I wish I could have recorded it. The woods echoed back her prayer-song, as she gave honor to the burials of ages past. She told me the burial ground was Delaware, and that the person who owned the land was a Delaware mixed-blood. This tribe, for reasons long forgotten or, more likely, still secret, buried their warriors in a most curious way. A large, granite boulder would be laid out in the manner of a serpent's head. Then, the deceased were interred head-to-foot, leading out and away from the large boulder (the head), like a snake coiling through the woods. These serpentine burials are referred to as the "walls of the warriors." Singular burials of small stones placed atop the large boulders were not named.

We surmised that the serpent-like burials were representative of rebirth and renewal, just as the snake sheds its skin and begins afresh each year. But if the real reason for this mode of burial is still known today among the Delaware, they aren't talking.

CHAPTER 30

The Great Walls of
Texas and Iowa
by Frank Joseph

More than 150 years ago, an entire town was named after one of the most baffling discoveries in archaeological history. The mystery persists to this day, unlike a vanished, stone reservoir the first pioneers who crossed into the Hawkeye State found to their amazement.

A 30-minute drive from downtown Dallas, just north of Route 30, may be found the Texas town of Rockwall. Located close to the western shores of Lake Lavon, its name derives from a remarkable discovery made there in 1851 by three early settlers—Boyd Stun, Reg Stuvenson, and T.U. Wade. They were digging a well near what is now the town's city limits, and sank a shaft about 30 feet deep, when their picks hit solid masonry. Surprised, they excavated around the obstruction to reveal a stone wall, obviously man-made. Visitors flocked from all over the area to gawk at their subterranean anomaly, and someone suggested that the village, still nameless after its founding 10 years earlier, be christened in honor of the discovery. Today, Rockwall, Texas, is occupied by 10,500 residents, who are no less mystified by their town's namesake than Messrs. Stun, Stuvenson, and Wade when they first laid eyes on the underground rampart nearly 150 years ago.

Since then, incomplete excavations of the site showed that part of the mysterious structure bisects Rockwall's downtown area, and stretches nearly as far as the town of Lavon, about 7 miles to the north. Jane Gilbert, writing for *The Rockwall County Historical Foundation,* claims it extends further still, "running throughout Rockwall County and into Hunt and Kaufman Counties," approximately 10 miles altogether.[1] Thorough geological or archaeological surveys of the site in its entirety have thus far not been undertaken.

"According to some calculations," wrote Frank X. Tolbert in *The Rockwall Community Shopper,* "the walls are four miles square, and sometimes forty feet in height. Blocks in the walls are often strikingly symmetrical, and held together by a mortar-like substance."[2]

Opinion, professional or otherwise, is still divided over the find's real identity. Gilbert writes that "the wall has been interpreted by geologists as being a series of clastic dikes, caused by liquid material being forced up through cracks in the Earth's crust, and becoming hardened into a wall-like formation."[3]

This theory stems from cursory examinations of the site undertaken by W.L. Stephenson (Smithsonian Institution, Washington, D.C.) and Robert T. Hill (University of Texas) performed in 1927 and 1975, respectively. Martin Kelsey (Dallas) and Harold Denton (Beaumont) published a monograph during the early 1980s, when they similarly referred to the Rockwall structure as "a sandstone dike," composed of 55 percent zircon, 17 percent garnet, 13 percent tourmaline, 10 percent titanite, 2 percent saurolite, and 1 percent brookite, with about 2 percent unknown material.[4] The soil surrounding the walls is Taylor chalk, except for some 2 feet of black, waxy substance composing the topmost layer. Hill, Stephenson, Kelsey, and Denton are the only geologists to have actually visited the site, however fleetingly. Their professional colleagues, who have at least heard about Rockwall, dismiss it as an underground extension of the Balcones Escarpment. But even they admit that it is "a freak of nature" without parallel anywhere else in the world. And there are some troubling questions about Rockwall for which geologists still lack answers.

Dr. James Lafayette Glenn, a former agent for Florida's Seminole Indians, author of *A Photographic Essay of the Rock Walls in Rockwall, Texas,* and decades-long researcher at the site, observes that

> the rocks, which are large and flat, are standing on their edges. What breed of wall builders would build a wall like that? If a rock were six inches thick and eighteen inches in circumference, would you lay them on their sides? Also, there appears to be a mortar of yellow sand between each rock, a type of cement. Yet, there is no sand in the area, especially yellow sand. As a matter of fact, the wall is set in solid clay. In 1897, a farmer by the name of Deweese was digging a well near the town, when he discovered a two-foot square window in the wall. This was at a depth of forty-two feet, I believe. It was supposedly a perfect window with a cap-rock or keystone at the top of the window.[5]

Twenty years later, according to Tolbert, "a well was hand-dug on the T.H. Meredith farm, east of Rockwall town. Mr. Meredith said the digging went along what he took for a masonry wall with what appeared to be an arch over a gate or doorway."[6]

Composite image re-creation of Rockwall.

Although no human artifacts have thus far been discovered at the site, the carving of a serpent's head plainly appears on the wall, and townsman Raymond B. Cameron claimed "that four large stones taken from the wall segments had some form of writing in them, and he said the stones appeared to be beveled around the edges," wrote Tolbert.[7] Alfred D. Hartman, Rockwall County librarian, spoke with an Egyptologist recently returned from the Nile Delta, where he had been excavating a Ptolemaic burial chamber. "He told me Rockwall was the same type as used in the king's tomb," said Hartman.[8]

Tolbert described a French archaeologist, Count Byron De Prorok, who studied the subterranean walls in the early 1930s: "De Prorak was in Dallas lecturing on his recent excavations among the ruins of Carthage in North Africa. The count viewed some outcroppings of the Rockwall County phenomenon. He peered into hand-dug water wells, where the walls show best, if you don't mind the chance of falling in. He said the walls looked remarkably like those in North Africa and in the Middle East."[9] De Prorak also examined a series located northeast of the town. "This section is laid in the manner of a stone wall, with shaped edges and a substance resembling mortar holding the stones together," observed Gilbert. "The wall is jointed, with the stones laid as a mason would lay them."[10]

Although born in France, Count Francis Byron Khun De Prorok (1896–1954) was actually Hungarian, educated at the University of Geneva, later inducted into the Royal Geographical Society and Archaeological Institute of Great Britain and Ireland, and, after becoming a U.S. citizen, held the Archaeological Institute of America's prestigious Norton Lectureship in 1922–1923. "Gifted with energy and determination, and speaking several languages," according to *Archaeology* magazine, "De Prorok was no intellectual slouch," although his prodigious accomplishments in the pursuit of a highly adventurous life have been virtually forgotten, in part due to his belief in the former existence of Atlantis, tantamount to the worst scientific heresy.[11]

After excavating the ruins of Carthage at Tunis, North Africa, from 1920 to 1925, he headed numerous, very often hazardous excavations from East Africa to the Amazon jungle, and was the first archaeologist to document his research with motion picture cameras. Says archivist and cinematographer Michael Tarabulski, who has studied De Prorok's career, "I admire Byron's many talents—painting, writing, and having the presence of mind to have film shot.... But the films, if they exist, would give him a legacy. He would have made a contribution to world culture."[12] Tragically, none of the Count's numerous archaeological movies are known to have survived, although his books have been re-published.

Geologists argue that the Texas walls' prodigious length—at least 10 miles and almost certainly longer—negates their man-made provenance. But Dr. Glenn's associate, an oil well employee just returned from Andean South America, said he saw a similar, pre-Inca wall more than 100 miles long in the mountains of Bolivia. A Florida archaeologist who preferred anonymity "concluded the wall was man-made, constructed while this area of Texas was near the gulf. He stated houses were built on top of the wall, projecting over the water," said Dr. Glenn.[13] This would explain how the walls came to be buried under ground, as the waters retreated over time, but leaves us with a disturbing time sequence for the structures, because geologists believe the Gulf drained from the Dallas area about 10,000 years ago.

Though it is difficult to imagine the existence of any civilized people sophisticated enough to have raised stone ramparts in Texas so long ago, a more likely scenario has Lake Lavon (near which Rockwall is located) somewhat larger than its present area retreating within more workable time parameters—say, within the last 2,000 years. Such an interpretation of the evidence compliments both geology (which shows that Lake Lavon shrank to its current limits about 20 centuries ago) and archaeology; independent comparisons made by De Prorok and Hartman's Egyptologist both suggested a general date sometime during the first century AD for Rockwall.

A section of excavated Rockwall demonstrating its man-made character.

Indeed, if it is artifactual, the courses of its masonry might be Roman stonework, or, at any rate, stonework influenced by Roman models—another point in favor of its 2,000-year-old origins. As such, the Texas site could join other, suspected evidence from ancient Italy in pre-Columbian America, including Roman masonry marks allegedly appearing on Maya brickwork at Mexico's Comalcalco; Rio de Janeiro's third-century Roman amphorae authenticated by University of Massachusetts classical history professor Elizabeth Will; Roman-minted coins found in Wisconsin and Kentucky; plus numerous, similar artifacts discovered throughout the Americas.

"Man-made or natural?" asks Gilbert. "Remains of an ancient civilization, or natural formation? What is the rock wall? There has never been an effort to define which formations are natural and which are man-made. Perhaps the mystique of the rock wall lies in the fact that it cannot be said with absolute certainty that it is either."[14]

Texas, however, is not the only state featuring enigmatic, stone walls. Another example, but unquestionably man-made, was found in the Middle West. According to a front-page story in the April 19, 1884, issue of the *Pointe Coupe'e Democrat* (New Roads, La.):

> The greatest wonder in the state of Iowa, and perhaps any other state, is what they call 'Walled Lake,' in Wright County, twelve miles from the Dubuque and Pacific Railway, and about one-hundred-fifty miles west of Dubuque City. The water is from two to three feet higher than the earth's surface. In most places, the wall is ten feet high, fifteen feet wide at the bottom, and five feet wide at the top. Another fact is the size of the stone used in its construction; the whole is of stone, varying in weight from three tons down to 100 pounds.
>
> There is an abundance of stones in Wright County; but surrounding the lake, to the extent of five or ten miles, there are none. No one can form an idea as to the means employed to bring them to the spot, or who constructed it. Around the entire lake is a belt of woodland half a mile in width, composed of oak; with this exception, the country is a rolling prairie. The trees, therefore, must have been placed there at the time of building the wall. In the spring of 1856, there was a great storm, and the ice on the lake broke the wall in several places, and the farmers in that vicinity were obliged to repair the damages to prevent inundation. The lake occupies a ground surface of 1,905 acres, with depth of water of 25 feet. The water is clear and cold, soil sandy and loamy. It is singular that no one has been able to ascertain where the water comes from and where it goes to, yet it always remains clear and fresh.[15]

During summer 1997, on my way to Utah's *Ancient American* conference, I went in quest of Iowa's Walled Lake. There never appeared to have been any such thing in Wright County, but two counties over, in Sac, I did find a "Wall" Lake. Perhaps county boundaries changed since the 19th century. In any case, Wall Lake loosely corresponded to the *Pointe Coupe'e Democrat*'s 113-year-old description, minus, unfortunately, its encircling ramparts. Also, the lake appeared shallow enough to walk across, unlike the 25-foot depths described in the old magazine article.

No one in the area could tell me how or why this body of water, now seldom visited, received its name, let alone anything about some great wall.

Nor could anyone at the Fort Dodge Historical Museum add anything. I visited Wall Lake nonetheless and, finding nothing suggesting former stonework, was about to leave, when a row of uniformly arranged rocks protruding from the water's edge near the eastern boat access caught my attention. Wading down among the thick overgrowth of bull rushes and cattails, I partially uncovered a much longer arrangement of undressed, but fitted stones. They seemed to go on farther than I could uncover them.

Were they part of a foundation, all that remained of a 10-foot-high wall that once held back its waters? If it collapsed since the *Pointe Coupe'e Democrat*'s article was published (or, more likely, dismantled by turn-of-the-century developers), then the lake would have spilled most of its volume, resulting in the present shallowness of Wall Lake. Naturally, more than this cursory examination of the apparently arranged stones would be needed to confirm their identification with a pre-settlement structure. But finding them at this site with its evocative name implied a possible connection that justifies further investigation.

While in western Iowa, I was surprised to learn of another place called Little Wall Lake. Seventy-five miles due east of Wall Lake, in Hamilton County (southern neighbor of Wright County, mentioned by the *Pointe Coupe'e Democrat*), its description was closer to that reported by the old Louisiana magazine, because Little Wall Lake is located the 150 specified miles from Davenport. As before, no one locally knew why or how the lake got its name. In area, it compares with the 1884 description, although its depth is supposedly greater by 15 feet. In any case, Little Wall Lake, being a popular recreational spot, is more easily accessible than its Sac County counterpart and better maintained, its shoreline relatively free from obscuring weeds.

Poking among the tall grass, I soon found level courses of rough stonework, but this time was able to follow them entirely around the perimeter of the lake. The stones went down into the water and stood less than 2 feet above the surface. How old was this construction, I could not guess. But its man-made character was unquestionable. Little Wall Lake is, in fact, completely surrounded by a little wall. Is it all that remains of that engineered rampart on the lonely plains first encountered by early-19th-century pioneers during their trek westward? Who could have built such a structure, and when? Like the rock walls of Texas, Iowa has its own traces of unknown colonizers who passed through our continent so very long ago, leaving hardly more than faded memories behind.

Part III

Ancient American
Hi-Tech

<CHAPTER 31>

Prehistoric Aviators
of the Andes
by Frank Joseph

The following article first appeared in Fate magazine (Volume 48, Number 6, Issue 543, June 1995), republished with permission in revised form by Ancient American (Volume 15, Number 91, June 2011).

Our readers know that the Wright Brothers were the first men to fly a heavier-than-air craft. Another set of brothers—Jacques and Joseph Montgolfier—are credited with having successfully piloted the earliest hot-air balloon in late-18th-century France. Virtually every chronology of aviation is based on these two historic facts. One of them, however, is a fallacy.

Aircraft aficioandos are mostly unaware that the first fully documented, human flight took place 74 years before the Montgolfier brothers lifted off the ground at Annonay. The true honor, instead, goes to Bartolomeu de Gusmao (pronounced "Gooshmouw"). On August 8, 1709, he readied a small skiff made of woven reeds attached by thin, sturdy cords to a huge, triangular envelope made of cotton and paper that, when fully inflated, resembled an irregular pyramid. John V, king of Portugal, watched with his assembled court and a great crowd of spectators, as a small fire filled the envelope with smoke.

Gusmao hopped aboard *La Passarola* ("The Sparrow"), which, to the amazement of spectators on the ground, rose vertically and majestically to about 60 feet in the air, then drifted with a mild wind more than a mile from Lisbon's Castle of St. George to the House of India. Landing gently on the lawn of the colonial office to wild, popular acclaim and royal favor, the pilot was hailed as *El Voador,* "the Flying Man." King John personally granted him a patent for *La Passarola,* the military potential of which was even then apparent, and its debut was recorded by Vatican archives as the first successful flight in human history.

But *El Voador*'s glory was short-lived, as was he himself. Hounded by politically powerful religious fanatics who condemned his invention as a blasphemous device of the devil that enabled sinful man to storm heaven, Gusmao fled to Toledo, Spain, where he died impoverished and forgotten at age 38. Not until the advent of the Wright brothers' first heavier-than-air flight was the Portugese Flying Man's achievement rediscovered, ironically enough, by French researchers, who found a conflicting claim to the world's first aviation honors held by their own national heroes, the Montgolfier brothers. The story of 1709's previously neglected exploit became so popular that the Aeronautical Academy of Bartolomeu de Gusmao flourished in Paris from the turn of the century through the 1920s.

Until the economic "crash" of 1929, its members raised substantial funds for commission of a large monument to *El Voador,* then shipped it to his Brazilian birthplace, where it stands to this day, neglected. An elaborate bronze plaque commemorating the flight shows a large, triangular-shaped balloon flying over old Lisbon. Beneath are inscribed the words "The Empire of the Skies was reserved for the Gods Until It Was Conquered by Man on August 8, 1709."

Academy members underwrote two additional memorials: one in Lisbon to honor the date and place of *The Sparrow*'s inaugural flight, the other in Toledo at the aero-pioneer's grave. They even had a medal struck to celebrate the bicentennial of his unprecedented achievement. The Academy could not survive the worldwide financial depression of the 1930s, however, and turbulent events of the following decade consigned Gusmao once again to oblivion, except for a commemorative stamp issued by the Brazilian government in 1944.

Not until 33 years later was his fame resurrected by an American balloonist, James Woodman, whose work in South American archaeology brings us to a far greater mystery than the disregard still surrounding his 18th-century predecessor's singular accomplishment, with which it is nonetheless strangely linked.

During the early 1970s, Woodman became fascinated with the so-called "Nazca Lines," the largest art gallery on Earth. This collection of outsized designs—some geometric, others portraying a variety of animals—was created by removing dark grey top-cover to reveal faint yellow sand just beneath the Peruvian Desert. Uncertainly bracketed within the parameters of the third-century BC and fifth-century AD, pre-Inca Nazca Civilization is poorly understood by archaeologists. Their only clues are vividly decorated pottery remnants; massive, sophisticated, subterranean aquifers associated with its people; and colossal geoglyphs scattered across the arid plain. These images were not discovered until the early 1930s, and then by accident, when a local pilot happened to fly over the figures, which had gone unnoticed until then. All are superbly executed in perfect proportion—some several miles in length—demonstrating an exceptionally high degree of skill in surveying techniques, social cooperation, and the ability to accurately transfer artwork from normal-sized sketches to a gigantic scale. The Nazca Lines were popularized by Erich von Daniken, the ancient-astronaut theorist, who insisted they had been laid out many thousands of years ago by visitors from another planet, as runways for space ships. Although Woodman dismissed this juvenile fantasy, he nonetheless believed that the terraglyphs could only be appreciated from an aerial perspective. At the other extreme, mainstream scholars assumed that they were sacrificial offerings only, not made to be seen by their creators, but meant for viewing exclusively by the gods, who lived in the sky.

Such conventional speculation, as baseless as it is unconvincing, did not sit well with Woodman, who was unable to shake off the logical, no less officially impossible conclusion that ancient South Americans had somehow achieved manned flight, the only means by which they could observe their gargantuan art tableau spread across the Peruvian Desert. It did not make sense to him that they should have gone to the immense trouble of executing such a huge collection, only to deny themselves any opportunity of ever seeing it, no matter how deep their devotion to the gods. The very notion seemed contrary to fundamental human nature, regardless of cultural and temporal differences separating our times from the prehistoric Nazca.

Woodman began researching possibilities, however unlikely, for pre-Columbian aviation, an investigation that led him to the forgotten story of Bartolomeu de Gusmao, a no-less-mysterious figure, it turned out, than El Voador's own, early 18th-century balloon.

Born 1685 in Brazil of Portugese parents, Gusmao was educated at his native city of Santos by Jesuit fathers. He completed his advanced education with them at their seminary in Belem, where he excelled in languages, mathematics, and physics. It is important to understand that the Jesuits were great explorers of Brazil and the rest of South America. Motivated by missionary zeal, they traveled throughout the continent where no modern Europeans had ever gone before, and got to know many tribal peoples firsthand. The Catholic fathers studied native myths, customs, and behavior, then passed the information on to their students as aids to successful evangelism.

As part of his schooling, Gusmao not only heard cultural news from the friars, but participated in several jungle expeditions himself. Either during one of these missionary forays or from veteran Jesuit accounts, young Bartolomeu learned some very peculiar details about the natives of the rain forest. He was told that several, otherwise-backward tribes in Brazil and Peru were skilled in the manufacture of curious objects. These were 5-foot-tall envelopes of paper that could fly. Filled with smoke rising from small, clay pots of smoldering cane suspended underneath a single opening, the contraptions actually rose into the air of their own accord. When questioned by the astounded friars, the Indians explained that the little hot-air balloons comprised a legacy from their most ancient ancestors and were flown only for religious purposes, bringing small offerings to the sky-gods.

In spring 1709, Gusmao appeared in Lisbon with his own flying model. Because of its successful performance before a royal committee, the Jesuit priest from Brazil was financially encouraged to proceed with the completion of a full-sized version that carried him aloft for the first time a few months later. When Woodman learned of this lost achievement, he was particularly intrigued, as an archaeologist, by *El Voador*'s apparent indebtedness to the Brazillian natives for the triumph of *La Passarola*. Further research disclosed that at least one Indian tribe, today in residence near the Honduran border, still makes ceremonial aerostats like those the Portugese missionaries saw fly 300 years ago.

Investigation of Peruvian myth revealed additional clues. The Incas, Woodman discovered, honored a deity they referred to as Orichan, who could fly to heaven and back in a vessel of golden flames—imagery implying a gondola equipped with its firepot suspended beneath a hot-air balloon. Even more suggestive was the ancient Andean hero Antarqui, the boy-god, who reconnoitered for Incan armies by flying high over battlefields, then returning to the Emperor with intelligence about enemy dispositions. The myth of Antarqui lends credence to the possibility that Andean lads—because of their light weight—were used to fly military observation balloons.

Boys actually did serve as military observers while strapped to large, leather-made kites for Greek armies in the field some 200 years before the advent of Nazca Civilization. The first such aerial reconnaissance had been invented by Archytas of Tarentum, a philosopher, mathematician, astronomer, statesman, and strategist, around 400 BC.[1] The following century, un-manned hot-air balloons were being flown over China.[2] It is possible, then, that similar, contemporaneous advances in aviation were undertaken by pre-Columbian South Americans.

Better known than Antarqui was Kon-Tiki-Viracocha, the Incas' red-bearded, light-complected, fair-eyed founding father, who fled as a flood-survivor from some natural catastrophe. "Sea Foam"—a reference to his white skin and oceanic origins—allegedly shared the high wisdom of his lost homeland with native peoples to create Andean Civilization. Among the cultural gifts he bequeathed was the aerostat, or hot-air balloon. A standard image in Nazca art may be a direct reference to and, in fact, a symbol of this gift. The likeness of a sea-eagle, or frigate bird, appears as the single most reproduced animal throughout Peru's Pacific coastal pottery remnants. The bird is remarkable for its ability to inflate its gullet to a grotesque size in mid-air, resembling a balloon in flight.

Most Nazca drawings depict birds, likewise suggesting flight. Of these, the most cogent to our investigation is a half-human image, the so-called Owl Man. Regarded as one of the oldest bioglyphs, it portrays a standing, 98-foot-long, anthropomorphic figure with the head of an owl incised into the sloping face of a cliff. Like its companions, the ground-drawing may be properly appreciated only from the perspective of altitude at several hundred feet. It gestures with his right hand lifted toward heaven, while its left points to the earth. It is as though the the figure were indicating something integrally important concerning all the Nazca Lines: "If you want to see us properly, you have got to go into the sky!"

"Owl Man" is a misconceived name, however, because it appears to have been originally associated with a sorceress similarly portrayed on Nazca pottery and still revered by mountain Indians. Often shown holding a San Pedro cactus in her left hand, she was and is worshipped as a supernatural guardian of the highland lagoons, where the plant grows. This hallucinogenic cactus, when ingested, makes possible the well-known "flight of the shaman," an out-of-body experience shamans use to soar up to the gods for healing and wisdom. Containing mescaline, the San Pedro plant does indeed produce convincing sensations of flight in anyone who ingests it. Whether the desert drawings imply drug-induced astral projection or balloon flight, an aerial experience related to the geoglyphs seems suggested.

Even non-avian depictions point to connection with the heavens. The dog and fox, both portrayed on the Nazca Plain, were symbolic messengers between divine spirits above in the sky and human worshippers below on the ground. Woodman was especially surprised to find that Quecha, the language spoken by the Incas, actually contains a pre-modern word for "balloon-maker." Moreover, some surviving examples of pottery recovered from the vicinity of the Nazca geoglyphs portray objects resembling balloons flying across the sky, trailing ropes or streamers. Nazca tapestries housed at Lima's National Museum of Anthropology and Archaeology unquestionably depict humans in flight, either through the agency of hallucinogenic pathogens or via balloons.

At the Nazca Lines themselves, broad patches of scorched earth may still be observed at the intersects of drawings or atop nearby, low rises. They are the results of intensely hot fires that burned when Nazca Civilization flourished in the area. Woodman wondered if these fires were originally ignited by pre-Columbian aviators to inflate their balloons with hot air.

Putting his speculations to the test, Woodman and his colleagues— fellow professional balloonists from the United States—built a hot-air balloon designed to resemble Gusmao's Sparrow and the deltoid miniatures still flown by Andean natives. The American scientists restricted their experiment to materials known to have been used by pre-Inca peoples. These included finely woven textiles, straw ropes, and a reed boat of the kind well-known from Bolivia's Lake Titicaca, which served as the most likely gondola. Even the ground-fires for providing hot air were stoked only with desert wood close at hand. Nothing belonging to modern times was included in the undertaking.

At dawn on November 25, 1975, the massive envelope of Woodman's balloon, *Condor-I,* inflated with 80,000 cubic feet of smoke, then ascended at 18 feet per second, bearing Woodman and a companion aloft to almost 400 feet above the Nazca Plain. From that altitude, the awe-inspiring drawings of a vanished, prehistoric race came into perfect perspective and proportion. As Woodman later wrote, "The sun had just cleared the mountains and now flooded the fantastic scene below.... Surely, I thought, the men who created these lines had to have seen them like this, with the shadows of dawn etching their magnificent art. For those two minutes, we were alone with Nazca. We had flown back in time, as much as we had climbed into the sky."[3]

After the 20th-century balloonists bumped down to a soft landing in the desert, one of them remarked, "[U]p there, just now, I had the feeling we weren't the first ever to have flown with the wind above Nazca."[4]

Woodman capably demonstrated that the ancient Peruvians could have manufactured and flown a hot-air balloon. That they actually did so was not proved. But *Condor-I*'s success; the model aerostats flown for unknown centuries by native South Americans (from whom Gusmao seems to have obtained the prototypes for his balloons); Andean traditions of human flight; the remains of ancient bonfires at the geoglyphs themselves; and the fact that the lines there may only be properly appreciated from several hundred feet above them, pursuasively argue on behalf of Peruvian flight during the ancient past. That a people sophisticated enough to create Andean Civilization should have possessed the ability to achieve human flight may lie outside the box of modern archaeology, but appears to have been nonetheless true.

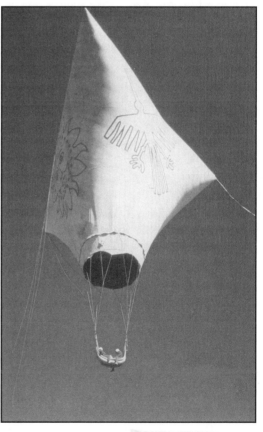

The Nazca hot-air balloons were certrainly the privilege of upper-class passengers, perhaps reserved exclusively for royalty. Flights

Condor-I *rises above Peru's Nazca Desert. Photo by and courtesy of Julian Nott.*

were probably undertaken for religious purposes during important, sky-worshipping ceremonies, in view of the geoglyphs' apparent astro-spiritual significance. Doubtless, such ventures were also regarded as an elite sport. Antarqui's myth likewise appears real enough, and we may believe that boys were indeed used additionally for airborne military reconnaissance by the Nazcans, just as history records they were by their nearly contemporaneous Greeks.

Though official critics continue to sell short the abilities of Prehistoric Man, and ancient astronaut theorists endeavor to deprive him of his early achievements by assigning them to anonymous extraterrestrials, the Wright brothers may not have been the first Americans to have flown after all.

CHAPTER 32

West Virginia's Ancient Highway to Nowhere
by David D. Cain

Although Rome was famous as the great road-builder of the ancient Old World, similar accomplishments in pre-Columbian North America have been forgotten.

Past president of the Marion County Historical Society, David D. Cain received the "West Virginia History Hero" award for his explorations and research into the state's pre-history. He is a prolific writer, whose articles have appeared in numerous periodicals, such as Wonderful West Virginia Magazine and The Times West Virginian daily newspaper, where he wrote a history column for 10 years.

When the first explorers and pioneers arrived in the Upper Monongahela Valley of present-day West Virginia, they found significant physical evidence that a mysterious, pre-Columbian race of people once inhabited the area. Of particular interest was the discovery of an ancient engineering site—a prehistoric road laboriously constructed from knapped stone, crushed mussel shells, and clay tamped into a hard surface.

The ancient road was 12 miles in length, 14 inches thick, and 9 feet wide, extending from the mouth of the Monongahela River, following the East bank to Catawba, Marion County. Also within about a mile radius on both sides of the river in and near present-day Fairmont were discovered extraordinary archeological sites consisting of stone structures, mussel-shell burial mounds, giant human skeletons, and an earthen fort with mound complex. Numerous artifacts ranging from copper bowls and jewelry to finely worked stone weapons and tools were likewise found here.

These prehistoric locations were not the products of human imagination. Evidence for their existence is well documented by credible sources.

Rev. Henry Morgan recalled many eyewitnesses, who told him of seeing sections of "the old Indian Road," and said it was made of small, broken stones and mussel-shell mortar.[1] In some places, it was still fairly solid, but mostly it came apart when uncovered and subjected to rain. The road was largely destroyed when grading was laid for the F.M. & P. Railroad. The upper section of coke ovens at Montana Mines was built on the site of the stone and mussel road.

"I remember the Indian Road well," wrote John J. Prickett. "It left the Monongahela River near Pricketts Fort, crossed the ridge, rejoined the river, and ran to Catawba, where it ended. It was plowed out on the Prickett land, but there has always been a path where it was."[2] A hiking path at present-day Pricketts Fort State Park was designated the "Mussel Shell Trail."

It was historian Adam O. Heck's opinion, after talking to 23 persons who remembered the stone-mussel shell enterprise, that laying of the road had begun just below the mouth of the Tygart Valley River, and ended at Little Creek (Catawba); and that, except for about half a mile on the Prickett land, it followed the east bank of the river, very near the water, from beginning to end, and almost all of it not destroyed by the railroad construction, had gone under water when the first locks were built.[3]

Local newspaper columnist and historian E.E. Meredith reported a train wreck on the day before Christmas 1894, of a locomotive and several coal cars at the Montana coke ovens. According to Meredith, Dr. Kramer, an amateur archeologist from Smithtown, arrived on the scene to help the injured. It was then he made a most interesting discovery. The train, in leaving the tracks, had torn great holes and gashes in the earth; in places the bedding-slag and top soil had been "skinned off" a space about 40 feet wide and 100 feet long. In this trench-like excavation, about 3 feet deep, lay revealed a section of the stone and mussel-shell road. Dr. Kramer, a student of prehistoric lore, instantly knew what stood revealed, and called attention to the "ancient wonder," asking the man in charge to "please make certain the site was not disturbed until pictures could be made of it."[4] Dr. Kramer returned with Fairmont photographer, Israel Foreman, who developed prints of the ancient construction's exposed remnant.

A section of the prehistoric road uncovered by the wreck was examined by Dr. Kramer and other investigators. They found that the mussel-shell mortar had lost its "hold," and it was impossible to remove intact any part much larger than a man's hand. Several local residents took their own photographs of the exposed section, but all copies have long since vanished. The last reported sighting of parts of the road was made in 1959.[5]

CHAPTER 33

The Incas, More Advanced Than Imagined
by Dr. Arlan Andrews

Dr. Arlan Andrews, Sr., is a Registered Professional Engineer with a 40-year career in high-tech fields at White Sands Missile Range, AT&T Bell Labs, Sandia National Laboratories, the White House Science Office, his own technology startup companies, and government service, as an environmental engineering supervisor. A professional member of the Science Fiction Writers of America, he is the author of more than 400 articles, stories, interviews, poems, and plays in published books, magazines, newspapers, and tabloids worldwide.

In support of his original argument, released for the first time by Ancient American magazine, the Sayhuite Stone he postulates as a model for urban water use is located at an Incan site "regarded as a center of religious worship focusing on water," 30 miles east from the city of Abancay, in Abancay province, in Peru's Apurímac region.[1] The bizarre monolith is covered with more than 200 geometric and zoomorphic figures. The latter include carvings of mountains, rivers, animals (particularly monkeys, pumas, and condors), and humans. It is at the center of a 149-acre archaeological zone dotted with the remains of Inca places of worship, houses, and, appropriately enough, irrigation systems.

A crowded party was being held during the 1986 World Science Fiction Convention at the futuristic Hyatt Hotel in downtown Atlanta, Georgia. Over the hubbub of writers and readers and fans, I overhead a young woman conversing about her experiences as an archaeologist in the Peruvian Andes. Drink in hand, I approached her and introduced myself as someone interested in Inca technology.

"Have you ever heard of the large carved stone that the Incas made," I asked, "their model of a topographical landscape, complete with streams and irrigation ditches? It looks like a hydraulic recreation."

The Sayhuite Stone, as it is known, had been featured on a recent television show about Peru, and, as an engineer, I was drawn to its implications. She said she was familiar with the carving and added, "There are several of them like that."

Peru's Sayhuite Stone.

"Have archaeologists ever found traces of mercury in any of those sculptured models," I asked, "in the channels?"

Surprised, she replied, "As a matter of fact, they have. We've always wondered what it meant. Why do you ask?"

"I know why the mercury's there," I told her. About that time, we were separated by others in the milling crowd, and never saw each other again.

Our conversation took place nearly 10 years after I read *Pharaoh's Pump,* a small book by Edward J. Kunkel and entered into a correspondence with the author, who gave me written permission to rewrite his tome into a more readable version.[2] Mr. Kunkel's thesis held that the inner galleries and rooms of Egypt's Great Pyramid on the Giza Plateau are the remnants of a water-pumping system originally used for supplying water to a series of locks that raised the colossal monument's ponderous, stone blocks during its construction.

To test his theory, Kunkel had built a 1/12th scale, plumbing-pipe model of how he thought the King's Chamber, Queen's Chamber, Grand Gallery, and various channels and valves and flaps would have performed more than 45 centuries ago. To his delight, the whole thing worked very efficiently, pumping more water than it wastes, the only version of its kind that does. Based on this early dynastic design, he was awarded a United States patent for a "Hydraulic Ram Pump."

As an engineer, with a long-term interest in ancient technologies and prehistoric civilizations, I was impressed by this "experimental archaeology" approach. Desiring to replicate Kunkel's theories on a tabletop, I envisioned building a Great Pyramid model that could be carried about and disassembled to show its hydraulic details, perhaps with a glass plate down the center plane, allowing the fluid flow and operation of the theorized pump-and-valve system to be observed.

But where water worked well enough at Kunkel's large scale, it would not perform identically on a tabletop model. Although I was able to drastically miniaturize the dimensions of the Great Pyramid and its features, I could not equally miniaturize the physical properties of water; it has non-scalable properties, such as density, viscosity, and surface tension. Within the tiny lines and small chambers of the model I planned, the subtle features of *Pharaoh's Pump* just would not function properly.

This is where the science and engineering of scale modeling come in. We have all seen pictures of model airplanes and model rockets inside wind tunnels, where variations can be modeled and results measured, and then applied to the full-scale item. Hydraulic engineers use similar methods to model the flow around ships, submarines, canals, locks, and other constructions, still using water. The important lesson here is that large, physical reality can be accurately scaled down to a smaller model of manageable size. In engineering terms, the applicable value is called the "Reynolds Number." This is a ratio of certain flow forces. Recalling a college course I'd taken on "dimensional analysis," I was able to calculate the properties of a fluid that would flow inside a 1:300 scale model the way water would in the real pyramid, about 35 times the density of water.

The only available fluid that came anywhere close to that density was liquid mercury. Mercury was not perfect, just 13.6 times the density of water, but it was the closest liquid that would work when scaling the Great Pyramid from 754 feet on a side down to 2.5 feet. If the ancient Egyptians, or whoever else may have built the Great Pyramid, had wanted to make models with liquid mercury simulating water to test their theories and their knowledge, the substance was available to them: "The oldest sample of mercury metal dates to about the fifteenth or sixteenth century BC It was found in an Egyptian tomb at Kurna, stored in a small, glass container."[3]

In my own case, after checking into the price of liquid mercury, and finding out about the health dangers in dealing with such a toxic substance, I put the project aside, although I never forgot about using liquid mercury to simulate water in hydraulic models.

Later, in 1985, when Chinese government officials announced the partial opening of Emperor Qin Shi Huangdi's tomb (he died in 221 BC), photographs were published for the first time of thousands of life-sized, terra-cotta warriors that had accompanied their leader into eternity. But what caught my interest was a statement in press coverage to the effect that historians reported the tomb also featured a large topographical model of China: "...with quicksilver, the various waterways of the empire, the Yangtze...and Yellow Rivers, and even the great ocean itself...created and made to flow and circulate mechanically."[4]

I recalled my pyramid fluid flow modeling attempts, and wondered if the ancient Chinese had reached the same conclusion—namely, that in order to simulate the flow of water accurately in small scale, they had to use liquid mercury. Perhaps it was just the fact that liquid mercury was beautiful and "living" ("quick" = "living" silver), would not readily evaporate, as water would, and made a much more attractive scale model of China. However, for an emperor who had spent his reign building canals and initiated construction on the Great Wall, it would not be surprising if his designers had made use of all the modeling technologies at hand for their plans. (In an interesting aside, Emperor Qin apparently died of mercury poisoning, which may well have been related to his tomb-building project, a connection pointed out in this article for the first time.)

During the intervening years, the remainder of the collapsed tomb site has not been excavated, but I will be waiting to see what the Chinese eventually tell us. If the ancient stories are true, and the tomb space itself remained well-sealed, ancient, liquid mercury could still be there, as well as whatever pumping mechanisms which may have been used. I now work in a government environmental group, and a colleague there used to live in Peru, where he studied archaeology. Recently, he answered my questions about the ability of the Incas to produce liquid mercury by going immediately to the Internet, and retrieving articles about mercury production in ancient and modern times.

He stated that one of the two major sources of mercury in the Western Hemisphere was still in Peru, and that mercury itself can be derived by baking the mineral cinnabar. "In fact," he said, "they used liquid mercury to separate gold from ore, which has been done all over the world since ancient times. They had access to lots of it." Since before the 16th-century Spanish Conquest, Peruvian cinnabar and mercury have come from a town now called Huancavelica.

With this information, I was newly energized about ancient Andean technology. After a few minutes of googling various terms relating to "Inca," "stone sculptures," et cetera, I uncovered photographs of the Saihuite Stone, located in the village of Conchasa, in the Apurimac Department, or province. True to my memory, there it was: the top half of a stone some 13 feet in diameter, elaborately carved with model villages, waterways, canals, and irrigation ditches. I examined its details. If this had been intended merely for passive show, as the fabled Chinese hydraulic relief map may have been, it would be essentially two-dimensional. However, I could see that there were many channels for downhill flow, waterfalls, lakes, catchments, and finally, a depressed rim around the entire perimeter, with outlets where the liquid could be caught and reused.

To an engineer with some knowledge of fluid flow and a specific knowledge of ancient modeling, this was it: a working, productive, hydraulic model that could demonstrate how invaluable water could be directed where it was needed, captured for lakes, slowed for irrigation, impounded for other uses. Additionally, one of the Internet travelogues specifically cited the Sayhuite Stone: "...this wonderful monument contains a hydraulic system that allows [sic] the deposited water in its superior (higher) parts, flows through channels and halls, watering all the stone sides."[5] In other words, the model continues to show off its utility: It still works!

Detailed inspection of available photographs and drawings of the Sayhuite Stone reveals many hydraulic features carved into the model, along with somewhat cartoonish representations of human and animal figures. These figures of living creatures may represent designations for different parts of the Inca Empire, much as we today may represent states or regions by vegetation, animals, or large monuments (for example, cactus, buffalo, the Golden Gate Bridge, and so forth). Some Internet sources speculate that the Sayhuite Stone details represent various sites in the Inca

Empire. This may be true, and truer than they realize, being engineered models of the Empire's advanced irrigation systems. Details include terraces, which may stand for the incredible waterworks of Macchu Picchu; waterfalls built into many Inca structures; and stepped causeways, which may have been intended to control the velocity of flowing water.

The Sayhuite Stone evidences interlocking "fingers" or *camellones* (raised agricultural beds in flood-irrigated lands) that obviously represent the Incas' sophisticated irrigation layouts. It is well established that these ancient waterwork techniques were far superior to those of the invading Spaniards, and, in fact, have been re-adopted lately for greatly increased yields. The next steps in this analysis of ancient technology and technique will require accurate, three-dimensional renderings, preferably CAD (computer aided design) models of the entire surface of the Sayhuite Stone and any similar Inca sculptures. It is likely that even more advanced features will be discovered, and this would be proof enough even for hardened skeptics and professional archaeologists. I would expect, at the least, to find tiny fountains, gate (shut-off) valves, and other means of diverting, separating, and mixing flows.

Given the advanced concepts the Inca engineers employed, I would not be surprised to find expressions of the Bernoulli Principle, which governs the velocity and pressure in waterways. Such evidence could include widened corners for slowing down flows and thinner walls indicating reduced pressure in fast-flowing channels. Roman engineers used this knowledge in their advanced waterworks, some of which still stand today. Because of the Inca Empire's wide variety of topography, with its narrow valleys and high cliffs, I would also advise archaeologists to look for strange constructions on this Sayhuite model or elsewhere in the field, which might indicate that the Incas had their own version of the "hydraulic ram pump" that Kunkel favored as a means of building the Great Pyramid.

Hydraulic ram features would take the form of narrow channels or tubes running down into the bottom of hollow carved stones, and smaller tubes that exit from these stone domes. Such pottery or stones may exist today, their functions ignored and completely unknown. Whether or not a "Pharaoh's Pump" was actually used to build Egypt's Great Pyramid, Kunkel may have been onto something: Ancient engineers all over the world, in all cultures, were intelligent, practical, and experienced in handling water, the one, truly essential resource.

This article represents the first time that hydraulic modeling with liquid mercury has been proposed as an ancient technology, as opposed to a purely ornamental feature. It is also the first time that mercury modeling has been proposed as the cause for residue traces of mercury found on the Sayhuite Stone. To my knowledge, liquid mercury for such hydraulic modeling has not been used since. I am finally convinced, however, that the ancient Incas used their knowledge of liquid mercury in conjunction with hydraulic modeling to create and study the flow of water. They would have done this to design, improve, and optimize their advanced irrigation techniques and their incredible waterworks systems with their characteristic waterfalls, baths, and fountains.

CHAPTER 34

Did Pre-Columbian Americans Master Electricity?
by Larry Brian Radka

Thomas Alva Edison is credited with the discovery of applied electrical power. But other American inventers may have preceded him by many centuries.

Larry Brian Radka is a graduate of the University of the State of New York and retired broadcast engineer. His Astronomical Revelations on 666 was released in 1997, followed nine years later by The Electric Mirror on the Pharos Lighthouse and Other Ancient Lighting.

Although conventional scholars emphatically resist the notion that advanced technologies could not have existed in pre-modern cultures, a growing body of evidence nonetheless suggests that the ancient Egyptians and other ancient peoples employed electricity to light their temples, tombs, and lighthouses during the pre-Christian era. Even years later, but still centuries before discoveries made by Thomas Alva Edison, Jerusalem was bathed in the briliant glow of eight electric searchlights casting their beams from windows in the distant Christian Church of the Ascension on the Mount of Olives.

The late seventh-century Frankish bishop, Arculf (Arculfus) of Prigueux, who visited and explored the Holy Land accompanied by Peter, a Bergundian monk and guide, described the details and effects of those eight, carbon-arc lights. In the words of the *Catholic Encyclopedia*:

St. Bede relates (Hist. Eccles. Angl., V, 15) that Arculf, on his return from a pilgrimage to the Holy Land about 670 or 690, was cast by tempest on the shore of Scotland. He was hospitably received by Adamnan, the abbot of the island monastery of Iona, to whom he gave a detailed narrative of his travels to the Holy Land, with specifications and designs of the sanctuaries so precise that Adamnan, with aid from some extraneous sources, was able to produce a descriptive work in three books dealing with Jerusalem, Bethlehem, the principal towns of Palestine, and Constantinople. Adamnan presented a copy of this work to Aldfrith, King of Northumbria in 698. It aims at giving a faithful account of what Arculf actually saw during his journey. As the latter "joined the zeal of an antiquarian to the devotion of a pilgrim during his nine months' stay in the Holy City, the work contains many curious details that might otherwise have never been chronicled."[1]

The following two excerpts, from *The Pilgrimage of Arculfus in the Holy Land* (circa AD 670), translated in 1895 by Rev. James R. MacPherson, reports: "The translation has been made as literal as possible in passages where the exact rendering was of any controversial or archaeological importance, as in the description of the sites and buildings."[2] Here follow the two excerpts, wherein Arculf continues to describe one of those buildings, a church on the Mount of Olives:

In the western side of the church, we have mentioned above [before], twice four windows have been formed high up with glazed shutters, and in these windows there burn as many lamps placed opposite them, within and close to them. These lamps hang in chains, and are so placed that each lamp may hang neither higher nor lower, but may be seen, as it were, fixed to its own window, opposite and close to which it is specially seen. The brightness of these lamps is so great that, as their light is copiously poured through the glass from the summit of the Mountain of Olivet, not only is the part of the mountain nearest the round basilica to the west illuminated, but also the lofty path which rises by steps up to the city of Jerusalem from the Valley of Josaphat, is clearly illuminated in a wonderful manner, even on dark nights; while the greater part of the city that lies nearest at hand on the opposite side is similarly illuminated by the same brightness.

The effect of this brilliant and admirable coruscation of the eight, great lamps shining by night from the holy mountain and from the site of the Lord's ascension, as Arculf related, is to pour into the hearts of the believing onlookers a greater eagerness of the Divine love, and to strike the mind with a certain fear along with vast inward compunction.[3]

Arculfus went on to add:

> This also we learned from the narrative of the sainted Arculf: That in that round church, besides the usual light, of the eight lamps mentioned above as shining within the church by night, there are usually added on the night of the Lord's Ascension almost innumerable other lamps, which by their terrible and admirable brightness, poured abundantly through the glass of the windows, not only illuminate the Mount of Olivet, but make it seem to be wholly on fire; while the whole city and the places in the neighborhood are also lit up.[4]

The ancient electric searchlights had to cover nearly a mile to light up the far side of Jerusalem. Other examples of such bright lights are portrayed on crypt walls under the temple at Denderah, which still serve as reliable witnesses to the accomplishments of ancient Egyptians in the field of electric lighting.

Battery-powered searchlights and filament lamps in the crypts of the Temple of Hathor at Denderah.

Did the pre-Columbian inhabitants on this side of the Atlantic likewise enjoy its benefits? Described as "the French Isaac Asimov," popular science writer, Robert Charroux (1909–1978) postulated that ancient Americans may have advanced even beyond Egyptian electric battery technology, as described at length in "An Electric Lamp." In his *Forgotten Worlds, Scientific Secrets of the Ancients and Their Warning for Our Time,* he wrote that

> there is abundant evidence showing that in Brazil, and all over South America, including Peru, Inca Civilization was preceded by an unknown culture, equally powerful and probably more advanced.

> During 1601, the Spanish writer and traveler, Barco Centenera, visited the ruins called El Gran Moxo near the sources of the Rio Paraguay, that is, in the vicinity of the *Siete Lagos* ("Seven Lakes"), in the middle of the Matto Grosso, near the modern town of Diamantino, in Brazil. He found a kind of large, non-flaming light in good working order. It was certainly not powered by batteries, but it gave light uninterruptedly and there is reason to believe that the source of the light was chemical and electrical. This is what appears from its description: "A column surmounted by a moon or large sphere, which brightly illuminated the surrounding area."[5]

After describing yet another, similarly spherical lamp comparable to our neon or mercury vapor versions, he wrote of the *Radiant Rock of Ylo*:

> The archaeologist, Harold T. Wilkins, discovered an extraordinary monument that seems to be related to the ancient spherical lamps. At Ylo, on the Pacific coast south of Arequipa, Peru, stands the *Tombo del Ynca* (Tomb of the Inca). It bears an ancient inscription that is said to reveal the location of the entrance to a tunnel leading to the "Ancient Lost World [of] mysteries and gold," whose hidden door lies fouled with gases behind one of the Los Tres Picos (The Three Peaks). Wilkins believed that the tunnel is at the southern end of the Atacama desert, in southern Chile. The indecipherable description in phosphorescent and the top of the rock itself gives off a light like that of the lamp in El Gran Moxo.[6]

Educated at Cambridge University in journalism, Harold T. Wilkins (1891–1960) was a renowned investigator, among whose outstanding reportage was coverage of early television experiments during the 1920s.

His histories of piracy and British public schools were widely read and honored after publication, but his *Mysteries of Ancient South America* (1945) and *Secret Cities of Old South America* (1952) are particularly valuable, because Wilkins spent many years in South America, as a very active and original researcher. As such, his firsthand description of luminous spheres in Peru underscores the American application of electricity during pre-Columbian times.

CHAPTER 35

The Mystery in the Sphere
by Frank Joseph

The creation of Central America's monumental stone balls by a pre-modern people is, in itself, a technological feat of the highest order. But if their suspected function, as posited by the following article, is correct, they could only have been produced by a society in at least some respects scientifically superior to our own.

Beginning in the mid-1930s, soon after United Fruit Company workers began clearing hundreds of acres in the hitherto-unexplored Costa Rican jungle, they stumbled over a strange, dark shape curving out of the ground. Within minutes, their bulldozers excavated a 16-ton ball, 6.5 feet in diameter. Its smooth, black, perfectly round surface was unadorned by inscriptions, illustrations, or marks of any kind. Through the first half of the next decade, an estimated 330 similar stone spheres came to light. Treasure-hunters blasted dozens in half with dynamite caps, hoping that gold might be found inside. Instead, the broken spheres revealed only that they were solid rock through to their core.

They ranged in size from the first specimen discovered down to examples the size of a grapefruit, and mostly made of *gabbro*, a coarse-grained equivalent of basalt. Others were sculpted from sedimentary stone, andesite (quartz-feldspar rich, volcanic rock), about one dozen from shell-rich limestone, and another dozen from sandstone granite. Known locally as *Las Bolas*, they are very nearly perfect in roundness, varying no more than 2 inches in diameter. More often, that variation is far lower, especially among the largest of their kind. Florida's Dr. Tim McGuinness of the Society of American Archaeology, points out: "The maximum circumference error in one six-foot, seven-inch diameter sphere is only 0.5 inch, or 0.2% ..." and he goes on to quote from another researcher, "The best spheres are perhaps the finest examples of precision stone carving in the ancient world."[1]

The balls are so plentiful throughout the Diquis Delta region, covering the southern half of Costa Rica, that most of them have been set up as lawn ornaments at private homes or decorate banks and business establishments. A few are on display at the National Museum, in San José. Others appear in Papagayo on the Nicoya Peninsula, more than 190 miles north of the Diquis Delta. None anywhere show signs of ever having been engraved, incised, painted, or decorated in any way. McGuinness believes at least two "have uncharacteristic carvings," but what he takes for "celestial maps" more resemble natural accretion.[2]

A megalithic sphere displayed at Costa Rica's National Museum, in San José. Photo by David Hoffman.

During the late 20th century, writers Ivar Zapp and George Erikson tried to show that Costa Rica's lithic mystery was disclosed in its identity as a navagational aid for Bronze Age seafarers from the ancient Old World.[3]

Their hypothesis was rendered fundamentally untenable by a globe's self-evident unsuitability as a marker. Moreover, so far as is known, no stone orbs have been discovered near shore, where they might have been otherwise seen by sailors. On the contrary, the vast majority of them were deliberately buried much further inland, in the depths of the jungle, a location and condition that likewise makes their utility as "star charts" unlikely in the extreme.

One or two petrospheres have been found placed on mounted, cobbled platforms, and a few more were configured into triangular sets of three, spaced 88 feet apart, although many, maybe most, were deliberately buried, perhaps to preserve them against the deterioration of rain and alternating temperature extremes that have wreaked havoc on *Las Bolas* since their excavation and exposure to the elements. They were often grouped, but whatever general system or alignment mode that arranged them was lost when most were carried away from their original positions. The largest assembly known contained at least 45 balls.

The Costa Rican versions are the largest of their kind, although others occur at Zaculeu, in the Guatemalan Highlands, where the largest—15.5 inches across—was extracted from an Early Classic Maya strata, AD 200 to 600. Several older Vera Cruz petrospheres—at least one with a diameter of 3 feet—have been recovered from Mexican sites associated with the Olmec, America's earliest-known civilizers, going back to 1500 BC, although some researchers place their beginnings, not without cogent reasons, to around the turn of the fourth millennium BC. Olmec artifacts are displayed in the garden of Mexico City's Museo Nacional de Antropología. A single monumental ball has been reported atop a prominent cliff on a deserted islet off the coast of Haiti, and the Troy Museum, in Cannakale, west-coastal Turkey, features a line of similar, gray-granite spheres, each about 2 feet across. What relationship, if any, these various collections may have to each other is not known, but pre-modern stone spheres do not appear at any other locations.

Mainstream archaeologists assumed the Costa Rica specimens were made by members of the Aguas Buenas and/or Diquis Cultures, because artifacts from either have been found in the orbs' immediate vicinity. This form of inferential relationship dates creation of *Las Bolas* from 200 BC to AD 1500, with emphasis on the eighth to 15th centuries, due to a predominance of Diquis materials, particularly pottery shards, recovered from around the stone balls. However, as McGuinness quotes another investigator, "One very disturbing mystery emerges in examining the Diquis culture: The superb stone-carving skill necessary for the creation of the spheres was not applied to any other object."[4]

Indeed, none of the many hundreds of preserved tools employed by the Aguas Buenas or Diquis were designed to work in stone. They were used exclusively for far more menial tasks, such as scaling fish, stripping bark, or scraping deer hide. These primitive implements never evolved during the 1,700 years of Aguas Buenas-Diquis existence, nor have any pre-Columbian stone-working tools been found throughout the region. An abundance of surviving Aguas Buenas-Diquis artifactual evidence reveals a materially unsophisticated society, relative to contemporaneous Maya Civilization, which flourished alongside in Costa Rica.

Nor did the Aguas Buenas-Diquis build or operate more than primitive watercraft for mostly riverine fishing. Yet, petrospheres have been found at several off-shore islands, such as Isla del Caño and Isla del Coco, which lies 330 miles southwest of the Pacific mainland. Transporting 15-ton, 6-foot-wide globes in wood dug-outs or reed skiffs over hundreds of miles of open ocean does not seem likely. Something more in the way of a real, sea-going, cargo-carrying ship would have been required. Moreover, the granite from which many of the balls were made was not available locally, but had to have been transported from the other side of lofty mountain peaks, some 11 miles away. Everything known about the Aguas Buenas and Diquis suggests they never engaged in the kind of social cooperation necessary to haul what amounted to many thousands of tons of rock over challenging terrain, nor that they ever, in fact, did so.

Smaller stone balls, 10 inches to 2 feet across, have been removed from some native burial mounds, and a pre-Columbian cemetary was laid out around a group of spheres, implying their mortuary significance. But they appear to have been thus revered by the Indians after inheriting them from a former people. Indeed, concluding that the Aguas Buenas or Diquis were the sculptors, based only on observation that these indigenous peoples dwelled in the same area with the spheres is tantamount to assuming that a Model T Ford parked at an Apache reservation must have been built by local Indians.

But if so, who actually made the stone balls, and when, how, and why? Their creators must have been in possession of a higher culture beyond anything known to the Aguas Buenas or Diquis, as logically deduced from the petrospheres at Caño and Coco—objects that could only have been carried to these islands by an ocean-going vessel, something neither Indian group possessed. So, too, their precision of craftsmanship bespeaks a sophisticated civilization, the identity of which cannot be identified with any known culture throughout the ancient world. Consequently, their age likewise cannot be determined.

McGuinness tried to show that Diquis workers could have cut the wooden template of a semi-circle, within which to sculpt a rock boulder to size. But results of his experiment were crudely unimpressive, and nothing exists to indicate that the natives ever employed such a method. Among all the many thousands of illustrated pottery shards from pre-Columbian Middle America, not one of them so much as alludes to a petrosphere or the wood template supposedly used to create it. For a better appreciation of Costa Rica's prehistoric achievement, try asking a modern stone-cutter to sculpt the circumference of a 15-ton, solid granite globe to within a 0.2 percent margin of error. He would probably need something more than a wood template and the kind of tools used by Diquis natives to scale fish. As such, no physical evidence exists—including the stone balls themselves—that can tell us anything about them. As Thomas Mann observed, "Distance in a straight line has no mystery. The mystery is in the sphere."[5]

If the who, when, and how of the great globes utterly escape us, trying to answer the why may broach conclusions conventional scholars refuse to consider. Putting aside all their archaeological references, they do share some common denominators: They all contain veins of quartz and are located in one of the world's most seismically active areas. Far to the south, along the mountain ridge-tops of Peru and Bolivia, a natural phenomenon known as the "Andes' glow" sometimes flits in waves of azure light immediately prior to the onset of major earthquakes. Moving tectonic plates squeeze the mountains' quartz-rich granite to generate a piezo-electric discharge composed of negatively charged ions that radiate blue light, an effect, geologists suspect, that may release and dissipate at least some seismic energy.

Perhaps a similar corelation was made centuries or millennia ago by Andes' glow observors, who endeavored to reproduce it in quartz-banded balls, the spherical shape of which would have evenly diffused tectonic pressure. When thus charged, the stone orbs would have been enhaloed with the Andes' glow effect. If so, then the El Gran Moxo lamp and *Radiant Rock of Ylo* witnessed, respectively, by Barco Centenera and Harold Wilkins (described in Chapter 34) may have been the same kind of luminous petrospheres found in Costa Rica. In any case, counterparts in Brazil and Peru might be explained by a prehistoric harnessing of piezo-electricity. Seeding the stone orbs throughout the soil of Costa Rica might have been aimed at mitigating the worse effects of that country's frequent earthquakes by highly advanced civilizers, long since lost to time.

Until other investigators can offer better evidence to the contrary, *Las Bolas* stand as mute testimony to the monumental greatness of a vanished people.

Part IV

Foreigners in Prehistoric America

CHAPTER 36

Genetics Rewrites American
History Textbooks
by Patrick C. Chouinard

The false paradigms of Establishment archaeology are based on the unswerving conviction that what is official is incontestable. But this intellectual snobbery is being taken down a peg by the revelations of hard sciences, over which Academia's living fossils fortunately exercise no control.

When Johann Friedrich Blumenbach (1752–1840) first used the term *Caucasian* in 1795 to describe the white population of Europe, he could scarcely imagine the epic story about to unfold. He was a German physician, physiologist, and anthropologist, among the first scientists to study mankind as an aspect of natural history, and whose teachings in comparative anatomy were applied to the classification of human races. Blumenbach adopted the term *Caucasian* from native inhabitants of the Caucasus Mountains in southeastern Europe, a race he believed to be the most beautiful and vigorous on Earth. His arguments are no longer fashionable, but there was much more to the story of ancient Caucasians than Blumenbach or anyone else of his time could have imagined.

For centuries, there have been reports of ancient, Caucasoid peoples thriving in remote corners of the world, and then vanishing mysteriously from history. These accounts speak of white, red-haired giants and yellow-haired barbarians in countries now almost exclusively populated by non-Caucasian peoples. In time, modern archaeologists found traces of their existence. Millennia-old corpses found preserved in desert sands or frigid glaciers would ultimately be discovered. In addition to such physical remains, a wealth of historical and mythological evidence, both in written form and oral tradition, spoke of lost civilizations consisting of fair-skinned gods and light-eyed benefactors, who helped establish new cultures. According to numerous Native American accounts, at the dawn of their society, they were visited by a Great White God who arrived from a faraway land located across the sea, established their new mode of life, then departed, promising to return someday.

The discovery of light-skinned mummies in New Guinea and New Zealand, and persistent references to godlike, light-skinned peoples inhabiting a now-sunken landmass in the Pacific Ocean, raised some interesting possibilities of just such a primordial race. But the presence of lost Caucasian peoples in the Americas is but the capstone to a much broader reality. Today, there exists an overwhelming body of evidence suggesting a now-lost population of Caucasians. The last decades of the 20th century saw a revolution in our understanding of the depth and magnitude of prehistoric Caucasian migration and influence.

In 1959, for example, hard, physical evidence of primitive, proto-Caucasoid peoples in the Americas during prehistory began to surface. Archaeologists digging at Santa Rosa Island, off the California coast, unearthed a number of skeletal remains dating back to 10,000 BC, with apparent Caucasian features. During the 16th century, as Spanish explorer Juan Rodriguez Cabrillo skimmed the same coastline, he found that native Chumash Indians possessed physical attributes that set them apart from the rest of the Channel Island Indians. He reported that the women had "fine forms, beautiful eyes, and a modest demeanor," and their children were "white, with light hair, and ruddy cheeks."[1]

Also in the New World, the 1990s saw the discovery of the most controversial archaeological find in North American history: Kennewick Man, a 9,000-year-old Native American with clearly Caucasian, not Mongoloid, traits. Forensic reconstructions of the recovered skull show a face akin to Patrick Stewart, the actor who portrayed Captain Jean-Luc Picard in *Star Trek: The Next Generation.* Additional discoveries throughout the Americas hinted at a primordial, Caucasoid population that roamed freely across much of the Western hemisphere.

Such discoveries by hard-science were not confined to the Americas alone. In the late 1980s, Chinese archaeologists unearthed hundreds of Caucasian Mummies along the Western frontier of China. Similar, ancient corpses, located in Mongolia, Siberia, and Central Asia, were also discovered. These mummies date back to at least 3500 BC, and still others appear to be far older, circa 5000 to 4000 BC. Not only did they belong to Chinese prehistory, they showed no evidence of Asian ethnicity.

Bearded profile of Kukulcan, the Mayas' "Feathered Serpent," in bas relief at the ceremonial ball-court of Chichen Itza, Yucatan, Mexico. Amerindian males cannot grow facial hair.

The corpses had been dressed and interred in Western-style clothing and closely resembled Europeans. Later, C-14 dating established their original age, placing them at 3,500 years before the advent of the Han Dynasty (206 BC to 220 AD). They are related to an Indo-European-speaking group of Caucasians known as the Tocharians. These prehistoric Chinese remains were unknown to much of the outside world until a security break led to their announcement in 1994.

In March 2010, the archaeological community was stunned by the discovery of yet another Caucasian skeleton, this time in Mongolia. DNA extracted from this individual's bones confirmed a direct genetic link to the West. In essence, these remains were clearly European, if not Western Eurasian. This time, however, the ancient corpse was not as old, dating to the first century AD.

The period of prehistoric Western arrival or habitation in China and East Asia is continually being pushed backward in time to an even earlier date. The origins of some Caucasian mummies trace back to some 6,000 years ago; some are even older. But the Mongolian individual was apparently held in high regard by his peers, as a major player in the Xiongnu Empire, a multi-ethnic melting pot of former Eurasian nomads who challenged Han Dynasty supremacy. This ancient conglomeration of foreign tongues and non-Mongoloid races no doubt consisted of many Indo-European speaking peoples.

During 2007, Peruvian investigators found literally dozens of Caucasian mummies in a vaulted tomb buried 82 feet beneath the forest floor of the Amazon jungle. These belonged to a pre-Inca race known as the Chachapoyas, or "Cloud-People." Their discovery complimented 16th-century Spanish reports of "strange, white Indians" with beards in the same region.[2]

Even the giant statues of Easter Island, 2,180 miles off the Chilean coast, bear witness to the arrival and passage of an ancient Caucasoid race. In 1915, British archaeologist Katherine Routledge learned from a native islander the true nature of the Long Ears, "men who came from far away in ships. They saw they had pink cheeks, and they said they were gods. The last real *ariki,* or chief, was said to be quite white. "White like me?" I innocently asked.

"'You!' they said, 'you are red,' the color in European cheeks." Red is "the term generally applied by Easter Islanders to Europeans. And urukeku is often translated 'red-haired'." Indeed, the towering statues obviously displayed something other than Polynesian physiognomy, "and if the fine, oval faces, the large eyes, the short upper lip and the thin, often Apollo's bow lips, are any guide to race, they indicate a Caucasoid race."[3]

Anthropologists are baffled by the apparent presence of Caucasoid peoples in the prehistoric Pacific. Genetic testing conducted during the 1990s showed traces of Basque DNA in the people of Rapa Nui and Greater Polynesia. These age-old, oral traditions are not only being underscored by the latest strides being made in genetic research, but combining to show that the prehistory of America is far richer in its human background than previously suspected.

CHAPTER 37

Anasazi Chocolate
by David Allen Deal

Chaco Canyon's fabulous achievements in colossal architecture, urban planning, and astronomy are world famous. Lost in the shadows of its monumentality, however, residue of a humble pleasure incidentally points to thousand-year-old connections far beyond the American Southwest.

The earliest known use of chocolate in North America above the Rio Grande River has been found amid the ruins of Chaco Canyon, New Mexico. Dated between 1000 and 1125 AD, residue of theobromine, a chocolate trace-element, was removed from ceramic pieces of broken cylinder jars used by the Anasazi at their foremost ceremonial structure. Known as Pueblo Bonito, the "Beautiful Town" is a colossal, five-story, D-shaped building housing some 500 rooms and chambers, mostly for arcane ritual purposes.

The Anasazi (Navajo for "Ancient Enemy") were a red-haired race of civilizers who built an immense network of roads and astronomically oriented monuments in the Four Corners Region of the American Southwest, beginning around the turn of the 11th century, until they were overthrown by native tribal peoples less than 200 years later, finishing up as the renowned Cliff Dwellers, circa 1350 AD.

The discovery of chocolate at Pueblo Bonito proves that the Anasazi engaged in long-distance trade with Central America, because the nearest cacao plantation was more than 1,000 miles away. A recent investigation found that the Anasazi themselves were not natives of the American Southwest, but originally a people remembered as the Huari, from Pacific coastal Peru, where they built a prosperous, pre-Inca civilization.[1] The Huari were forced by their enemies to emigrate aound 1000 AD, coincidental with the sudden rise of the Anasazi in New Mexico. The Huari and Anasazi shared enough diagnostic culture traits to reveal their common identity.

Chocolate was a luxury drink enjoyed exclusively by the upper classes, used in rituals, and invented by the Olmecs, America's first civilizers, on the Atlantic coast of Mexico, 3,000 years ago. It was sometimes mixed with hot peppers or, possibly honey. Cacao beans were so valuable they were used by the Maya as legitimate currency.

Archaeologist Patricia L. Crown from the University of New Mexico discovered theobromine on the Anasazi ceramic fragments. Her research was published in the January 27, 2008 issue of *Proceedings of the National Academy of Sciences*.[2]

CHAPTER 38

Genocide in Ancient Kentucky
by William Conner

Most modern Midwesterners do not realize that their peaceful farming country was long ago soaked with the blood of the very people who introduced agriculture into North America. Author William Conner is an autodidactic expert in this little-known holocaust. After serving with the United States Air Force and graduating from Ohio University in the 1950s, he became a newspaper reporter and science columnist for The Springfield Daily News (Ohio), was a public relations staff member of New Jersey's Bell Laboratories, and was editor of The Satellite News, Washington, D.C.'s telecommunications' periodical. Today, his articles—mostly about Ohio archaeology, including pioneering research into prehistoric iron-working—are published by the Midwest Epigraphic Society's quarterly Journal.

In May 1773, a representative of Lord Dunmore, the governor of Colonial Virginia, visited the Native American town of Chillicothe on the Little Miami River in what would later become the southwest corner of the state of Ohio. Thomas Bullit was seeking permission from the Shawnee for his fellow Virginians to settle throughout Kentucky. In his re-creation of this meeting, Allan W. Eckert, known to closely base his novels on actual oral and written history, relates how Chief Black Fish told Bullit that the land was not the Indians' to give away, because it did not belong to them:

> The Shawnees cannot tell you that you are allowed to settle in the Can-tuc-kee lands. We have never owned that land. It belongs to the murdered ghosts of the murdered Azgens—a white people from the eastern sea. Their bones and their ghosts own and occupy

every hill and valley of the country. Long ago, our fathers and our grandfathers killed off the Azgens, but we now fear the spirits of these people more than our fathers and grandfathers feared them when they were flesh.[1]

Chief Black Fish's expression "their fathers and grandfathers" implies a long period. How long? Was it several hundred years, 500, or 1,000? Celtic sea-farers could have arrived in North America around 500 AD, and/or the Norse appeared circa 1000 AD. But definitive association of either people with the Azgens is lacking.

The surviving evidence of some three-score pit iron furnaces nevertheless attests to the presense here of pre-modern Western Europeans. Iron-making is an economic activity based on a demand for goods or services by consumers, existence of the means of production, and the creation of a workforce to respond to that demand. Before white settlers arrived around 1800, the economic conditions for iron manufacture simply did not exist in the Middle West.

Yet, the story of the Azgens may reveal a forgotten people that furnished the economic conditions suitable for the production of iron from the extensive bog ore deposits in the rolling terrain of glaciated south-central Ohio. These natural conditions end abruptly just north of Chillicothe, where the Scioto River Valley begins winding through the hills of the southern part of the state. The prehistoric Azgens would not find ore deposits in northern Kentucky, and especially not among the rugged hills across the Ohio River, south of the mouth of the Scioto.

Iron tools and weapons produced by Azgen work parties in south-central Ohio could have reached their homeland in Kentucky by boat, via the Scioto and Ohio rivers. With iron and steel-edged weaponry, the minority Azgens defended themselves until superior technology succumbed to overwhelming numbers of native enemies in the final attack by Black Fish's "fathers and grandfathers."

CHAPTER 39

A Giant's Hand in Michigan
by Jay Stuart Wakefield *and*
A Worldwide Race of Prehistoric Giants
by Patrick C. Chouinard

A Giant's Hand in Michigan
by Jay Stuart Wakefield

Early-19th-century treasure-hunters often dug into so-called "Indian mounds" of the American Middle West, hoping to find gold or precious jewels. Instead, they sometimes broke into ancient burials containing the skeletons of giants.

For nearly 200 years, scientists explained that these oversized human remains only appeared as such, because bones proportionately disarticulate in the soil over time. Beginning in the 1960s, however, improved excavation techniques and forensic procedures determined that the mounds' skeletal evidence did, in fact, belong to individuals of extraordinary stature. Even mainstream archaeologists came to admit that first millennia BC Americans academically referred to as the "Adena" were at least occasionally given to physical height far above the modern average. Men stood about 7 feet tall; their women, around 6 feet, 8 inches. The tallest, professionally measured Adena male reached 7 feet, 2 inches, although unoffical sources report other specimens as high as 8 feet.

None of this came as a surprise to Native American record-keepers, who have long told of the Ron-nong-weto-wanca, or "Fair-Skinned Giant Sorcerers," that once strode across the American plains.

Jay Stuart Wakefield is a Washington State zoologist, who owns a world-class collection of antiquities from around the world. His original research into European megalithic connections with the Americas have been presented at national conferences of the Ancient American Artifact Preservation Society and Midwest Epigrapic Society. He is the co-author of When the SunGod Reached America and the encyclopedic Rocks and Rows, Sailing Routes Across the Atlantic and the Copper Trade, the most comprehensive study of its kind published so far.

The cover of *Ancient American*'s December 2009 issue (Volume 13, Number 85) features an image on a Michigan rock outcropping I found on September 29, 2008. The petroglyph is located 6 feet above what might have been a beach in Copper Harbor, when Lake Superior was higher, probably when ancient miners were working the area for copper, between 2400 BC and 1200 BC. I took the photo myself, with my own hand in it. I am 6 feet tall, and my hand is 7 1/2 inches long. My middle finger

Jay Wakefield's hand compares with the Upper Michigan petroglyph.

is 3 1/2 inches long, so I calculate the glyph has fingers extending nearly 2 inches beyond mine.

The depth of the carving and its details need study, but it may be evidence for individuals of extraordinary stature among the crews of sea-faring miners who excavated half a billion pounds of copper ore from the Upper Peninsula during prehistory.

In *Rocks and Rows,* to illustrate connections between their monuments inscribed with navigation directions to America and Europe's so-called "Bell Beaker" pottery people, I wrote, "For a long time it was confidently believed that there was a physically separate group of people who made and used Bell Beaker pottery (2400 BC to 1500 BC) and the [metal] artifacts found with it. Early work suggested that the men in particular were more robust than usual, their skulls larger and rounder."[1] The 1980 text goes on to predict that computer developments should enable better data recovery and analysis of this issue.

Innumerable "giant" skeletons have been found in mounds throughout the Midwest, as documented in many original sources, and summarized in others. Kimball tells a Tuscorora legend the annihilation of giants around 1000 BC. More than seven pages of Childress's book are devoted to description of the 57, red-haired giant (seven-foot) mummies found in Nevada's Lovelock cave in Nevada by University of California archaeologist, Llewellyn Loud, during 1924.[2] Giants and their skeletons have been found all over North and South America. How may the very real existence of these giants be understood?

An explanation may lie in the nutrition and diet of megalithic people living along the coasts of Europe from circa 6500 BC to 1200 BC. Until then, the oceans had never been fished on a large scale, nor yet loaded with chemicals and plastic debris. Salmon ran in the rivers of Europe. Farming was expanding, but the people were probably not yet mineral-depleted. Two thousand years later, Vikings moved to Greenland, with its enormous marine resources.

According to Dr. Graeme Davis, a specialist in the medieval world and its language, literature, and culture, "Viking Greenland was a prosperous nation for five centuries.... Greenland to the Vikings was as California to the pioneers.... Skeletal remains of early Viking settlers in Greenland show them growing around two inches taller than their ethnically identical contemporaries in Norway, while there is much evidence of robust health and longevity."[3]

A Worldwide Race of Prehistoric Giants
by Patrick C. Chouinard

In 400 BC, the Greek poet Homer wrote, "On the earth there once were giants."[4] In Old Irish mythology, we learn of the *Formorach*, a giant "Sea People." Their leader, Balor, was said to have guided them to the shores of Ireland following the Great Flood. They then became the native inhabitants of the Island. While some scholars positioned the Formorach point of origin in Spain or North Africa, still others claimed the original homeland of these pre-Celtic giants was Atlantis, some 200 miles west of Gibraltar.

More tales of giants were told by the Norse and other Germanic peoples of northwestern Europe. According to the *Eddas*, the ancient Norse scriptures, there once were two races of giants: the children of Thrud, descended from the frost giant, Ymir, and the children of Bor, who included the Aesir, the gods of Valhalla. Though tremendous in size, the Aesir were distinctly Nordic in appearance. For reasons unknown, they battled with giants in endless combat.

Finally, Odin, Vili, and Ve, the first Aesir, ambushed Ymir and killed him. When they slit his throat, a great deluge rushed forth to drown most of the giants. Some escaped in a boat to a new realm later known as Jotunheim, home of the giants. The world as we know it, Midgaard, was formed from the body of Ymir. His salty, watery blood became the oceans, rivers, and lakes; his flesh formed the Earth; his bones, the rocks and mountains; his hair, the forests. Maggots from inside his stomach evolved into dwarves.

According to Genesis (6:4), "There were giants in those days; and also after that, when the sons of God came into the daughters of men, and they bore children to them: the same mighty men, who were of old, men of renown." In the fifth book of the Pentateuch, the biblical narrative speaks of a giant sarcophagus: "For only Og, king of Bashan, remained of the remnant of giants; behold, his bedstead was a bedstead of iron.... Nine cubits was the length of it, and four cubits the breadth of it, after the cubit of a man. (Deuteronomy 3:11)." The Hebrew *amah* or *amot* (commonly translated as "cubit") is generally, if not universally, accepted at 17 inches. As such, Og's iron bed would have been 12.9 feet long and 5.8 feet wide.

The Old Testament also describes one of the most famous giant encounters ever: "And there went out a champion from the camp of the Philistines, named Goliath, whose height (8.6 feet) was six cubits and a span (nine inches)...and he was armed with a coat of mail; and the weight of the coat was five thousand shekels (more than 150 pounds) of brass...and the staff of his spear was like a weaver's beam; and his spear's head weighed six hundred shekels (about twenty pounds) of iron." (Samuel 1-4:7)

Greek myth was also populated by giants. In their most common form, they were known as the *Gigantes.* Eons ago, they attempted to overthrow Zeus and the other gods of Mt. Olympus, but ultimately failed. They were grotesque creatures, huge humanoids, with snake-like legs. A Greek saga, the *Agronautica,* described the giants in the following manner: "Their bodies have three pairs of nerved hands, like paws. The first pair hangs from their gnarled shoulders, the second and third pairs nestle up against their misbegotten hips...."[5]

The seventh-century BC mythographer Hesiod stated that the Titan Kronos, wielding a sickle, severed the genitals of his father, Uranus, allowing drops of fresh blood to trickle down to Earth Mother Gaia, who became impregnated, and thereafter gave birth to the Erinyes (Furies), the "great giants, shining in their armor and holding long spears in their hands."[6] Hesiod describes them as "great," but they are often not huge at all, instead in possession of unusual strength and hubristic aggression.

The *Gigantomachy* is the giant's primary myth, and relates a war with their main opponents, the Olympian gods. This was perhaps the most widely depicted struggle in Greek art and literary tradition. The Giants bombarded the gods with boulders and the flaming trunks of burning trees. An oracle foretold how the gods themselves would be unable to finish off the Giants, but, if aided by a powerful mortal, the task could be completed. That hero was Heracles.

It is important to understand that the Gigantes were not the only large beings in Greek mythology. The gods themselves were giants. Unlike the Gigantes, they were blond-haired, fair-skinned, and highly Nordic in appearance. Their description is consistent with worldwide traditions of ancient Caucasians, some depicted as giants, others of normal stature, that long ago prevailed in areas long deemed to have been the sole domain of non-European peoples.

Non-Western giants appear throughout Indo-European mythology. The Sanskrit *Daitya* were water-giants cited in the *Vishnu Purana* and the *Mahabharata,* the most ancient and highly revered of Hindu sacred texts. The *Daitya* were equivalent to the Titans in Greek mythology, including Atlas and the other kings of Atlantis.

Some of the earliest surviving written and oral accounts tell of fierce, light-skinned peoples who were once the central force of a lost civilization. Science writer Terrence Aym described a series of events in two unpublished articles dealing with the presence of giants in ancient America.[7] He also wrote of several encounters between European explorers and various, giant-sized, Caucasian aborigines in Central and South America. The Paiute tribe of present-day Nevada tell of an ancient war they waged against a primordial race of white, red-haired giants. The Indians called these imposing Caucasians the *Si-Te-Cah,* a name referencing *tule,* a fibrous plant that the giants used to construct assault rafts. According to tribal lore, this race was already living in North America when the ancestors of the Paiute arrived 15,000 years ago.

Although today's scientific dogmatism dismisses such traditions as sheer fantasy, Aym states such perennial accounts cannot be so easily discarded. The physical remains of giant-sized Caucasian peoples have been found on almost every continent. Across North America, dozens of sites yielding over-sized human bones were excavated, including those in Virginia, New York State, Michigan, Illinois, Tennessee, and Arizona. Hard, scientific evidence supporting the Paiute folk-memory of a war with giant, red-haired Caucasians first came to light in 1924 at Nevada's Lovelock Cave. Some 10,000 years ago, a massive fresh-water body, called Lake Lahontan, covered the region. It was beneath this vast body of water that the original cavern was positioned, and remained submerged until the lake eventually dried-up.

According to Paiute accounts, the giants practiced cannibalism, as did early Neanderthals, whose campsite remains include human bones marred with butcher-marks. In the Paiute version, the giants stood 12 feet tall, perhaps exaggeration of a naturally tall, Caucasoid race. In any case, the Indians' ancestors pursued the giants into a cave, where the giants took sanctuary and continued to resist their enemies. The cave entrance was stuffed with dry bush, then ignited to smoke out the giants. Those who emerged were immediately overwhelmed and slaughtered, while any remaining inside died of smoke asphyxiation. Tribal legend became archeological fact in 1911, when outsized human remains were found in Lovelock Cave. These included two mummies; one, a 6.5-foot-tall female, the other, male, supposedly more than 8 feet tall. Both were red-haired. Scattered haphazardly around them was a profusion of arrowheads, testimony to the massacre mentioned by the Paiutes.

A 16th-century mestizo chronicler, Fernando de Alva Ixtlilxochitl, wrote:

> In this land called New Spain, there were giants, as demonstrated by their bones that have been discovered in many areas. The ancient Toltec record keepers referred to the giants as *Quinametzin*; and as they had a record of the history of the *Quinametzin*, they learned that they had many wars and dissensions among themselves in

this land that is now called New Spain. They were destroyed, and their civilization came to an end, as a result of great calamities and as a punishment from the heavens for grave sins that they had committed.[8]

Western European explorers, such as Magellan, Sir Francis Drake, Desoto, and Commodore Byron, the famous poet, Lord Byron's grandfather, all submitted reports of having personally encountered living giants in North America. A well-documented sighting by Magellan occurred in 1520 near the harbor of San Julian, Mexico, where he and his crew confronted a red-haired giant allegedly standing nearly 10 feet tall and with a "voice like a bull."[9] Later, Magellan learned from natives that the giant belonged to a neighboring tribe. Remarkably, Magellan's logs claim that he and his mates captured two of these living giants and brought them aboard ship for transportation to Europe. Neither survived the voyage, however, and both were buried at sea.

Numerous earthworks associated with red-haired giants dotted the Middle West from as far south as Tennessee and north into Wisconsin. Most were obliterated by early-19th-century farmers. According to author Frank Joseph in *Advanced Civilizations of Prehistoric America,* "The Mound Builders stood out like aliens in the midst of tribal America's far more multitudinous native population."[10]

It seems clear, then, that an actual race of red-haired giants dominated our continent during prehistory, perhaps thousands of years before the ancestors of today's Native American arrived over the Bering Straits.

CHAPTER 40

Native Americans From
Europe and the Near East
by Wayne May

Curious cultural comparisons between Native American tribal peoples and Western Europeans have been noticed and commented upon since pre-Colonial times. But only with the advent of modern advances in genetic testing and DNA research have those suspicious parallels been provided the kind of scientific support necessary to confirm their validity.

Whether a primeval migration came from the west or the east has yet to be determined concerning the DNA "X" markers found primarily in the native populations of North America. Recently, however, anthropologists and archaeologists have been considering the possibility of an east or Atlantic migration from some remote age. Algonquian native tradition speaks of just such a mass movement from "the direction of the rising sun," not from the west. Critics of an eastward migration are quick to dismiss a crossing either by boat or ice sheet. Ripan S. Malhi and David G. Smith from the University of Michigan, Ann Arbor, and University of Davis, California, argue DNA evidence to support the factual foundation of Algonquian oral history for a migration of eastern people:

> The wide geographic and linguistic distribution of haplogroup X in modern Native North American groups, and the predominance among those of a characteristic mutation in HVSI of the control region not found in European or Asian members of haplogroup X, imply that it is a founding Native American lineage. In addition, the presence of three (allegedly full-blood) Algonquian-speaking

Native Americans who exhibit both the haplogroup X with the transition...of the rare Albumin marker, Albumin Naskapi, also only found in North America due to recent European admixture. The most convincing evidence that haplogroup X is not the result of Viking or even more recent European admixture would be its presence in ancient Native Americans.[1]

"The new data from a genetic marker appropriately called Lineage X suggest a definite, if ancient, link between Eurasians and Native Americans," says Theodore Schurr, a molecular anthropologist from Emory University in Atlanta, who presented his findings in March 2007 at the annual meeting of the American Association of Physical Anthropologists in Salt Lake City (Utah). Schurr continues, "Researchers had already identified four, common, genetic variants, called haplogroups A,B,C, and D, in the mitochondrial DNA of living Native Americans.... Haplogroup X was different: It was spotted by Torroni in a small number of European populations.... We fully expected to find it in Asia, or Northeast Asia.... To their surprise, however, haplogroup X was only confirmed in the genes of a smattering of living people in Europe and Asia Minor, including Italians, Finns, and certain Israelis. The only time you pick it up is when you move west into Eurasia."[2]

Masterfully created reed boats still made by native Andeans at Lake Titicaca, Bolivia, are identical to counterparts constructed by Pharaonic Egyptians. The faithful re-creation of a reed boat built by Thor Heyerdahl in 1970 successfully sailed from North Africa to America, proving that ancient seafarers did indeed possess the capability to successfully complete trans-Atlantic voyages.

Clearly, the roots of Native America are not found exclusively in Siberia. The presense of population groups from Europe and the Near East at the dawn of our continent's human occupation are beyond question.

CHAPTER 41

Odysseus Sailed to America
by Victor Kachur

Although the Odyssey, along with Homer's Iliad, was retold throughout all the centuries of Classical Greece, neither epic belonged to that period. Instead, both were rooted in the Late Bronze Age that ended abruptly around 1200 BC, followed by a 400-year Dark Age, until the Athenian awakening of the ninth century BC. Accordingly, the author looks for pre-Classical motives that prompted Odysseus to undertake his long sea voyage, and, in the process, finds them in ancient America.

Copper mining in the Keweenaw Peninsula of Lake Superior has been dated by radiocarbon to nominally 5,000 years ago.[1] Naturally formed ingots of this red metal were available in those days by surface mining, and were loaded aboard vessels for transport eastward. The rich copper ore was of secondary importance, as long as the large, metal nuggets were available. Smelting of the copper ore with charcoal was not a complicated technology, and the required temperature was somewhat less than that needed for the smelting of iron ore into pig iron.

The molten copper was cast into ingots of standardized size and weight. The weight was nominally a talent—around 60 to 90 pounds, and the shape was in the form of a fat X that permitted four positions for hand-holds when moving the cast ingot manually. Given its reddish color matching a sunset, and the nominally ox-hide shape, copper became poetically referred to as the "cattle of the sun." The ingots could be re-smelted for alloying and casting into utilitarian shapes, but the bulk weight of the metal remained seemingly indestructible.

From the Early Bronze Age on, a single ship could return from its voyage carrying home a treasure's worth of trade goods, and sailing maps were equivalent to covert information belonging to the local city-state. These prehistoric copper-mining and sea-faring connections between Michigan's Upper Peninsula and the ancient Old World through daring sea-farers seem suggested by subtle references found in one of the greatest epics of Western literature.

The *Odyssey,* by the venerable, blind poet, is filled with religious symbolism, not geographical knowledge. Even so, Homer's energetic hero starts out with a small fleet, leading it into new waters against terrible hazards, only to be mostly destroyed by unfriendly natives. One vessel survives, the flagship under his personal command, which sails on, because there was no treasure to bring home.

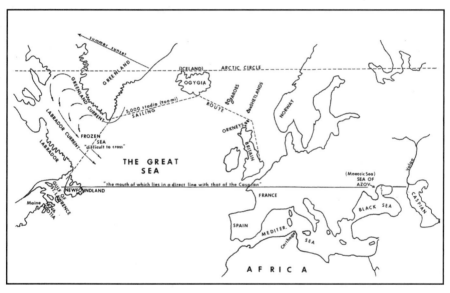

Homer's Odyssey *is a template for North Atlantic geography.*

The storyline is convoluted, but Odysseus plays the geographical cards close to his chest. His far-flung journey passes between the six-headed Scylia monster and the sun-god's cattle. Homer tells us that there were seven herds of cattle with 50 heads each, and seven flocks of sheep with a similar 50 heads each, a remarkably detailed example of record-keeping for a piece of fiction. Odysseus was forewarned to leave the sun-god's cattle alone and get off of the island as soon as possible for a safe journey.

The flagship would typically load up with fresh food and water, then continue its journey. Along came a storm, and Odysseus and crew were stranded on a mysterious island. Rough weather lasted for a month, suggesting that the sailing season was over. Food provision on the flagship ran low, and when Odysseus was away, hunting up a meal, his men started butchering the sun-god's cattle for supper. Odysseus was unhappy with the way the situation had gotten out of control, but the damage had been done. At a break in the storms, they shoved away from the island, but soon their ship was destroyed by a bolt of lightning sent by an angry sun-god.

The Classical Greeks referred to particularly prosperous islands as *Thrinacia,* implying a triangular shape. They were usually associated with profitable commercial routes, and the details of their location were not public knowledge during ancient times, but valuable trade secrets. Several triangular-shaped islands include Sicily and Britain, but they possess no copper to be mined and exported. On the other hand, Newfoundland Island off eastern Canada has a roughly triangular shape, distorted by bays and secondary peninsulas. It is nevertheless a large island situated on the ancient copper route. The St. Lawrence River passes eastward into the Gulf of the St. Lawrence, with a further connection to the Gulf Stream flowing eastward from nearby Nova Scotia to the distant lands of Western Europe.

In terms of regional geography, Newfoundland Island is large enough to be between 47 and 52 degrees North latitude, so nominally at 50 degrees north latitude. A single degree of latitude corresponds to about 60 miles of distance, or roughly the maximum distance seen on a clear day by a keen-eyed lookout atop a ship's mast. Coincidentally, cattle herd numbers given in the *Odyssey* tell us that the sun-god's island is nominally at 50 degrees north latitude, and large enough to be spread out over nearly 7 degrees of latitude, when sailing approaches are considered.

Another factor in the location is Homer's longitude, which corresponds to the seven flocks of sheep at 50 heads each. The longitude degree as an east/west distance is smaller than the latitude degree of about 60 miles, and becomes smaller, as one moves further north from the equator. The east/west spread of Newfoundland Island is nominally 52 to 59 degrees West longitude, accounting for the seven flocks. Modern longitude is measured from the Greenwich Observatory near London in England, but during ancient times its reference was the city of Alexandria, in far-off Egypt, some 30 degrees further east.

The Pillars of Hercules (or Straits of Gibraltar) are nominally 5 degrees westward of London, and so Newfoundland is about 50 degrees westward of the Pillars as a natural reference site for sailing into the Atlantic Ocean. Accordingly, Odysseus was a mythical personification of Classical and even Pre-Classical Greek seafarers, who regularly sailed across the Atlantic Ocean to North America for the high-grade copper that made them rich, because Homer's epic is rooted in the Late Bronze Age.

CHAPTER 42

Earliest Americans and Mayas, Older Than Imagined
by Fred Rydholm

C. Fred Rydholm was widely known and respected as "Mr. Copper," a professional educator and foremost authority on the immense mining operations that occurred in the Upper Great Lakes Region of the American Middle West from roughly 3100 BC to 1200 BC. His Michigan Copper, released three years before his death in 2009 at 75 years of age, is the greatest published resource concerning those ancient excavations. He argued that they did not comprise some freak archaeological anomaly, but were part of a panorama of American antiquity diametrically opposed to standard versions of the deep past repeated and taught today. The roots of our prehistoric re-orientation, Rydholm emphasized, are sunk not only in the Upper Peninsula of Michigan, but in the Brazilian jungles and entwine the Maya ruins of Mexico.

    Official insistence that men first crossed some hypothetical land-bridge at Alaska's Bering Straits into North America 12,000 years ago has been dealt yet another serious blow by recent discoveries. Petroglyphs depicting animals, humans, and even what appears to be buildings at the Pedra Furada rock shelter, in Brazil's Sierra da Capivara National Park, yielded charcoal from a camp-fire dated 56,000 years old.

    Dr. Guaciara dos Santos and his colleagues at Australia's National University used an acid-base, wet oxidation technique that chemically scours a fine layer from its charcoal surface, which allows investigators to go beyond the 40,000-year barrier limited to standard Carbon-14 testing.

Five of the seven charcoal samples removed by Dos Santos and Dr. Michael Bird from the Pedra Furada site yielded dates in excess of 56,000 years. Two additional samples yielded dates to 53,000 and 55,000 years ago.

"These dates are good and reliable," said Dr. Bird, who developed the new technique. "And there's no reason to doubt them."[1] The Brazilian find was not the first correctly dated by his ABOX methodology. It was used successfully two years earlier at archaeological locations in South Africa and Western Australia, where an Aboriginal site, known as the Devil's Lair, was credibly back-dated to 50,000 years Before Present.

Sierra da Capivara National Park, and particularly its Pedra Furada area, is rich in sandstone rock shelters, many of them filled with tools, weapons, human remains, evidence of hearth fires, and cave art tens of thousands of years old. They demonstrate that Man was already settled in South America more than 40,000 years before mainstream scholars claim the so-called "Clovis people" first arrived from Siberia.

Complementary finds there likewise undermine a 12,000-year date for the first Americans. In January 2009, a human settlement at Eastern Siberia's Yanu River was carbon-dated to twice the age of the oldest previously known site in the region. Excavated by archaeologists from Russia's Institute for the History of Material Culture, in Saint Petersburg, director Vladimir Pitulko reported that their analysis of man-made hearth fires showed that lands north of the Arctic Circle were occupied about 30,000 years ago. "There was nothing to prevent these early pioneers from migrating into North America at this time," he said.[2] Pitulko and his colleagues made their discoveries while following up on the work of geologist Mikhail Dashtzeren, who found a 30,000-year-old rhino-horn fore-shaft to a spear near the Yanu River in 1993. A "fore-shaft" is the detachable piece between the main part of a spear and its point. This rhino-horn fore-shaft, together with a pair of smaller versions made from mammoth ivory, are virtually identical to weapons used by the Clovis people, who spread across North America, supposedly just 12,000 years ago.

Pitulko led his team to the same area, where they uncovered 383 stone artifacts, such as flaked stone tools, including mammoth, reindeer, bison, and woolly rhinoceros bones. The occurrence of these skeletal remains demonstrates that Eastern Siberia enjoyed a temperate lapse during the last Ice Age, when open meadows attracted these large animals, which were themselves pursued by early hunters. Apparently, the preferred meat was reindeer, judging from a majority of bones collected at the site.

Though the Yanu River finds show the Clovis people began entering North America long before conventional archaeologists believed, they were but one of several waves of immigration that arrived on our continent, some long before, as indicated by the 56,000-year-old Pedra Furada rock art, as far south as Brazil. If their creators took the Bering Strait route, they could have begun their trek into America more than 60,000 years ago.

Although not nearly as old, both the age and scope of Maya Civilization were expanded by the discovery in May 2003 of a center for the mass-production of ceremonial columns near the Atlantic coast of Nicaragua, 2,700 years ago. Archaeologists held that the Maya spread as far south as Honduras, beginning around 200 BC. But the El Cascal de Flor de Pino site shows that Maya Culture was already flourishing 500 years earlier, and beyond its accepted geographical parameters.

Dr. Ermengol Gassiot, who headed up the excavation for Spain's Universitat Autonoma de Barcelona, reported that his team recovered monuments, petroglyphs, pottery, and numerous pillars of prodigious size. "These columns resemble those found at Mexican sites, where they had ritual uses," he said, adding that El Cascal de Flor de Pino shows the Maya influenced a much larger geographical area than supposed until now.[3] The Nicaraguan pillars resemble those used in the construction of important sacred buildings at Tikal, in Guatemala, Mexico's Palenque, and Copan, in Honduras.

Jeremy Sabloff, Williams Director of the University of Pennsylvania Museum of Archaeology and Anthropology, commented on the Nicaraguan site: "[T]his discovery greatly extends the range of these pre-classical civilizations."[4]

Such recent finds from the Arctic Circle to Brazil are confirming what writers for *Ancient American* have been arguing for the last 11 years—namely, that Man's antiquity in America goes back much further than students are still taught in school by mainstream academics.

CHAPTER 43

Kelts in Pre-Columbian Ohio
by Fritz Zimmerman

The Kelts were great travelers. Beginning more than 3,000 years ago, they wandered out of their homelands in the Steppes of Central Russia, across the entire European Continent, unto the ends of Portugal and Ireland. They did not lack the will or the means—capacious, sea-worthy ships—to follow their restless instincts even further westward.

Born in Knox, Indiana, Fritz Zimmerman spent 13 years personally searching out more than 700 prehistoric earthworks across five states in the American Middle West. A presenter at Wisconsin's Vortex Conference (Burlington), his original findings have been published in the two-volume Nephilim Chronicles: Fallen Angles in the Ohio Valley and A Travel Guide to Ancient Ruins in the Ohio Valley.

Did ancient Britons cross the seas more than 3,000 years ago to become our country's mysterious mound builders? More specifically, were cultural traits of the so-called "Bell Beaker People" of Western Europe shared in common with North America's "Adena"? The former is an archaeological name for a people better remembered as the "Celts," while the latter, likewise a scientific term, applies to our continent's first agriculturalists, referred to by some native tribal peoples of the Ohio Valley as the "Allegwi," or "Alleghany."

The contemporaneous emergence of these two peoples precipitated a change from the Stone Age to the Bronze Age in Britain, and the copper age in North America. So, too, woven textiles made their first appearance,

Forensic reconstruction of head from an Adena skull.

along with the wide use of earthenware. Houses built by both cultures were round and, in some instances, identically rested atop subsequent burial sites. Physical characteristics shared by either folk comprised exceptionally tall stature and Brachycephalism, for human skulls wider than they are long. Their rounded skulls featured a prominent brow ridge and a larger jaw.

In writing of early migrations to the British Isles, historian M.C. Burkett, observed:

The invaders differed somewhat from the former inhabitants of the land. The Neolithic folk seem to have been of moderate stature, long-headed, oval-faced, narrow-nosed, with small features. They were not at all [a] powerfully built race. The newcomers on the other hand were characterized by [a] short, square skull, showing a great development of the superciliary ridges and eyebrows. The cheek-bones, nose and chin were prominent, and the powerful, lower jaw was supplied with large teeth. They were a tall, strongly built race, and must have presented—at any rate as far as men were concerned—a fierce, brutal appearance. The dead were buried in round barrows, inhumation being practiced. They knew about the use of copper, and introduced into England the beaker type pot.[1]

A similar migration of a large people with brachycephalic skulls occurred in North America around 1000 BC. Their arrival separated "Archaic Cultures" from the so-called "Early Woodland." They were familiar with the use of copper tools and weapons, which included tanged daggers and socketed spearheads. The European Celts and American

Allegwi likewise buried their dead in conical earth mounds, many surrounded by a moat. Their ceremonial centers were alike circular henges.

A "henge" is defined as a circular earthwork with an interior ditch and an outer, earthen wall. Accordingly, it would appear that both peoples belonged to a kindred stock and undertook similar religious practices. Allegwi burials typically involved cremation or extending the corpse in a burial vault. Pottery was not generally included. But the ceramic vessels they did use were similar to the Bell Beakers in having a sort of tulip shape to them. Allegwi pottery finds its match in Michelsberg, where a type of rough pottery, daing to circa 3500 BC, shares the same "tulip" design. Earthworks near the German town suggest a connection with England's Windmill Hill, in Wiltshire.

Both Western European sites are Neolithic hilltop forts or settlements pierced by numerous entrances and quite similar to the Adena Fort Ancient and Fort Hill in Ohio. At Windmill Hill, the skeleton of a man was found that was encased in a certain kind of clay, unlike any clay ever found in this country, and had been burned after it was adjusted to the subject, some of the charcoal still remaining. This person was supposed to have been taller in life than 6 feet in height, with large bones, and a broad under-jaw; the front of the head receded so much as to leave no forehead.

A burned, clay vase or urn, of about 3 feet in height, was found standing upright, into which the whole skeleton of a man had been compressed, the top of the urn being covered with burned clay. Resting against the outside of the urn was a similar skeleton, supposed to be that of a female. Pipes were found with the skeletons which had been molded from some plastic material and glazed and burned, on which were skillfully portrayed the likeness of different human faces, and other fancied or real objects. Although each pipe has several faces exactly alike, yet they are entirely unlike those on the other pipes. The entire group represents broad, round, oval, oblong, and conical shaped faces, not caricatures, but careful, skillful, and truthful representations after nature.

Stone tubes, and stones that had been wrought into many curious and beautiful forms—many of them perforated, a process requiring great skill and patience—were found in mounds with the previously described skeletons. Comparisons between second millennium BC Bell Beaker people and contemporaneous Americans are so close in many particulars, a relationship of at least some kind seems undeniable. Further research may yet prove beyond a shadow of a doubt that the Allegwi may, in fact, have been the Celts of Roman Era Europe.

fasces   *Thomas Jefferson*

<hr>

⬡ CHAPTER 44 ⬡

<hr>

Werewolves in the Ancient Old World and Pre-Columbian America
by Frank Joseph

Early rituals aimed at inducing an altered state of consciousness were similarly employed by shamans or medicine men worldwide. Was their common practice an instinctual kind of spirituality fundamental to human nature? Or was it a pre-Columbian legacy introduced by shape-shifters from beyond?

To modern Americans, werewolves are nothing more than silly images trotted out by Hollywood moviemakers every few years in new films on a familiar theme. But long before Michael Landon or Lon Chaney, Jr., underwent their cinematic transformations, the political, military, and, most significantly, spiritual origins of human civilization itself were rooted in werewolf energy.

The foundation myth of ancient Rome told how Romulus and Remus were human twins suckled by a she-wolf, the *lupa romana*. They grew up to become invincible warriors, overcoming and then uniting all Italian tribes to create Roman Civilization. The symbol of their unification was a bundle of wooden sticks bound together by a leather strap, a mighty axe at its center.

This was the *fasces*. It signified that, while the various tribes could be individually beaten, just as single sticks were easily broken, united around a central authority, they were unconquerable. This concept made Rome great, and it was the same imagery used successfully more than 2,000 years later by Thomas Jefferson when he selected the ancient *fasces* to identify the new American Revolution. Fasces still emblazon the U.S. House of Representatives, although they were also used by Benito Mussolini as the emblem of his Fascist movement.

a logo?

The Romans consecrated a southern constellation near the Milky Way, east of Centaurus, as Lupus the Wolf, related perhaps to the Norse cosmic wolf Fenris. Their attraction to wolfish imagery pointed up the militaristic dynamism of this people during the centuries before their decline into self-indulgent materialism. With the collapse of their society, all the spiritual values of preceding millennia were demonized by the Christian Church Triumphant.

Despite rigorous oppression, some of the earlier cults managed to survive, mostly as underground movements. But they occasionally made themselves known in popular folk holidays, like *Samhain* (Halloween) or *Beltane* (May Day), and in some of the greatest literature of the Middle Ages, such as stories of the Grail-knights and King Arthur. Even among the masonry of churches and cathedrals appeared subtle "heathen" themes, such as sculpted images of the Green Man, a Keltic variant of the Roman Lupercus.

Keltic holy men, the Druids, believed they could infuse themselves and their initiates with the spirit of the wolf to become invincible in battle. These elite troops were known as the *Ulfheonar*, literally "werewolves," who transformed themselves in much the same manner that the later Norse of Scandinavia underwent special training as *berserkers*, or "were-bears," human warriors with the strength and fury of a wild bear.

In a Medieval Russian folk custom, anyone desirous of becoming a werewolf invoked the moon-goddess with the words: "Toward the dull herd wanders the shaggy wolf. Moon, moon, gold-horned moon, check the flight of bullets, blunt the hunters' knives, break the shepherds' cudgels, cast wild fear upon all cattle, on men, on all creeping things, that they may not catch the grey wolf! My word is binding, more binding than sleep, more binding than the promise of a hero."[1]

As late as AD 435, Saint Patrick complained that his efforts to Christianize Ireland were opposed by many families of werewolves; that is, practitioners of the Old European nature-cult. He and his New World Order won out, however, and the old religion, while incapable of being extirpated, was nevertheless forced deeper underground as a Dark Age fell over the Western mind. Around AD 950, however, a repressed "paganism" suddenly broke forth to publicly reassert itself in Mercia, a former Anglo-Saxon kingdom in southern England. The audacious revolt was led by a pair of unrepentant Druid priests, one of whom called himself "Werwulf."

Predictably, Church authorities reacted against their attempt with torture and pulpit propaganda. The very name *werewolf* became synonymous for "outlaw," and "spirit-wolf" was applied to all damnable opponents of the dominant Christian paradigm. Competition from a resurgence of folkish mystery-religions was not to be tolerated. From the Middle Ages down to the Industrial Age, wolves were demonized to the brink of extinction, upsetting the natural order of wildlife and leading to a population explosion of deer and other former prey, resulting in the spread of hitherto virtually unknown communicable pathogens, such as Lyme disease.

Werewolf cult followers were simultaneously condemned as agents of Satan and/or the doomed victims of an evil curse. Well into the 1940s, Hollywood perpetuated this characterization in numerous "wolfman" movies, with memorably melodramatic doggerel such as: "Even a man who is pure in heart/and says his prayers by night/may become a wolf when the wolfsbane blooms/and the moon is full and bright!"[2]

According to the great Roman epic poet Virgil, the first werewolf was Moeris, wife of the fate-goddess Moera, who taught him how to bring the dead back to life. Romans knew the werewolf itself as *versipellis*, or "turn-skin."

Standard-bearers in the ancient Roman Army wore a long, draping headgear of wolfskin, symbolizing the lupine nursing of Romulus and Remus and the "wolf-spirit" fierceness of Rome's invincible armed forces. This head-gear was the *galea lupina*, a helmet shaped like a wolf-head, as first worn by Romulus when he led his followers in wolf-skins to establish the foundation of Rome against their outnumbering enemies. The Roman Lupercalia demonstrated Roman veneration of the animal's powerful qualities. The name derives from the Latin *lupercal*, or "wolf's den," where initiation rituals took place. These were conducted by *Luperci*, priests who became werewolves, their faces smeared with the blood of sacrifice, for the duration of the "Wolf Festival" in order to personally identify with Lupercus, and receive his blessings and protection.

Late-19th-century German philosopher Friedrich Nietzsche excoriated some would-be revolutionaries "who have the courage of the knife, but not of the blood."[3] The purpose of the Lupercalia was to make its followers familiar with both. These Luperci formed secret fraternities, in which dogs and goats were sacrificed, because they symbolized the protectors of the flocks and the flocks themselves preyed upon by wolves.

Celebrated every February 15th in a cave at the foot of Mount Aventine, it was an important fertility holiday honoring Lupercus, or Luperca, the god of agriculture, crops, prophecy, and (surprisingly perhaps) cattle and herds. These are some of the same features divinely patronized by Rome's war-god Mars, recalling his Teutonic equivalent, Tyr, who was likewise associated with the wolf. Both reveal the ancestral Indo-European background from which the Romans and Norse sprang.

An even older festival was the *Feronia* (philologically suggestive of the Norse Fenris) celebrated in Italy by the Sabines before the foundation of Rome itself, and named after their tribal Wolf-Mother. Her consort was Soranus, a primeval god who dwelled in forests, where he was revered as the underground Lord of Death. Soranus reincarnated with each sunrise, a theme found throughout wolf myth, wherein the beast and the sun are closely affiliated and sometimes interchangeable. The annual *Feronia* was faithfully observed throughout Roman times, its rites performed by members of a sacred clan famous for its profound antiquity.

Priests and followers were allegedly capable of prodigious psychic accomplishments, such as walking in barefooted processions over burning coals. The secrets of these and other miraculous deeds of self-mastery were passed down in initiation rituals through successive generations going back to Stone Age times and long before. Here, as in other blood-related cultures, the leading motifs of death, rebirth, lone courage, and fighting endurance were personified in the wolf and spiritually transferred to the warrior. These were "mystery cults" in the sense that their practices were sacred and available only to suitable initiates willing to undergo trials and instruction.

An Egyptian war-god with lineage going back to pre-Dynastic times was Apu-At, "The Opener of the Way," so-called for his ability to break through the enemy's ranks, and portrayed in temple art as a werewolf. His body was entirely black, signifying death to the foe, but his headdress and loin-cloth were gold, as were the *Ankh,* or Cross of Life, he held in his right hand at his side; with his left he grasped a golden scepter topped with the head of a bird of prey, a stylized talon at the scepter's base. From the neck down, Apu-At resembled a man, but his head was that of a wolf.

Throughout time, as Egyptian society grew less threatened by outside aggression and settled into stable prosperity, Apu-At's original military identity gave way to mortuary duties. Now, he had the head of a jackal, deemed more suitable to his role as the divine patron of embalming and mummification, because the scavenging beast was notorious for snooping around cemeteries, and known to dig up freshly buried corpses if given half a chance. He is best remembered in the West by his Greek name, Anubis.

Second-century geographer Pausanias observed that the god's original incarnation—Apu-At—gave his name to the Greek sun-god Apollo. He was, in fact, worshiped as "Wolfish Apollo," Apollo Lycaeus, from which the word *lycanthropy*, or "werewolfism," derives. Socrates taught at the famous Lyceum or "Wolf Temple." The sacred werewolf goes back in Greek history at least as long ago as the Bronze Age (2000 to 1200 BC), when Zeus Lycaeus, or Lycaeon, was the divine wolf-king of the Pelasgians, or "Sea Peoples," pre-Hellenic inhabitants of the Peloponnesus.

The barbaric Scythians instituted a religious group, the *Neuri*, who annually transformed themselves into werewolves during a cultic warrior festival. The Scythians were widely feared for their ferocity in battle.

To the ancient Teutons and Norse, Fenris (or Fenrir) was a cosmic wolf chained by the gods, the Aesir, as part of their attempt to bring order to the world. While he was being fettered, Fenris bit off the left hand of Tyr, the war-god. Ever since, the left hand has been known as *sinistrose*, or "unlucky." The ancients believed that when the Aesir's world-order begins to fall apart just before doomsday, Fenris will break free from his bonds to swallow the Sun, and bring upon mankind an age of darkness.

In fact, the Vikings called the first and darkest month after the winter solstice *Fenrir*. The deep antiquity of this imagery likewise demonstrates the common origins of diverse peoples: The Norse Fenris and Lupa of the Etruscans (the pre-Roman inhabitants of Western Italy, who dominated much of the Mediterranean Sea from 1200 BC to 200 BC) were virtually identical. Significantly, Lupa devoured the Sun every winter solstice, as a necessary part of its annual rebirth.

Werewolves are known as far away as the Philippines and China, where they are still revered as the Aswang and Lang Ren, respectively. Often, they are regarded with a mixture of terror and veneration, particularly in the Baltic, where the Finnish *Ihmissusi*, Lithuanian *Vilkatas*, and Latvian *Vilkacis* will sometimes lead his courageous followers to hidden treasures—an apparent folk memory of werewolf cult practices from pre-Christian times. Even today, the Portuguese *Bruxa* and Serbian *Wurdalak*, for all their awful ferocity, are synonymous with justifiable homicide and honor-bound revenge. A somewhat common Slovakian family name is *Vlkodlak*—literally, "Werewolf."

The vast scope of this cultural phenomenon, extending continuously back through several millennia and among disparate peoples unknown to each other, implies its primal rootedness in a dark but integral region of human consciousness. In fact, clinical lycanthropy is a mental disorder, in which afflicted persons are convinced they can transform themselves into another animal, often a wolf. Such a rare condition may partially account for the persistent, worldwide belief in werewolves. More importantly, they are the therianthropic results of shamanism, wherein a man or woman achieves an altered state of consciousness to spiritually identify with the soul of a non-human animal. In Turkish, for example, the *Kurtadam* is not only a werewolf, but also a shaman. In fact, the totemic ancestor of the Turks is the wolf.

Werewolves are still taken very seriously in many parts of the modern world. Indigenous tribal peoples throughout the Americas are firm believers in "skinwalkers," known across Canada as *Wendigo* or *Witiko,* and to the Mohawk Indians of the continental United States as *Limikkin.* South of the Rio Grande, the werewolves became were-jaguars, survivors of a potent cult that was the spiritual centerpiece of America's first civilizers, the Olmecs, 3,500 or 5,000 years ago. The cult spread from the Valley of Mexico to South America, and lives today among the Runa-Uturungu of Argentina and Ecuador's Kanima. Were-beast imagery profusely covers the stone ruins of Peru's seminal Chavín de Huántar, going back at least to the 13th century BC, across the continent to the San Agustín ceremonial centers of Colombia.

Retrieved from Kentucky's Ayers Mound on Eagle Creek, near New Liberty, in Owen County, a spatula precisely cut from the upper jaw of a mature wolf belonged to one of the most bizarre finds yet made by American archaeologists. They found nearby the elongated skull of a big-boned, tall, adult male, whose incisors and canines of his upper jaw had been deliberately cut out in a careful, surgical operation to allow for neat insertion of the wolf spatula in the man's mouth. Apparently, he wore it in life as the component of a mask or headgear, part of a costume for impersonating a wolf, as part of some kind of shamanic activity. So precise was his dental work that infection never set in, as revealed by microscopic examination, and the procedure itself was followed by normal tissue and bone growth—a remarkable, surgical achievement for a pre-modern culture.

His was not the only surviving specimen of such strange attire. Other wolf spatulas and human jaws similarly cut for their insertion have been excavated from 10 more contemporaneous burial mounds throughout Ohio and Kentucky, suggesting that a respected werewolf cult was practiced by the Adena inhabitants. "Adena" is a purely archaeological term applied to a people remembered by Native American tribal elders as the

Allewegi or <u>*Alleghany*</u>. They appeared suddenly around 1000 BC on the Eastern Seaboard, spread rapidly to the Mississippi River, and settled primarily in the Ohio Valley. Credited with the introduction of agriculture, stone hill-forts, and iron foundries, they were eventually exterminated by ancestors of today's Plains Indians in the early eighth century AD.

Their earthworks containing werewolf regalia were self-evident burials for shamans belonging to a lupine cult. The Adena's elaborate headgear has been underscored by the discovery of related artifacts, including an effigy pipe, its stem fashioned to resemble a wolf's head, from the Englewood Mound, near Dayton, Ohio. Keltic artists likewise favored the portrayal of wolf heads, an outstanding example being the baked clay mouth of a trumpet, the creature's jaws agape, from the hill-fort of Numantia, Spain.

Artist's reconstruction of how the Adena wolf-shaman may have appeared in life.

Clearly, the relationship we share with the wolf is as psychologically intimate as it is profoundly ancient. Something kindred has always blurred otherwise-clear distinctions separating the beast from the human within us. Only that, perhaps, can explain our apparently endemic fascination for the werewolf. As such, the question arises: Are close parallels between werewolf worship in the ancient Old World and the pre-Columbian New World explained by a univeral impulse intrinsic to all mankind, or are they part of the evidence for overseas influences at work in the Americas during antiquity?

CHAPTER 45

Who Were the First Americans?
by Patrick C. Chouinard

Though the Siberian ancestors of today's Plains Indians undoubtedly migrated over the Bering Straits during the last ice age some 16,000 years ago, they were not the only people to inhabit North America. Nor, it now appears, may they have been our continent's earliest residents.

Scientists of the recently formed North Atlantic Bio-Cultural Organization (NABO) have made it clear that Asiatic migration via the Bering Straits was not the only possible path taken by prehistoric peoples into the New World. If so, could Kennewick Man, the 10,000-year-old, Caucasian-like skeleton found Washington State's Columbia River, be related to the oldest cultures of Western Europe? A definitive answer may be forthcoming in a new theory concerning North America's human origins. It also addresses the dispersal of peoples across our country from a circumpolar culture, which was responsible not only for mass-migration between the two major continents, but also the interbreeding and establishment of hybrid cultures.

The possibilities prompted directors of the Center for the Study of the First Americans at Oregon State University to process genetic testing of human remains found both in Eastern North America and Western Europe.

Further examination of the human mitochondrian cells may prove a Caucasoid link to the origins of the first Americans, dating as far back as 28,000 BC. Known as the "power packs" of DNA, these cells helped scientists develop four categories of ancestral groups or lineages that are viewed as the founding genetic material for Native Americans. Congruent with existing dogma, and fueling arguments in favor of Asiatic origins for the New World population, they could be traced back to Siberia and northeast Asia, specifically in the Baikal and Altai-Sayan regions.

However, there is a fifth lineage also credited among the founding genetic strains of present-day Native Americans. Known as the "haplogroup X," this genetic signature is the vestige of either a later population found in Europe and the Middle East, or a primeval population of Caucasoid ethnic groups that inhabited Asia. Most Americans, taught the Bering Strait theory as the sole explanation for the peopling of our continent, are unaware that it is no longer entirely accepted, even by scientific dogmatists. Archeological finds in South America and along the North American Eastern Seaboard show conclusively that there were several distinct and separate migrations of different racial groups to the Americas during prehistory.

Furthermore, recent studies point to the hypothesis of a North Atlantic Crescent, composed of water and ice to serve as a "bridge" between the two land masses that connected Europe with the Americas. In December 2000, archaeo-cartographers of the National Geographic Society mapped a "European Theory" for the possible migration of at least some Native American peoples. *Scientific American, Discovering Archaeology,* with its January 2, 2000 issue, already broached an "Atlantic route."[1] It depicted northern island-hopping possibilities from Iceland to Greenland, then Labrador, which is still possible today by following present ice-cover.

Arctic waters provide abundance of seafood and enable travelers to eat as they go, as witness Inuit "Thule Eskimo" migration from Alaska to Greenland. This sudden turn-about—the admission of a possible alternate diffusion to the Americas, followed hard on the discovery of a "rare X-factor" in mitochondrial DNA among indigenous peoples of both northern Europe and North America—demonstrates a fundamental shift in mainstream scientific opinion. The "X pattern," or "European X lineage" joins the already well-known linkage of "O" blood type among North American natives (should be "B" type, if it came from Asia) and modern aboriginal populations along the Atlantic fringe of Europe (the mountain border of Norway-Sweden, west-coastal Ireland, and Pyrenees Mountains).

Referred to variously as "Old European," "modern Cro-Magnon," or "Palaeo-Atlantid," they were tall, heavy-browed, ruddy-complected, and brunette, sometimes light-eyed, with a high Rh-negative factor. Transatlantic migrations involving these deeply ancient genotypes are enumerated by a growing frequency of genetic comparisons with North American aboriginal tribes. In Newfoundland, survivors from at least one of these migrations persisted until their forcible extinction in 1829. They spoke a linguistic isolate bearing no connection to nearby mainland peoples, whether Inuit (Eskimo) or Algonquian.

Genetic sequencing of haplotypes reveals that more than one migratory event took place. As one DNA study stated, "The notion of a homogeneous, Amerindian genetic pool does not conform with these and other results."[2] Mummies of Caucasoid persons have been found at South America's pre-Columbian cities, some of which appear to have been populated by more than 50,000 residents. As these ruins continue to yield such atypical evidence, it appears that many of America's ancient civilizations were founded by sea-faring peoples with long traditions of open-water voyages. Rather than walking 10,000 miles from Mongolia to Chile, the first Americans may have sailed first class. And where they came from will soon be firmly resolved by DNA testing.

From red-headed mummies in Peru's pre-Inca graves to blond-headed Toltec warrior-priests in central Mexico, this is not the history of our father's generation. Pre-Columbian tombs are shattering the adage that "dead men tell no tales." Great steps in understanding the real origins of America are being made. They are striding over the academically dead corpses of fearful, politically correct social historians, who now find themselves haunted by the long dead bodies of Stone Age Americans. Some archaeologists have built their own academic and financial empires based on theories invalidated by modern genetics.

DNA research has placed all upholders of the old paradigm under siege. And when the lab returns are in, they will be out looking for job retraining.

Notes

Introduction

1. Shaw, George Bernard. *George Bernard Shaw: Four Books of Essays in a Single File* (Kindle edition) (West Roxbury, Mass.: B&R Samizdat Express, 2010).
2. Gordon, Cyrus H. *Before Columbus: Links Between the Old World and Ancient America* (New York: Crown Publishers, 1971).

Chapter 1

1. Perry, Tom, "In Lebanon DNA May Yet Heal Rifts," Reuters Website, *www.reuters.com/article/2007/09/10/us-phoenicians-dna-idUSL0559096520070910.*
2. Wikipedia. *en.wikipedia.org/wiki/Lebanese_people#Ethnic_Groups.*
3. Attridge, H.W., and R.A. Oden, Jr. *Philo of Byblos: The Phoenician History*: Introduction, Critical Text, Translation, Notes (Washington, D. C.: The Catholic Biblical Association of America, 1981).
4. Markoe, Glenn. *Phoenicians* (University of California Press, 2000).
5. Hillinger, Charles. "Mazes Remain Enigmas of Ancient Indian Art," *The Los Angeles Times, articles.latimes.com/1991-06-11/news/mn-515_1_hemet-maze, June 11, 1991.*

Chapter 2

1. Fell, Barry. *America B.C.: Ancient Settlers in the New World, Revised Edition* (New York: Pocket Books, 1989).
2. *Ancient American, Volume 14, Number 87,* June 2010.
3. "'Exceptional' Roman Coins Hoard," *Coin Collecting News, www.coinlink.com/News/ancients/exceptional-roman-coins-hoard/.*

4. *Current Antropology, Volume 22, Number 10* (University of Chicago Press).

5. Ibid.

6. *Ancient American, Volume 2, Issue 7,* November/December 1994.

7. McCulloch, J. Huston. " Roman Coins from Breathitt Co., Ky.," *www.econ.ohio-state.edu/jhm/arch/coins/breathit.htm.*

8. Dorado, Miguel Rivera. *La Ciudad Maya: Un Escenario Sagrado* (Madrid: Tapa blanda, 2001).

9. Ancient Kentucky Historical Association, *www.razoo.com/story/Ancient-Kentucky-Historical-Association.*

10. Henson, Michael Paul. "Mysterious Swords," *Lost Treasure*, January 1993, pp. 26, 28.

11. Ibid.

12. Ancient Kentucke Historical Association, *www.razoo.com/story/Ancient-Kentucke-Historical-Association.*

Chapter 3

1. Mertz, Henriette. *The Mystic Symbol: Mark of the Michigan Mound Builders* (Wisc.: Hay River Press, 2004; reprint of the 1970 original).

2. Harrold, Francis B., and Eve, Raymond A. *Cult Archaeology and Creationism: Understanding Pseudoscientific Beliefs about the Past, Revised edition* (University of Iowa Press, 1995).

3. Thomas, Cyrus. *The History of North America: Volume 2. The Indians of North America in Historic Times* (Chestnut Hill, Mass.: Adamant Media Corporation, 2001).

4. Jameson, John H., Jr. *The Reconstructed Past: Reconstructions in the Public Interpretation of Archaeology and History* (Lanham, Md.: Altamira Press, Rowman & Littlefield Publishing Group, 2004).

5. Gordon, Cyrus H. *Before Columbus: Links Between the Old World and Ancient America* (New York: Crown Publishers, 1971).

6. Wolter, Scott, and Richard D. Stehly. "Report of Archaopetrography Investigation on the Bat Creek Stone of 1889," *Ancient American, Volume 14, Issue 88*, September 2010, p. 1.

7. Gordon, Dr. Cyrus. "Stone Inscription Found in Tennessee Proves that America was Discovered 1,500 Years Before Columbus," *Argosy Magazine, Volume 22, Issue 102,* January 1971.

Chapter 4

1. Thompson, Dr. Gunnar. *American Discovery, The Real Story* (Seattle, Wash.: Misty Isles Press, 1992).
2. Ibid.
3. Ibid.
4. White, J.J. "The Pig-Soldier Figurine from Moche Appears to Be a Fox After All," *Midwestern Epigraphic Journal, 22 (3)*, 2007, pp. 12, 13.
5. *The Complete Museum of Pre-Columbian Gold* Website, *www.precolumbiangold.com/moche.htm*.
6. Leicht, Hermann. *Pre-Inca Art and Culture* (New York: Orion Press, 1960).
7. Thompson, *American Discovery.*

Chapter 5

1. Irwin, Constance. *Fair Gods and Stone Faces* (New York: St. Martin's Press, 1963), p. 347.
2. White, J.J., and B.H. Moseley. "Burrows Cave: Fraud or Find of the Century? (aka, 'Men of Tyre in Ancient Illinois and Other Worldwide Destinations')," *Ancient American, 1 (2)*, 4–15 (1993).
3. White, J.J. "Tyre—Circle Cross Connection Found at Burrows Cave," *Midwestern Epigraphic Journal, 7, 91* (1993).

Chapter 6

1. Nielsen, Richard, and Scott F. Wolter. *Kensington Rune Stone: Compelling New Evidence* (Minn.: Lake Superior Agate Publishing, 2006).
2. Mertz, *The Mystic Symbol.*
3. Deal, David Allen. "Michigan's Ancient Coptic Christian Picture-Library," *Ancient American, Volume 3, Number 18,* May/June 1997.
4. Von Harnack, Adolf. *History of Dogma, Volume 1* (Charleston, S.C.: Nabu Press, 2010).
5. Mead, G.R.S. *Pistis Sophia: The Gnostic Tradition of Mary Magdalene, Jesus, and His Disciples, Book I, Chapters 8 and 11* (CreateSpace, 2010).

Chapter 7

1. Davidson, H.R. Ellis. *Gods and Myths of Northern Europe* (New York: Penguin, 1965).

2. *Directory of Designations of National Historic Significance of Canada, Serpent Mounds National Historic Site of Canada,* 2005, *www.pc.gc.ca/ apps/lhnnhs/det_E.asp?oqSID=0518&oqeName=Serpent+Mounds&o qfName=Tumulus+Serpent.*

3. Kenyon, W.A., *Aboriginal Canada* (Toronto, Ontario: River Run Press, 1959).

Chapter 8

1. Isbitts, Steven. "Discovery Could Rock Archaeology," *The Tampa Tribune,* June 25, 2006, *tboblogs.com/index.php/opinion/comments/ whats_up_with_the_rocks/.*

2. Rydholm, Fred. *Michigan Copper: The Untold Story; A history of Discovery* (Mich.: Winter Cabin Books, 2006).

Chapter 9

1. Hall, Yancey. Interview. "'Inca Mummy Man' Johan Reinhard," *National Geographic News,* June 21, 2005, *news.nationalgeographic. com/news/2005/06/0621_050621_incamummy.html.*

2. Ibid.

3. Ibid.

4. Prescott, William Hickling. *History of the Conquest of Peru, with a Preliminary View of the Civilization of the Incas: Volume 3* (Chestnut Hill, Mass.: Adamant Media Corporation, 2001).

Chapter 11

1. Wilson, Alan, and Baram Blackett. *Artorius Rex Discovered* (UK: King Arthur Research, 1986).

Chapter 12

1. Reichel-Dolmatoff, G. "The Loom of Life: a Kogi Principle of Integration," *Journal of Latin American Lore, 4-1,* 1978, p. 15.

2. Totten, Norman. "King Juba Remembered," *ESOP 21,* 1992, p. 173.

3. Herberger, Charles F. "The Quincunx as an External and Internal Orientation Symbol," *ESOP 23,* 1998.

Chapter 13

1. Thompson, *American Discovery.*
2. Colton, Harold Sellers. "In the House of Tcuhu, the Minoan Labyrinth," *Science, 45*:667–668, 1917.
3. Haury, Emil W. *The Hohokam: Desert Farmers and Craftsmen* (The University of Arizona Press, 1978).
4. Colton, "In the House of Tcuhu."
5. Thompson, *American Discovery.*

Chapter 14

1. Long, Asphodel P. "Asherah, the Tree of Life and the Menorah." Lecture, The College of St. Mark & St. John, Plymouth, Massachusetts, 1996.
2. Hestrin, Ruth. "Understanding Asherah—Exploring Semitic Iconography," *Biblical Archaeology Review, 17,* Sept.–Oct. 1991.
3. Patai, Raphael. *The Hebrew Goddess* (Detroit, Mich.: Wayne State University Press, 1990), pp. 34–49.
4. Yardin, L. *The Tree of Light: A Study of the Menorah* (Ithaca, N.Y.: Cornell University Press, 1971), pp. 4–14.
5. Patai, *The Hebrew Goddess,* pp. 13–33.
6. Stuckey, Johanna H. *Asherah, Supreme Goddess of the Levant* (Toronto: York University MatriFocus, 2004), pp. 1–4.
7. Long, "Asherah."
8. Yardin, *The Tree of Light,* pp. 36–53.
9. Patai, *The Hebrew Goddess*, pp. 50–61.
10. Kingsley, Sean. *God's Gold: The Quest for the Lost Temple Treasure of Jerusalem* (Calif.: HarperCollins, 2007).
11. Feron, James. "Depiction of a 2,200 Year Old Menorah of the Second Temple Discovered by Archaeologists in Old Jerusalem," *The New York Times*, December 3, 1969.
12. Meshorer, Ya'akov. *Jewish Coins of the Second Temple Period* (Tel Aviv: Am Hassefer, 1967).
13. Patai, *The Hebrew Goddess.*
14. Hestrin, "Understanding Asherah."

15. *Israel Exploration Journal 37,* 212–222; *AND* Meshel, Ze'ev, Kuntillet Ajrud. "An Iron Age Way-Side Religious Center in Sinai," *The Shelby White-Leon Levy Program for Archaeological Publications,* 2006, *www. bib-arch.org/news/white-levy-recipeints-2007.*

16. Stuckey, *Asherah*; Long, "Asherah"; Hestrin, "Understanding Asherah." Also see Hadley J. *The Cult of Asherah in Ancient Israel & Judah* (New York: Cambridge University Press, 2000).

Chapter 15

1. Flint, Richard and Flint, Shirley Cushing. *The Coronado Expedition to Tierra Nueva: The 1540-1542 Route Across the Southwest* (University Press of Colorado, 2004).

2. Mallam, R. Clark. *Site of the Serpent: A Prehistoric Life Metaphor in South Central Kansas* (Kansas: Coronado-Quivira Museum, 1990).

3. Ibid.

4. Ibid.

5. Douglas, Ronald M. *Scottish Lore and Folklore* (NY: Beckman House, 1982), p. 94.

6. Ibid, p. 95.

7. Buxton, Richard. *The Complete World of Greek Mythology* (London: Thames & Hudson, 2004).

Chapter 16

1. Burke, John, and Kaj Halberg. *Seed of Knowledge, Stone of Plenty: Understanding the Lost Technology of the Ancient Megalith-Builders* (Tulsa, Okla.: Council Oak Books, 2005).

2. Squier, Ephraim G., and Edwin H. Davis. *Ancient Monuments of the Mississippi Valley* (Washington, D.C.: Smithsonian Institution Press, 1998, reprint of 1848 edition).

Chapter 17

1. May, Wayne. *This Land: They Came from the East, Volume 3* (Wisc.: Hay River Press, 2005).

Chapter 18

1. Carlson, Suzanne. "Loose Threads in a Tapestry of Stone: The Architecture of the Newport Tower," *The NEARA Journal, Volume 35, No.1,* Summer 2001.

2. Barstad, Jan. "The Newport Tower Project, An Archaeological Investigation into the Tower's Past," Chronognostic Research Foundation, Inc., 2007, *www.chronognostic.org.*

Chapter 19
1. Fell, *America B.C.*
2. *History of the Ohio Falls Cities and Their Counties with Illustrations and Biographical Sketches, Vol. I* (Cleveland, Ohio: L.A. Williams & Co., 1882; a reproduction by Unigraphic, Inc., Indiana, 1968).
3. Ibid.
4. Ibid.
5. Ibid.
6. Ibid.
7. Ibid.

Chapter 20
1. McMahan, Basil. *The Mystery of Old Stone Fort* (Nashville, Tenn.: Tennessee Book Company, 1965).
2. Ibid.
3. Ibid.
4. Ibid.
5. Caesar, Julius. *The Gallic Wars* (St. Petersburg, Fla: Red and Black Publishers, 2008).

Chapter 21
1. Fell, *America B.C.*

Chapter 22
1. Joseph, Frank. *The Lost Pyramids of Rock Lake* (Lakeville, Minn.: Galde Press, Inc., 1992).
2. Ibid.
3. The spring expedition did not take place.

Chapter 23
1. Brooks, William. *On the Lucayan Indians* (Washington, D.C.: National Academy of Sciences, 1889).

Chapter 24

1. Allen, J.M. *Atlantis: The Andes Solution* (London: Weidenfeld Nicolson Illustrated, 1998).
2. Plato. *Timaeus and Critias,* translated by Desmond Lee (N.Y.: Penguin Classics, 1972).
3. De Gambóa, Pedro Sarmiento. *Narratives of the Voyages of Pedro Sarmiento de Gambóa to the Straits of Magellan,* translated by Clements R. Markham (Cambridge University Press, 2010).

Chapter 25

1. Derleth, August. *Father Marquette and the Great Rivers* (Calif.: Ignatius Press, 1998).
2. Hildebrand, Norbert. "The Monster on the Rock," *Fate,* May 1950.
3. Greenly, Albert Harry. *Father Louis Hennepin: his travels and his books* (New York: Bibliographical Society of America, 1957).
4. Hildebrand, "The Monster on the Rock."
5. Russell, Professor John. "The Piasu," *The Evangelical Magazine and Gospel Advocate*, 1848.
6. Armstrong, P.A. *The Piasu, or the Devil among the Indians* (Ill.: Morris, 1887), *www.earlychicago.com/biblio.php.*
7. Ibid.
8. Hildebrand, "The Monster on the Rock."
9. Ibid., p. 19.

Chapter 26

1. The oldest known New World pottery is the Amazonian of eastern Brazil. Shards found at Taperinha have been dated to about 5600 BC. The next oldest pottery sites are in Columbia, which have been dated to about 4500 BC. Valdivia pottery comes next with dating to about 3200 BC. The earliest Peruvian and Mesoamerican pottery dates to 2500 and 1800 BC, respectively. See the relevant articles in Barnett and Hoopes, editors. *The Emergence of Pottery* (Washington, D.C.: Smithsonian, 1995).
2. Jomon, Japan's oldest pottery tradition, has its origins about 10,700 BC. See Aikens, Melvin. "First in the World: The Jomon Pottery of Early Japan," in *The Emergence of Pottery*. See also Rice, Prudence M. "On the Origins of Pottery," *Journal of Archaeological Method and Theory, 6, no. 1* (1999): 1–54.

3. Meggers, Betty J., Clifford Evans, and Emilio Estrada. *Early Formative Period of Coastal Ecuador: The Valdivia and Machalilla Phases, Volume 1*, December 20, 1965 (Washington, D.C.: Smithsonian Contributions to Anthropology).

4. Needham, J. *Science and Civilization in China, Vol. 4* (Mass.: Cambridge University Press, 1971).

5. Meggers, Betty J. *Prehistoric America: An Ecological Perspective, 3rd expanded edition* (Piscataway, N.J.: Transaction Publishers, 2010).

6. Thompson, *American Discovery.*

7. Menzies, Gavin. *1421: The Year China Discovered the World* (London: Bantam Press, 2002).

8. Heyerdahl, Thor. *Early Man and the Ocean* (New York: Doubleday & Co., Inc., 1979).

9. Von Daniken, Erich. *The Gold of the Gods* (New York: G.P. Putnam's Sons, 1972).

10. Wingate, Richard. *Lost Outpost of Atlantis* (New York: Everest House, 1980).

11. Malmstrom, Vincent. *Cycles of the Sun, Mysteries of the Moon* (University of Texas Press, 1997).

12. Anawalt, Patricia Rieff. "Traders of the Ecuadorian Littoral," *Archaeology, Volume 50, Number 6*, November/December, 1997.

13. Prescott, William Hickling. *History of the Conquest of Peru, with a Preliminary View of the Civilization of the Incas, Volume 3* (Chestnut Hill, Mass.: Adamant Media Corporation, 2001).

14. Means, Philip Ainsworth. *Ancient Civilizations of the Andes* (New York: Charles Scribner's Sons, 1931), and Heyerdahl, *Early Man and the Ocean.*

15. Anawalt, "Traders of the Ecuadorian Littoral."

16. Alsar, Vital. *La Balsa: The Longest Raft Voyage in History* (New York: Reader's Digest Press, 1973).

17. Heyerdahl, Thor. *Kon-Tiki* (New York: Ballantine Books, 1950).

Chapter 27

1. *Ancient American, Volume 4, number 26,* November/December 2000.

Chapter 29

1. *Ancient American, Volume 8, Number 51*, May/June 2003.

Chapter 30

1. Gilbert, Jane. "City's Name Baffles Rockwall Residents," *The Victoria Advocate*, August 7, 1986, *news.google.com/newspapers?nid =861&dat=19860807&id=IrddAAAAIBAJ&sjid=5F0NAAAAIBAJ& pg=6426,1453449/*.

2. "Man-made or Geological Phenomenon," *www.pcmann.net/ wordmann/rockwall.html*.

3. Gilbert, Jane. "City's Name Baffles Rockwall Residents," *The Victoria Advocate*, August 7, 1986, *news.google.com/newspapers?nid =861&dat=19860807&id=IrddAAAAIBAJ&sjid=5F0NAAAAIBAJ& pg=6426,1453449*.

4. Steger, O.L. *History of Rockwall County, 1842–1968* (Rockwall, Tex.: Rockwall County Historical Foundation, 1999).

5. Glenn, Dr. James L. "Photographic Essay on the System of Rock Walls in Rockwall, Texas" (Rockwall, Tex.: Rockwall Chamber of Commerce, Rockwall County Historical Foundation, 1950), *www. rockwallcountyhistoricalfoundation.com/wall.htm*.

6. Steger, *History of Rockwall County, 1842–1968*.

7. "Man-made or Geological Phenomenon," *www.pcmann.net/ wordmann/rockwall.html*.

8. Ibid.

9. Steger, *History of Rockwall County, 1842–1968*.

10. Gilbert, "City's Name Baffles Rockwall Residents."

11. Count Byron De Prorok pioneered, among other innovations, the use of aircraft and automobiles in archaeology during the first third of the 20th century, although his memory is despised today by orthodox scholars for his unconventional methods. De Prorok's bestselling books—*Digging for Lost African Gods* (1926), *Mysterious Sahara* (1929), and *Dead Men Do Tell Tales* (1934)—were republished in the early 21st century by Narrative Press (Torrington, Wy.). His *In Quest of Lost Worlds* (1935) has been re-released by Adventures Unlimited (Kempton, Ill.).

12. Rose, Mark. "Tales of the Count," *Archaeology, Volume 54 Number 5*, September/October 2001, *www.archaeology.org/0109/abstracts/books. html*.

13. Glenn, "Photographic Essay on the System of Rock Walls in Rockwall, Texas."

14. Gilbert, "City's Name Baffles Rockwall Residents."
15. About *Pointe Coupee Democrat* (False River [i.e. New Roads],
    Parish of Pointe Coupee, [La.]) 1858–1862, Library of Congress,
    chroniclingamerica.loc.gov/lccn/sn86053686/.

Chapter 31

1. Huffman, Carl. *Archytas of Tarentum: Pythagorean, Philosopher and Mathematician King* (Mass.: Cambridge University Press, 2010).
2. Schomp, Virginia. *The Ancient Chinese* (London: Franklin Watts, 2005).
3. Woodman, Jim. *Nazca: Journey to the Sun* (New York: Pocket Books, 1977).
4. Ibid.

Chapter 32

1. Dunnington, George A. *History and Progress of theCcounty of Marion, West Virginia, from its Earliest Settlement by the Whites, Down to the Present, Together with Biographical Sketches of its Most Prominent Citizens* (Charleston, S.C.: Nabu Press, 2010).
2. Omanson, B.J. "Tales of the Early Pricketts," 2011, *prickettsfort. wordpress.com/2011/01/10/tales-of-the-early-pricketts/.*
3. Ibid.
4. Dunnington, *History and Progress of the County of Marion, West Virginia.*
5. Williams, John A. *West Virginia: A History* (Morgantown, W.V.: West Virginia University Press, 2003).

Chapter 33

1. Engl, Lieselotte, and Theo Engl. *Twilight of Ancient Peru* (New York: MacGraw Hill, 1969).
2. Kunkel, Edward J. *Pharaoh's Pump* (Ohio: Five Star Final Edition, 1977).
3. "Characteristics And Harmful Effects Of The Only Liquid Metal," Article Base Website, 2010, *www.articlesbase.com/education-articles/ characteristics-and-harmful-effects-of-the-only-liquid-metal-1979080. html.*
4. Andrews, Dr. Arlan. *Atlantis Rising, Issue 58*, July/August 2006.

5. Gartner, William Gustav. "Mapmaking in the Central Andes," in *The History of Cartography, Volume 2, Book 3* ("Cartography in the Traditional African, American, Arctic, Australian, and Pacific Societies"), edited by David Woodward and G. Malcolm Lewis (Chicago, Ill.: University of Chicago Press, 1992).

Chapter 34
1. *Catholic Encyclopedia* (Nashville, Tenn.: Thomas Nelson, 1990).
2. MacPherson, James Rose, translator. *The Pilgrimage of Arculf in the Holy Land, about the year A.D. 670* (London: Palestine Pilgrims' Text Society, 1895).
3. Ibid.
4. Ibid.
5. Charroux, Robert. *Forgotten Worlds; Scientific Secrets of the Ancients and Their Warning for Our Time* (N.Y.: Popular Library, 1973).
6. Ibid.

Chapter 35
1. McGuinness, PhD, Tim. "Costa Rican Stone Spheres," *www.mysteryspheres.com*.
2. Ibid.
3. Erikson, George. *Atlantis in America, Navigators of the Ancient World* (Kempton, Ill.: Adventures Unlimited Press, 1998).
4. McGuinness, "Costa Rican Stone Spheres."
5. Mann, Thomas. *Joseph and His Brothers* (New York: Everyman's Library, 2005).

Chapter 36
1. Kelsey, Harry. *Juan Rodriguez Cabrillo* (San Marino, Calif.: Huntington Library Press, 1998).
2. Savoy, Gene. *Antisuyo: The Search for the Lost Cities of the Andes* (New York: Simon & Schuster, 1970).
3. Routledge, Katherine. *The Mystery of Easter Island* (New York: Cosimo Classics, 2007, reprint of the 1917 original).

Chapter 37
1. Joseph, Frank. *Advanced Civilizations of Prehistoric America* (Rochester, Vt.: Bear and Company, 2011).

2. "Chocolate Drink Used In Rituals In New Mexico 1,000 Years Ago," *Science Daily,* February 3, 2009, *www.sciencedaily.com/releases/2009/02/090203173331.htm.*

Chapter 38

1. Eckert, Allan W. *The Frontiersmen: A Narrative.* (Ashland, Ky.: Jesse Stuart Foundation, 2001).

Chapter 39

1. De Jonge, Reinoud, and Jay S. Wakefield. *Rocks & Rows, Sailing Routes across the Atlantic and the Copper Trade* (Kirkland. Wash.: MCS, Inc., 2009).
2. Childress, David Hatcher. *Lost Cities & Ancient Mysteries of the Southwest* (Kempton, Ill.: Adventures Unlimited Press, 2009).
3. Davis, Dr. Graeme. *Vikings in America* (Edinburgh, Scotland: Birlinn, Ltd., 2011).
4. Homer. *The Odyssey,* translated by Robert Fagles (New York: Penguin Classic, 1997).
5. Apollonius Rhodius. *The Voyage of Argo: The Argonautica,* translated by E.V. Rieu (New York: Penguin Classic, 1959).
6. Hesiod. *Theogony and Works and Days*, translated by M.L. West (Oxford University Press, re-issue edition, 2009).
7. Terrence Aym, personal e-mail correspondence, January 22, 2011.
8. Peterson, Marshall N. *The Highland Maya in Fact and Legend: Francisco Ximenez, Fernando Alva de Ixtlilxochitl, and Other Commentators on Indian Origins and Deeds* (Essex, UK: Labyrinthos, 1999).
9. Caso, Adolph. *To America and Around the World: The Logs of Christopher Columbus and of Ferdinand Magellan* (UK: Branden Books, 2001).
10. Joseph, *Advanced Civilizations of Prehistoric America.*

Chapter 40

1. "Haplotypic Background of a Private Allele at High Frequency in the Americas," *Oxford Journals,* 2009, *mbe.oxfordjournals.org/content/early/2009/02/12/molbev.msp024.*

2. Schurr, Theodore. "Mitochondrial DNA and the Peopling of the New World Genetic variations among Native Americans provide further clues to who first populated the Americas and when they arrived," *American Scientist, Volume 88, Number 3*, May–June 2000, p. 246.

Chapter 41
1. Rydholm, *Michigan Copper.*

Chapter 42
1. Beale, Bob. "Ancient Hearth Tests Carbon Dating," *ABC Science,* November 17, 2003, *www.abc.net.au/science/ articles/2003/11/17/990775.html.*

2. Hecht, Jeff. "Ancient Site Hints at First North American Settlers," *New Scientist*, January 2, 2004, *www.newscientist.com/article/dn4526-ancient-site-hints-at-first-north-american-settlers.html.*

3. Black, Richard. "Ancient Nicaraguan Society Found," BBC News Website, May 19, 2003, *http://news.bbc.co.uk/2/hi/sci/tech/3035113.stm*

4. Ibid.

Chapter 43
1. Harrison, R.J. *The Beaker Folk, Copper Age Archaeology in Western Europe* (New York: Thames & Hudson, 1980).

Chapter 44
1. Walker, Barbara G. *The Woman's Encyclopedia of Myths and Secrets* (San Francisco, Calif.: HarperOne, 1983).

2. "Memorable quotes for *The Wolf Man*," 1941, IMDB Website, *www.imdb.com/title/tt0034398/quotes.*

3. Nietzsche, Friedrich. *Thus Spoke Zarathustra: A Book for Everyone and No One*, translated by R.J. Hollingdale (New York: Penguin Classics, 1961).

Chapter 45
1. "Once We Were Not Alone," *Scientific American*, January 2000, *www.sciamdigital.com/index.cfm?fa=Products.ViewIssue&ISSUEID_CHAR=82D7E940-CBFE-4BD2-989F-A47BDEAACE1.*

2. Callegari-Jacques, SM, FM Salzano, J Constans, P Maurieres, "Gm Haplotype Distribution in Amerindians: Relationship with Geography and Language," *American Journal of Physical Anthropology, 90(4)*: 427–44, April 1993, *www.ncbi.nlm.nih.gov/pubmed/768276.*

References

Alexander, William. *North American Mythology* (New York: Harcourt Brace, 1935).

Ashraf, Jaweed. "Maize In India: Introduction or Indigenous?," in *Annals, NAGI, Vol. XIV, No. 2*, December 1994.

Bailey, James. *The God-Kings and the Titans* (London: Hider & Stoughton, 1973).

———. *Sailing to Paradise* (New York: Simon & Schuster, 1994).

Baldwin, John. *Ancient America* (New York: Longstreet Publishers, 1998).

Blackett, W.S. *A Lost History of America* (London: Treubner & Co., 1883).

Burtt-Davy, Joseph. *Maize* (New York: Longmans, Green & Co., 1914).

Casson, Lionel. *Ships and Seafaring in Ancient Times*. (London: British Museum Press, 1994).

Corliss, William R. *Ancient Man: A Handbook of Puzzling Artifacts* (Glen Arm, Md.: The Sourcebook Project, 1980).

Daniel, Glyn. *The Illustrated Encyclopedia of Archaeology*. (New York: Thomas Y. Crowell Company, 1977).

De Jonge, R.M., and J.S. Wakefield. *How the SunGod Reached America, A Guide to Megalithic Sites* (Kirkland, Wash.: MCS, Inc., 2002).

Doran, Edwin J. "The Sailing Raft as a Great Tradition," in *Man Across the Sea* (Austin, Tex.: University of Texas Press, 1971).

Duff, Professor U. Francis. "Prehistoric Ruins of the Southwest," *Ancient American, Vol. 9, No. 55*, February 2004.

Evans, Arthur J. *The Palace of Minos, vols. 1, 2 & 3* (London: Macmillan, 1935).

Fagan, Brian M. *Ancient North America: The Archaeology of a Continent* (London: Thames and Hudson Ltd., 1995).

Farley, Gloria. *In Plain Sight* (Columbus, Ga.: ISAC Press, 1994).

Fingerhut, Eugene. *Who First Discovered America?* (Claremont, Calif.: Regina Books, 1984).

Fitting, James E. *The Archaeology of Michigan: A Guide to the Prehistory of the Great Lakes, 2nd ed.* (Bloomfield Hills, Mich.: Cranbrook Institute of Science, 1975).

Gallegos, Fernando S. "Beyond History: An Alternative Historical Perspective," research paper, San Jose State University, 2009.

Gardner, Percy. *Coins of Greek and Scythic Kings of Bactria and India* (Chicago, Ill.: Argonaut Inc., 1966).

Gill, Sam D., and Irene F. Sullivan. *Dictionary of Native American Mythology* (Santa Barbara, Calif.: ABC-CLIO, Inc., 1992).

Grant, Michael. *The Roman Emperors* (New York: Barnes & Noble, 1997).

Hamilton, Ross, with Patricia Mason, "North American Warfare and a Tradition of Giants," *Ancient American, Vol. 5, No. 36,* December 2000.

Hansen, L. Taylor. *The Ancient Atlantic* (Amherst, Wisc.: Amherst Press, 1969).

Harrison, R.J. *The Beaker Folk: Copper Age Archaeology in Western Europe* (New York: Thames & Hudson, 1980).

Hemming, John. *Conquest of the Incas* (New York: Harcourt, 1970).

Heyerdahl, Thor. *The Ra Expeditions* (London: George Allen & Unwin, 1971).

Hiemer, Paul. *Caribbean Mythology* (London: Thackery & Sons, Ltd., 1961).

Hinsdale, W.B. *Primitive Man in Michigan* (Ann Arbor, Mich.: University Museum, University of Michigan, 1925; reprint Au Train, Mich.: Avery Color Studios, 1983).

Hobhouse, Henry. *Seeds of Change: Five Plants that Transformed the World* (London: Sedgwick & Jacks, 1985).

Hollstein, Alfred, "Carthaginian Seamanship," *Ancient World Magazine, vol. 1, no. 1,* June 1980.

Huyghe, Patrick. *Columbus Was Last* (New York: Hyperion Books, 1992).

Jairazbhoy, R.A. *Ancient Egyptians and Chinese in America* (Rowman & Littlefield, 1974).

Johannessen, Carl L., and Anne Z. Parker. "Maize Ears Sculptured in 12th and 13th Century A.S. India as Indicators of Pre-Columbian Diffusion," in *Economic Botany, Vol. 42 (2)*, 1989.

Johnstone, Paul. *The Sea-craft of Prehistory* (Cambridge, Mass.: Harvard University Press, 1980).

Joseph, Frank. *Atlantis in Wisconsin* (Lakeville, Minn.: Galde Press, Inc., 1995).

——. *Discovering the Mysteries of Ancient America* (Franklin Lakes, N.J.: New Page Books, 2005).

Joseph, Frank, editor. *Unearthing Ancient America* (Franklin Lakes, N.J.: New Page Books, 2008).

Kaiser, Rudolf. *The Voice of the Great Spirit, Prophecies of the Hopi Indians,* translated by Werner Wuensche (Boston, Mass.: Shambala Publishers, 1991).

Krupp, E.C. *In Search of Ancient Astronomies* (New York: Doubleday, 1977).

Kunkel, Edward J. Patent, "Hydraulic Ram Pump, 2,887,956." U.S. Patent and Trademark Office, May 26, 1959.

Leach, Maria, editor. *Funk &Wagnalls' Standard Dictionary of Folklore, Mythology and Legend* (New York: Harper & Row, 1972).

MacCullow, Canon John. *Myths of All Races, vol. 2* (London: Marshall Jones Co., 1930).

Martin, John Bartlow. *Call It North America* (New York: Alfred A. Knopf, 1944).

Martin, Susan P. *Wonderful Power: The Sign of Ancient Copper Working in the Lake Superior Basin* (Detroit, Mich.: Wayne State University Press, 1999).

Matthew, William Diller. "Plato's Atlantis in Paleogeography," in *Procedures of the National Academy of Sciences, Vol. VI*, 1920.

McCarthy, Silvia. *Ancient Copper Miners of the Upper Midwest* (Detroit, Mich.: University of Michigan Press, 1952).

Mercatante, Anthony S. *Who's Who in Egyptian Mythology* (New York: Clarkson N. Potter, Inc., 1978).

Mercer, Robert. *The Phoenicians* (New York: Daily Books, 1978).

Mertz, Henriette. *Atlantis, Dwelling Place of the Gods* (Chicago, Ill.:Mertz, 1976).

Millar, Fergus. *The Roman Empire and its Neighbours, 2nd edition* (London: Gerald Duckworth and Co., 1981).

Newberry, J.S. "Ancient Mining in North America," *American Antiquarian* (1889) in *Ancient Man: A Handbook of Puzzling Artifacts* by William R. Corliss (Glen Arm, Md.: The Sourcebook Project, 1978).

Nuttall, Zelia. *The Fundamental Principles of Old and New World Civilizations, vol. II* (Cambridge, Mass.: Peabody, Harvard University, 1900).

Olsen, Brad. *Sacred Places North America: 108 Destinations.* (San Francisco, Calif.: Consortium of Collective Consciousness, 2003).

Owen, Weldon. *Old World Civilizations, the Rise of Cities and States* (Australia: McMahons Point, 1995).

Peale, T.R. "Prehistoric Ruins of the Southwest," *Ancient American, Vol. 9, No. 55,* February 2004.

Phelps, Louise, editor, *Early Narratives of the Northwest, 1634–1699* (New York: Charles Scribner's Sons, 1917; reprint New York: Barnes and Noble, 1967).

Postel, Rainer. *Katalog Der Antiken Munzen in Der Hamburger Kunsthalle* (Hamburg, Germany: Hans Christiens Verlag, 1976).

Quimby, George Irving. *Indian Life on the Upper Great Lakes: 11,000 B.C. to A.D. 1800* (Chicago, Ill.: The University of Chicago Press, 1960).

Radin, Paul. *The Winnebago Tribe* (Lincoln, Neb.: University of Nebraska Press, 1970).

Ricky, Donald B., editor. *Encyclopedia of Ohio Indians* (St. Clair Shores, Mich.: Somerset Publishers, Inc., 1998).

Riley, Carrol, et al. *Man Across The Sea* (Austin, Tex.: University of Texas Press, 1971).

Schoolcraft, Henry Rowe. *History and Statistical Information Respecting the Indian Tribes of the United States* (Washington, D.C.: Society for the Investigation of North American Antiquities, 1859).

Short, John T. *The North Americans* (New York: Harper and Brothers, 1880).

Shute, Nancy. "Where We Come From: Recent Advances in Genetics Are Starting to Illuminate the Wanderings of Early Humans," *U.S. News and World Report,* January 29, 2001.

Sodders, Betty. *Michigan Prehistory Mysteries* (Gwinn, Mich.: Avery Color Studios, 1991).

Stengal, Marc K. "The Diffusionists Have Landed," *The Atlantic Monthly,* January 2000.

Sykes, Edgerton. *Who's Who in Non-Classical Mythology* (New York: Oxford University Press, 1993).

Thompson, Dr. Gunnar. *The Friar's Map of Ancient America* (Wash.: Argonauts, 1996).

Trento, Michael Salvatore. *The Search for Lost America: The Mystery of the Stone Ruins* (Chicago, Ill.: Contemporary Books, 1978).

Urton, Gary. *At the Crossroads of Earth and Sky: An Andean Cosmology* (Austin, Tex.: University of Texas Press, 1981).

——. *Inca Myths* (Austin, Tex.: University of Texas Press, 1999).

Waters, Frank. *The Book of the Hopi* (New York: Viking Press, 1974).

Wells, Spencer. *The Journey of Man: A Genetic Odyssey* (New York: Random House Paperbacks, 2003).

Williams, Richard. *Mysteries of the Ancients* (New York: The Readers's Digest Association, 1993).

Yoshida, Professor Nobuhiro. "Ancient American and Japanese Dragons: Related or Coincidental?" *Ancient American, Vol. 12, No. 76,* December 2007.

——. "Japan's Megalithic Links to America and Europe," *Ancient American, Vol. 3, No. 23,* April/May 1998.

Zimmermann, Fritz. *The Nephilim Chronicles: A Travel Guide to the Ancient Ruins in the Ohio Valley* (CreateSpace, 2010).

——. "Cultural and Physical Similarities of the Beaker People and the Adena," *Ancient American, Vol. 9, No. 58,* August 2004.

Index

About the Editor

FRANK **J**OSEPH was the editor-in-chief of *Ancient American* magazine from its inception in 1993 until his retirement 14 years later. He has published more books (nine) about the lost civilization of Atlantis than any other writer in history. His 16 other titles dealing with archaeology, military history, and metaphysics have been released in 31 foreign editions around the world. Joseph lives today with his wife, Laura, and Norwegian Forest Cat, Sammy, in the Upper Mississippi Valley.

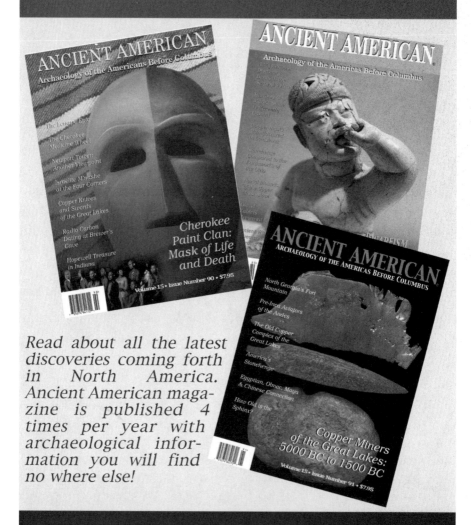